Pension Policies and Public Debt in Dynamic CGE Models

ETLA – The Research Institute of the Finnish Economy
Series A23 (ISSN 0356-7435)

The Research Institute of the Finnish Economy (ETLA) was founded in 1946 to conduct research in the fields of economics, business and social policy designed to serve financial and economic-policy decision making. At present the members of the association sponsoring ETLA are the central association of industry and employers, major banks and the central association of insurance companies. ETLA also conducts special studies financed from sources outside the association, for which a separate unit has been established. ETLA publishes monographs, reviews and forecasts in several different series.

Address: ETLA, Lönnrotinkatu 4 B, FIN-00120 Helsinki, Finland
Telephone 358-9-609900
Telefax 358-9-601753

Previous Volumes Published in Association with ETLA, Helsinki

Synnöve Vuori and Pentti Vuorinen (Eds.)
Explaining Technical Change in a Small Country

Rita Asplund (Ed.) Human Capital Creation in an Economic Perspective

D. Peter Broer
Jukka Lassila (Eds.)

Pension Policies and Public Debt in Dynamic CGE Models

With 33 Figures

ETLA 50

Springer-Verlag
Berlin Heidelberg GmbH

D. Peter Broer
Central Planning Bureau
P.O. Box 80510
NL-2508 GM The Hague
The Netherlands
and
Research Centre for Economic Policy (OCFEB)
Erasmus University
P.O. Box 1738
NL-3000 DR Rotterdam
The Netherlands

Jukka Lassila
Research Director
ETLA
The Research Institute of the Finnish Economy
Lönnrotinkatu 4 B
FIN-00120 Helsinki
Finland

ISBN 978-3-7908-0970-1

Die Deutsche Bibliothek – CIP-Einheitsaufnahme
Pension policies and public debt in dynamic CGE models/D. Peter Broer; Jukka Lassila (ed.). In assoc. with ETLA, Helsinki.

(Series/ETLA – The Research Institute of the Finnish Economy: A; 23)
ISBN 978-3-7908-0970-1 ISBN 978-3-662-01660-2 (eBook)
DOI 10.1007/978-3-662-01660-2
NE: Broer, D. Peter [Hrsg.]; Elinkeinoelämän Tutkimuslaitos ⟨Helsinki⟩: Series/A

Originally published by Physica-Verlag Heidelberg in 1997

SPIN 10550968 88/2202-5 4 3 2 1 0 – Printed on acid-free paper

PREFACE

In recent years, increasing attention has been devoted to the economic consequences of population ageing. The prospective increase in the share of elderly in the population in developed countries will have important consequences for the distribution of the net burden of government expenditure and social security provisions over generations. This raises a number of issues regarding the impact of current public debt policy and the system of public pension provisions on the efficiency and the distribution of welfare in these countries.

To study these issues, a workshop on "Pension Systems, Taxation, and Public Debt in Dynamic CGE Models," was organized by ETLA, The Research Institute of the Finnish Economy, in Helsinki, Finland, on April 6-7, 1995. At this workshop, papers were presented that addressed these questions using Computable General Equilibrium models. This book contains updated versions of these papers. *The financial support from the Yrjö Jahnsson Foundation, both for the workshop and for the preparation of this book, is gratefully acknowledged.*

Contents

1 Introduction and Summary . . . 1
D. Peter Broer and Jukka Lassila
1.1 The Basic Issues . . . 1
1.2 Public Debt . . . 2
1.3 Social Security Reform . . . 4
1.4 Evaluating Reform Proposals . . . 5
1.5 The Use of Computable General Equilibrium Models . . . 6
1.6 The Papers in this Volume . . . 9
References . . . 13

2 The Future of Public Pensions in the Seven Major Economies . 16
Thierry Chauveau and Rahim Loufir
2.1 Introduction . . . 16
2.2 Demographic Trends and Institutional Aspects of Public Pension Systems in the Seven Major Economies . . . 19
2.2.1 Demographic Trends in the Seven Major Economies . . . 19
2.2.2 A Brief Overview of Public Pension Systems in the Seven Major Economies . . . 24
2.3 Modelling the Seven Major Economies . . . 26
2.3.1 The Model . . . 26
2.3.1.1 Firms . . . 26
2.3.1.2 Households . . . 27
2.3.1.3 Public Sector . . . 29
2.3.1.4 Main Assumptions . . . 32
2.3.2 Calibration . . . 33
2.4 Simulation Results . . . 36
2.4.1 The Case of Closed Economies . . . 38
2.4.1.1 Output . . . 38
2.4.1.2 Prices . . . 41
2.4.1.3 Saving Rates . . . 43
2.4.1.4 Pensions . . . 44
2.4.1.5 Taxes . . . 49
2.4.1.6 Actuarial Fairness . . . 53

2.4.1.7 Social Welfare . . . 55
2.4.2 The Case of Open Economies . . . 58
2.4.2.1 Investment and Savings . . . 59
2.4.2.2 Per-head Output . . . 60
2.4.2.3 Pensions . . . 62
2.4.2.4 Taxes . . . 63
2.4.2.5 Actuarial Fairness . . . 65
2.4.2.6 Social Welfare . . . 66
2.5 Conclusion . . . 68
References . . . 70
Appendix . . . 71

3 Pension Systems in Europe . . . 74
Turalay Kenc and William Perraudin
3.1 Introduction . . . 74
3.1.1 The Pension Reform Debate . . . 74
3.1.2 General Equilibrium Analysis . . . 75
3.1.3 Related Research . . . 76
3.1.4 Structure of the Paper . . . 77
3.2 Pension Systems Heterogeneity . . . 77
3.2.1 Comparing Pension Regulations . . . 77
3.3 The Model . . . 79
3.3.1 Household Behaviour . . . 79
3.3.2 Firm Behaviour . . . 81
3.3.3 The Government . . . 82
3.3.4 Open Economy Aspects of the Model . . . 82
3.4 Simulations . . . 83
3.4.1 Summary of the Provisions to be Simulated . . . 83
3.4.2 The Baseline Parameters . . . 84
3.4.3 Baseline Simulations . . . 84
3.4.4 Components of the Reform . . . 86
3.4.4.1 Contribution and Replacement Rate Harmonization . . . 86
3.4.4.2 Retirement Age and Averaging Period Harmonizations . . . 87
3.4.4.3 Summary Results With and Without Capital Mobility . . . 88
3.4.5 Sensitivity Analysis . . . 88
3.5 Conclusion . . . 88
Appendix . . . 89
References . . . 108

4 Pension Policies and Lifetime Uncertainty in an Applied General Equilibrium Model . . . 110
D. Peter Broer and Ed W.M.T. Westerhout
4.1 Introduction . . . 110

4.2	The Pension Sector	112
4.3	The Household Sector	114
4.4	The Rest of the Model	117
4.5	Widening the Income Tax and PAYG Premium Base	118
4.5.1	Levying PAYG Premiums on Pension Benefits	119
4.5.2	Reducing PAYG Benefits	120
4.6	The Role of the Survival Profile Assumption	121
4.6.1	Perpetual Youth	122
4.6.2	Age-dependent Mortality	123
4.7	Conclusions	124
	References	124
	Appendix	125
5	**Pension Policies and International Capital Mobility** Jukka Lassila, Heikki Palm and Tarmo Valkonen	**139**
5.1	Introduction	139
5.2	Some Related Studies	140
5.3	The Model	141
5.3.1	Main Features	141
5.3.2	Capital Movements and Interest Rates	142
5.4	Pension Policy Simulations	145
5.4.1	Justification and Description of the Pension Policy Measures	145
5.4.2	Reducing the Pension Benefit Level	146
5.4.3	Raising the Retirement Age	149
5.4.4	Temporary Increase in a Pension Fund	152
5.5	Concluding Remarks	155
	References	156
	Appendices	157
6	**Debt Reduction, Wage Formation and Intergenerational Welfare** Svend Erik Hougaard Jensen	**167**
6.1	Introduction	167
6.2	Debt Policy and the Real Economy	169
6.3	A Dynamic CGE Model	170
6.4	The Design of Fiscal Policy	177
6.5	Macroeconomic Effects	179
6.6	Welfare and Generational Redistribution	183
6.7	Conclusions	187
	References	188

1 Introduction and Summary

D. Peter Broer[1] and Jukka Lassila[2]
[1] OCFEB, Erasmus University, Rotterdam, and
CPB Netherlands Bureau of Economic Policy Analysis,
The Hague, The Netherlands
[2] ETLA, The Research Institute of the Finnish Economy,
Helsinki, Finland

1.1 The Basic Issues

The age composition of the population in developed countries is shifting rapidly in favour of the elderly. Projections by the United Nations indicate that for the OECD area as a whole the share of the elderly (people at an age of 65 or above) will increase from 15 % in 1990 to 22 % in 2040. At the same time, the old-age dependency ratio[1] is expected to rise from 20 % to 37 %. For individual countries, these ratios may develop in an even more dramatic fashion, *e.g.* for Japan a rise of the dependency ratio from 16 % to over 50 % is projected, and for Germany from 22 % to 48 %. For developing countries, a similar change is expected at a later stage (United Nations (1994)). In the last decade, it is increasingly being recognized that this worldwide change in the age structure of the population will have far-reaching economic consequences. The change should give rise to substantial shifts in the distribution of the net financial burden of the public sector across generations, mostly as a result of a declining labour force participation. Rising dependency ratios imply a decline in the size of the tax base that can be used to finance public expenditure and social security transfers. Without a substantial cut in public expenditure programs and transfers, the ageing process will therefore cause a substantial increase in the net tax burden for younger generations.

This prediction can be substantiated by tracking net taxes and transfers of different generations over their lifetime, given a baseline projection of future developments. The method of *intergenerational accounting* has been advocated by Auerbach *et al.* (1991) as an alternative to the use of the official government per capita debt to measure the extent of redistribution implied by public policy. Intergenerational accounting calculations for the U.S. show that the lifetime tax

[1] The old-age dependency ratio is defined as the ratio of the elderly to the working-age population.

Pension Policies and Public Debt in Dynamic CGE Models

rates[2] for future generations are expected to *double*, from around 35 % to around 70 %, under the current policy regime (see Auerbach *et al.* (1994)). This dramatic change in the net burden of different generations stems mainly from two sources, first, the level of public debt and the associated projections of the government budget deficit and, second, the expected increase in social security transfers associated with the ageing of the population. Calculations for Germany show a similar pattern for the intergenerational burden (Boll *et al.* (1994)). However, Ablett (1996) obtains a different conclusion for Australia, mostly as a result of a smaller Australian public debt.

In itself, shifts in the burden between generations need not be a cause for concern, as they may simply reflect the role of social security as a public insurance contract.[3] However, a social security system must be regarded as an *implicit* social contract, that is not strictly enforceable. This implies that large structural shocks may endanger the viability of the contract.[4] Furthermore, the original social security contract may not have been optimally designed. These considerations point to the basic policy issues to be dealt with in this book, *viz.* the potential for a reform of the old-age social security system in OECD countries to cope with the demographic shock and the scope for fiscal policy in this respect.

1.2 Public Debt

One way to prepare for the ageing of the population is to reduce the level of public debt. Among policy makers, the negative effects of a high and rising level of public debt are virtually undisputed. Among academic economists, the predominant neoclassical view holds that a rising level of government debt implies a shift of the tax burden towards future generations that will boost current consumption of heterogeneous agents and lead to crowding out of capital formation. In addition, the probability that the debt will be monetized increases, which boosts expected inflation. Under the competing Ricardian view, families of intergenerationally linked households will adjust their consumption in reaction to any imbalance in the tax burden across generations. In that case, the consequences of the

---

[2] Defined as the ratio of lifetime net payments into the system and lifetime labour income.

[3] On the lack of efficiency of private insurance markets in the presence of asymmetric information, see *e.g.* Eckstein *et al.* (1985).

[4] For a discussion of the political stability of existing old-age provisions, see Verbon (1989) or Tabellini (1991).

ageing process for the distribution of the intergenerational tax burden are already discounted in the behaviour of households.[5]

The possible existence of intergenerational linkages does not deny the importance of a proper management of government finance, however. The conditions for the existence of Ricardian equivalence[6] are unlikely to be met in reality, so that public debt will crowd out savings, even with intergenerational linkages. In a closed economy, this will directly affect the tax base, through a reduced accumulation of capital, but also in a small open economy the accumulation of foreign debt will crowd out consumption of future generations. Furthermore, lacking the availability of lump-sum taxation, both the neoclassical view and the Ricardian view stress the use of the public deficit as a means to achieve an optimal timing of taxes over the business cycle, to minimize the intertemporal distortions of taxation, see *e.g.* Barro (1986). The desirability of tax smoothing carries over to the case of anticipated demographic shocks (Bovenberg *et al.*, (1993)). To avoid increases in taxes or social security premiums, future deficits should be met by current surpluses. Such a policy may imply a direct reduction in government debt by increasing taxes or reducing public consumption, or a reduction in old-age social security, along the same lines.

Historically, control over the level of government debt has been difficult to achieve. Within the EC, the incentives for a reduction of government debt have increased substantially with the conclusion of the Maastricht agreement. However, the provisions of the treaty were formulated mainly with an eye on the requirements for a monetary union (see *e.g.* Buiter *et al.*(1993)). In fact, the asymmetric treatment of government debt and the burden of unfunded social security in the provisions of the Maastricht treaty suggests that issues of intergenerational redistribution are not yet high on policy makers's agendas. As it is well known that unfunded social security is by and large equivalent with government debt (see *e.g.* Auerbach and Kotlikoff (1987)), a difference in priority between both policy issues appears to be unwarranted.[7]

---

[5] This is not to say that the distribution of the tax burden cannot have any consequences for household behaviour. For an exposition of both views, see *e.g.* Barro (1989) and Bernheim (1989).

[6] *E.g.*, perfect capital markets, no bequest constraints, lump sum taxation, certainty over future taxes and income.

[7] Except to the extent that there may be implicit escape clauses in the social contract between generations, that allow for a reduction of social security in case of large adverse shocks.

1.3 Social Security Reform

Next to a reduction in government debt, a straightforward way to deal with the distributional consequences of the ageing process may be to reform the social security system. In fact, the problems associated with a rise in the old-age dependency ratio originate partly from the current organization of old-age social security. The public old-age social security system in most western countries is largely on a Pay-As-You-Go (PAYG) basis.[8] PAYG systems are by their very nature defined-benefit systems, so that the contribution rate in these systems is rather sensitive to demographic shocks. As a result, PAYG systems are usually not actuarially fair in the presence of demographic shifts, and the discrepancy can be substantial (see *e.g.* Nelissen (1987) for some illustrative calculations). The *linkage* between a dollar paid and the present value of a dollar received, which is never very high in defined-benefit systems, may therefore be rather low in a PAYG system. This causes the PAYG premium to act as a distortionary tax on labour, that adds to the distortionary impact of the income tax. Given the high taxes on labour in most OECD countries, the additional efficiency loss may thus be very serious, which makes it worthwhile to look for efficiency-increasing reforms of the standard PAYG social security contract. To this end, several options may be considered:

- One option is to reduce the amount of social security by increasing the statutory retirement age, or reducing the replacement rate between wages and pension benefits. This could be interpreted as a break of the social contract. However, it might be justified by an appeal to the increased longevity of the population, or to the increase in wages as a result of the decline in labour supply. Making the contract contingent on these events need not impair the basic insurance function of the system.
- A second option is a transition to a funded system. A funded system offers a buffer against demographic shocks, that can give a more equal distribution of the generational burden. In conjunction with this, it should cause less distortion of labour market decisions. Homburg (1990) and Breyer and Straub (1993) show that, departing from a steady state, such a transition can be made in a Pareto-improving fashion. However, if the demographic shock is well under way, as is the case at present, a Pareto-improving transition to a fully funded system may take too long to be of practical use.
- Instead of a transition to full funding, it may be possible to achieve a better intergenerational distribution by allowing the pension fund to run surpluses and deficits, that are financed on the capital market. In this way, the distributional

[8] Some countries also have a supplementary pension system that is completely or partially funded. This is the case in Denmark, Finland, and the Netherlands.

role of the pension fund becomes quite similar to that of the government in its use of public debt. The advantage over the previous option is that a change to a system with an *ex ante* constant contribution rate can be made even at a late stage in the demographic transition.

- Lastly, it is possible to abandon the defined-benefit character of existing public pension schemes and switch to a defined-contribution system. This would put the public pension system more on a par with existing private pension schemes, that are always defined-contribution. In comparison with the previous option of premium smoothing, this system also implies stable premium rates, but it does not guarantee any specific level of pension benefits. Thus the insurance role of a defined-contribution system falls short of that of a defined-benefit system.[9] The big advantage of defined-contribution schemes is that they can be made actuarially fair, thus allowing for a better linkage between contributions and pensions. This does away with the distortionary character of pension contributions. In comparison with private pension schemes, the added benefit of a public defined-contribution pension scheme is that its compulsory character ensures that no adverse selection on the basis of private information about longevity risks can take place (see *e.g.* Townley and Boadway (1988)).

1.4 Evaluating Reform Proposals

Any evaluation of reform proposals should involve two criteria, *equity* and *efficiency*. The application of these criteria to the consequences of population ageing is not without difficulties, however, as ageing may be expected to have a considerable impact on the future development of the economy. As a result, an evaluation of an existing scheme of social security by means of a simple extrapolation of existing trends may be highly misleading. Auerbach and Kotlikoff (1987) show that, within the framework of their life-cycle model, the demographic transition will have significant effects on savings rates, wages, and current accounts. In particular, the decline of the working age population will lead to a fall in labour supply, that results in higher wages and lower interest rates during the transition period. This will affect the relative position of generations both through their lifetime income and through the link between pension benefits and wages.

---

[9] In particular, there is no hedge against unfavourable demographic or macro-economic shocks, that may affect some generations more than others. On the impossibility of private insurance markets to engage in intergenerational risk-sharing, see Gordon and Varian (1988).

To account for the effects of ageing on the position of households, reliable predictions of the general macroeconomic effects of ageing appear to be required. However, straightforward application of generational accounting methods to these projections, to determine the degree of intergenerational equality, does not necessarily provide clear results. The differences in net tax payments of the successive generations emerge partly from changes in household behaviour, that affect factor prices and incomes. The question to what extent a possible *ex post* difference in treatment before taxes of generations can be regarded as inequitable is then no longer well-defined (see also Haveman (1989)).[10]

Obviously, what is needed theoretically is a (money-metric) indicator of the change in utility of the generations involved. To what extent generational accounts provide a good indication of this change in utility is still open to debate. Fehr and Kotlikoff (1995) provide examples of welfare effects of policy measures in the Auerbach-Kotlikoff Computable General Equilibrium (CGE) model, where the utility gain of generations is approximated satisfactorily by the change in the generational accounts. Buiter (1995) and Raffelhüschen and Risa (1995) provide examples of CGE models where the use of the generational accounts would provide a very misleading idea about the welfare effects of policy changes. This objection gains weight when the problem at hand is the evaluation of a policy reform in reaction to a structural shift, *e.g.* population ageing. In that case, it is less likely that substitution effects can be treated as of second-order magnitude, so that the change in the generational accounts caused by the policy change cannot be isolated from the change caused by the policy shock. As an example take the result that a transition from a PAYG system to a funded system may be welfare-improving in the presence of distortionary labour taxation (Breyer and Straub (1993)). With an expected decline in interest rates, as a result of the demographic shock, this result need no longer hold.[11]

1.5 The Use of Computable General Equilibrium Models

The discussion of the preceding section shows that conventional macro-economic measures are not well suited for the evaluation of demographic shifts, because they do not link events to preferences. Computable General Equilibrium (CGE)

[10] To carry the argument to its logical conclusion, the process of ageing itself may be an optimal reaction of intergenerationally linked households, that adjust their fertility in response to a changing environment (see *e.g.* Razin and Sadka (1995)). In that case it is clearly pointless to compensate generations for the changes in their own behaviour.

[11] In view of the predicted surplus of capital on the transition path, a shift to a funded system might be carrying coals to Newcastle.

models are better equipped because they derive the behaviour of agents from structural parameters of preferences and technology. This also gives them an advantage over macro-econometric models in the construction of policies designed to deal with the shock (Bovenberg (1987)). In addition they can be disaggregated more easily in the relevant dimensions because their empirical status is different. CGE models do not usually aim at a good description of a given set of macro-economic variables in the time domain. Instead they are calibrated on a small number of years, while many parameters are obtained from separate data sets.[12] This brings a considerable extra amount of flexibility in the specification of behavioral equations, and allows for a much lower level of aggregation than in fully data-based (*e.g.* macro-econometric) models.[13]

In comparison with analytical models too, CGE models offer definite advantages. Existing theoretical models are not able to handle any substantial degree of household heterogeneity. This implies that the insights offered by these models are only of limited value, if the composition of households is an important characteristic of the economy, as it is in the analysis of the consequences of ageing. In this respect, the general life-cycle model of household behaviour can be imbedded in CGE models in a much more general fashion than in theoretical models, taking into account the finite length of life. Compared to the length of business cycles, a human life is long, between 70 and 80 years in industrialized countries. This gives rise to a completely different time scale when one tries to evaluate the effects of policies such as changes in pension systems. The changes are long-lasting almost by definition. An average citizen will feel the effects in many phases: first possibly as a child, through the living conditions of parents, afterwards in the labour market and finally upon retirement. Ultimately, he or she will probably pass on some of the effects in the form of bequests. All these phases must be taken into account if we want to know whether the change in pension system was beneficial or disadvantageous to the person in question.

As a result of these advantages, CGE models can be tailored to a much larger degree to the policy issue at hand. In fact, the rise of CGE models as a tool for economic policy analysis coincides with a shift of attention from macro-economic stabilization to structural problems. CGE models are now routinely employed for the analysis of tax reforms and international trade liberalization (for a survey, see Shoven and Whalley (1992)). The general equilibrium character of these models allows for the calculation of the incidence of taxes or tariffs, in terms of a money-metric measure of welfare. This, together with the generally low level

[12] For a discussion of the use of calibration techniques in CGE models, see Shoven and Whalley (1992). A more general discussion and a critique can be found in Hansen and Heckman (1996).

[13] A fully data-based model can be defined as a model that has a non-degenerate likelihood function in terms of its free parameters on the data set that it claims to describe.

of aggregation, provides policy-makers with a tool for a detailed analysis of the distribution effects of policy measures for specific groups or sectors of interest.

The growing popularity of CGE models as an alternative to conventional macro-econometric models has not occurred without a fair amount of criticism, however. Some of the main objections are discussed below.

- *CGE models are unreliable because of a weak empirical base.*

CGE models indeed do not usually possess a well-defined probability distribution of the model forecasts. Also, in terms of within-sample performance, macro-econometric models certainly hold an advantage. However, it should be borne in mind that parameters in macro-econometric models are usually also underidentified, in the sense that arbitrary exclusion restrictions are needed to obtain parameter estimates (see Sims (1980)). This implies that their reliability cannot be determined from their goodness-of-fit.

- *CGE models do not take account of market imperfections.*

This objection is somewhat obsolete, as imperfections are being built into CGE models, *e.g.* labour market imperfections in Jensen *et al.* (1994), both labour market imperfections and product market imperfections in Gelauff and Graafland (1994), or portfolio behaviour in Goulder and Eichengreen (1989). However, neither of these models offers a fully satisfactory choice-theoretic analysis of real-world phenomena like unemployment, cartels, uncertainty, *etc.* It seems fair to say that here macro-econometric models have an edge in terms of descriptive power, but as they lack a structural explanation of market imperfections, this does not necessarily make them more useful for policy analysis on this account.

- *CGE models unrealistically assume perfect foresight.*

Although perfect foresight is not a realistic assumption, it is difficult to replace it with a more satisfactory one. It would be desirable to incorporate uncertainty into CGE models, as well as incomplete information about the structure of the economy. Both steps provide serious theoretical and computational challenges, however. Uncertainty in non-linear models implies that the entire distribution of the endogenous variables becomes the relevant entity to solve for in each separate time period. Except for simple cases, no solution methods are known.[14] The introduction of incomplete information calls for a theory of learning, which is not available. Furthermore, while economic agents are certainly not in possession of perfect foresight, they do display forward-looking behaviour, which cannot be captured by a simple adaptive expectations scheme. The distinction seems especially relevant in the case of population ageing, the consequences of which are widely discussed on television and in the newspapers.

In addition, the weight of these objections may shift over time. For instance, market imperfections may become less important, as the liberalisation of financial markets shows. Blundell-Wignall and Browne (1991) list three important

---

[14] In Real Business Cycle theory, approximate solutions are obtained by linearizing the model.

ingredients of this liberalisation. First, the role of liquidity constraints in private spending and portfolio decisions is reduced. Current income and the availability of money are less binding constraints on expenditure and portfolio behaviour. Second, new inefficiencies may arise in liberalised markets, *e.g.* asset price bubbles. Third, globalisation of financial markets enables domestic savings and investment to diverge over prolonged periods. Issues one and three will probably make the approach in this book more relevant in time, whereas the second issue emphasises the increasing importance of an element missing in all these models, *i.e.* risk.

1.6 The Papers in this Volume

Among the central policy issues in population ageing are the financial consequences of the current system of old-age social security provision in OECD countries. Are these current systems financially feasible in the face of a substantial increase in the share of the elderly or can they be upheld only by imposing unacceptable burdens on younger generations? To what extent does an answer to this question depend on the demographic structure of each individual country?

The first paper, *The Future of Public Pensions in the Seven Major Economies*, by Thierry Chaveau and Rahim Loufir, considers these questions for the PAYG pension schemes of the seven major OECD countries for two alternative financing modes of the PAYG scheme. The first is a defined-benefit rule, in which case current benefits as a percentage of current wages are held constant and the contribution rates adjust to maintain a balanced budget. The second scenario is a defined-contribution rule, in which case the contribution rates, also as a percentage of wages, are held constant and pension benefits adjust to maintain budget balance. The consequences of both pension schemes for economic developments over the next 60 years are studied within the context of a dynamic CGE model, separately calibrated for each of the seven economies.

The model used is constructed along the lines of the Auerbach-Kotlikoff (1987) model. An innovative feature is that the mortality rate of households increases with age (no sudden death). This enables a realistic calibration of the model on the historic time path of the economies (*i.e.*, the reference path is not the steady state). Public pensions are determined by applying a replacement rate to current wages and they are financed by a tax on current wage income.

The main conclusions that arise from the paper are

- Ageing of the population affects the different countries in much the same way, despite initial differences in age structure. The growth of output per head will slow down and the real interest rate will fall during the transition phase. The slow down of output growth will be most severe in Germany and Italy, and least in the U.S.

- A constant contribution rate (CCR) system yields more growth, but a constant replacement rate (CRR) system does not run into financing problems. In a CRR system, contribution rates are expected to rise most for Italy, and least for the U.S.
- The intergenerational accounts are much more fair under a CCR regime than under a CRR regime. In the latter case, future generations are always treated worse, in the former case they are treated better in the case of Japan, Italy, and Germany.
- Welfare effects of a change from a CRR system to a CCR system are negative for current generations and positive for future generations. The positive long-run effects are quite substantial for France, Germany, and Italy.

Pension systems are generally rather complex, and the rules vary between countries, making international comparisons difficult. Additional costs come from the possible distortions introduced by the pension systems. These distortions are the subject of the study *Pension Systems in Europe* by Turalay Kenc and William Perraudin.

The crucial question is the linkage between pension benefits and contributions from an individual agent's point of view. If an agent's benefit is independent of the level of contributions, the latter are equivalent to a distortionary wage tax. At the other extreme, there is no distortion whatsoever if the benefits are actuarially fair in relation to the contributions. In practise the benefit-contribution link varies not only between countries but also within individual lifecycles in each country. Benefits are calculated from the average wage earned in some part of the agent's life before retirement. The length of the averaging periods varies between countries. If the period is short, the additional discounted benefits an agent receives if he supplies an additional unit of labour within the averaging period may be so large that the effective tax rate on wage income is negative. Short averaging periods may thus be equivalent to a widely fluctuating labour income tax over the life cycle.

Kenc and Perraudin formulate an overlapping generations model of an open economy in which terms of trade are variable and the supply of savings from the rest of the world is imperfectly elastic. There are two domestic industries using labour and capital to produce respectively an exportable good and a non-traded good. Studying the public pension systems in Germany, France, Italy and the UK, they simulate what would happen in each country if it would change its contribution and replacement rates, retirement ages and averaging periods, to the average values of these countries. They find striking effects of this harmonization. In France the long-run gain in output would be in the order of plus 8 %, whereas in the UK output would fall by over ten per cent. As a result of the different starting points the harmonisation would mean more saving and labour supply in France and less saving and labour supply in the UK, where the current system relies much less on an unfunded PAYG system. Germany and Italy fall in between.

The authors conclude that the burden of population ageing and the resulting necessity to adjust pension levels provides a valuable opportunity to reconsider the design of pension systems.

The third paper, *Pension Policies and Lifetime Uncertainty in an Applied General Equilibrium Model*, by D. Peter Broer and Ed W.M.T. Westerhout, differs from the previous two in that it concentrates on a single country. It explores the potential of a reform of the Dutch system of PAYG pensions, by exploiting the special character of the Dutch system of old-age social security. This system integrates a flat-benefit basic PAYG system with a supplementary funded system, that is both income- and contribution related. The CGE model used is a small-open economy version of the Auerbach-Kotlikoff model, extended with a model of the integrated pension system. Like in the study by Chaveau and Loufir, household mortality rates are increasing with age. Retirement from the work force is voluntary. The paper explores two policy options to reduce the burden of PAYG contributions, first a broadening of the PAYG contribution base by levying PAYG premiums on supplementary pension benefits, and second a cut in PAYG pensions. It appears that both measures succeed in improving efficiency. A broadening of the PAYG contribution base yields lower PAYG contributions, which stimulates labour supply. In addition, the tax generates a redistribution from older generations to young and future generations. The measure is efficiency-increasing, because it acts partly as a lump-sum tax on pension rights accumulated in the past, but it redistributes welfare at the expense of the old. Its political feasibility may therefore be questioned.

The second policy option is to reduce PAYG benefits. Because PAYG pensions are integrated into the supplementary pension scheme, this reduction does not lower total pensions. Instead, the premium contribution rate of the supplementary pensions is raised. Because this scheme is funded, the premium increase can be levelled out over all future generations. In addition, the linkage between contributions and benefits is increased, as supplementary pension rights are based on the premiums paid out of labour income. The net result is a Pareto-improving change, that boosts labour supply and capital accumulation on the transition path.

The paper also conducts a sensitivity analysis with respect to the survival distribution of households, to investigate the role of lifetime uncertainty. It appears that the macro-economic outcomes of the different assumptions – perpetual youth, age-dependent mortality, or sudden death (the assumption used by Auerbach and Kotlikoff) – are very similar. Pension reforms affect the behaviour of individual generations rather differently, however. In particular, effects on labour supply and welfare are much larger for older generations under the assumption of age-dependent mortality than under sudden death.

The ongoing globalisation of financial markets is especially important for small economies. The link between investments and domestic saving weakens. The history of countries like Finland has shown that current account problems have created fluctuations both in the interest rates and exchange rates. Within the EMU, interest rate effects of foreign borrowing should become small, perhaps negligible. What are the consequences of this change for pension policies?

In their paper *Pension Policies and International Capital Mobility*, Lassila, Palm and Valkonen approach the question by simulating pension policies under three capital mobility regimes and comparing the results. They use an open economy model of the Auerbach - Kotlikoff type. Under perfect capital mobility the amount of foreign borrowing and debt does not affect the conditions of further borrowing. In the flow equilibrium regime domestic interest rates react to the rate of borrowing but not to the level of debt, and policies affecting saving or capital formation have temporary interest rate effects. In the portfolio adjustment regime the level of net foreign assets or debt is crucial, and policies changing that level cause permanent interest rate differentials between the domestic interest rate and international rates. Both temporary and permanent interest rate changes affect the capital stock and through that everything else in the economy, so there is no theoretical doubt that this has bearing also on the outcomes of different pension policies. The authors attempt to characterise the differences and to give insights on what differences are important and what are not. The policy measures they consider are a reduction in the pension benefit level, an increase in the retirement age and a temporary variation in the pension fund.

The long-run policy effects are the same under perfect capital mobility and flow equilibrium regimes. The crucial difference is the speed of adjustment in the transition to the new equilibrium. Interest rate reactions make the current account changes smaller, and the required long-run change in net foreign assets takes more time to accumulate, so transition period is longer under the flow equilibrium regime. This is directly reflected in the capital stock, which reaches the new equilibrium value quicker under perfect capital mobility. For practical purposes the regimes are in fact quite different, as 'temporary' changes can last several decades. The short-run policy reactions are similar under flow equilibrium and portfolio adjustment regimes, but the long-run effects differ (except with the temporary fund variation policy) as the under the latter the interest rate differentials prevail and correspondingly the capital stock converges to a different level.

Are these differences important for pension policies? In some respects, yes. The degree of capital mobility does not change qualitatively the intergenerational welfare effects of pension policies but affects the size of gains and losses of different generations. In some respects, definitively no. The effects on the pension contribution rate are almost independent of the interest rate reactions. Pensions are generally both earnings-related and financed by payroll taxes, and this link is sometimes strengthened by the indexation of pensions to current wages. Although the wage effects of pension policies are quite different under different specifications of capital movements, the contribution rate does not vary much as changes in wages affect both pension benefits and their source of finance. A minor effect comes from differences in pension funds' interest incomes.

The problems raised by unfunded PAYG social security are to a large extent the same as those of public debt. In both cases there is an implicit redistribution of the tax burden to future generations and a potential efficiency loss through distortionary taxation. A natural alternative to a restructuring of old-age social security may therefore be a reduction in the level of public debt.

This issue is taken up in the last paper, *Debt Reduction, Wage Formation and Intergenerational Welfare*, by Svend Erik Hougaard Jensen. The paper considers the problems of choosing a suitable long-run target for the level of debt and the choice of an optimal tax instrument to achieve this level of debt, in relation to the possible adverse effects of taxation on wage formation and the level of unemployment.

The model used is a dynamic CGE model for a small open economy with overlapping generations of households. The Blanchard assumption of perpetual youth is used to model mortality rates. The labour force consists of workers of a large number of imperfectly substitutable skill levels. Each skill level is organised in a monopsonistic labour union, that sets its wage unilaterally, subject to the labour demand curve of the firm. The net wage is now a mark-up on the marginal disutility of work and the net unemployment replacement rate. This implies that the sensitivity of wages to wage taxation depends on the size of the preference for leisure.

Two alternative policies for debt reduction are investigated. Under the first one government debt is reduced to zero in twelve years, under the second policy the same reduction is achieved in 36 years. The first policy is the official goal of the Danish government. The available tax instruments are the wage tax and an excise tax on consumption. The single most important result is the strong sensitivity of the outcomes to the assumed degree of wage rigidity. In the long run, if unions attach little weight to leisure, wages do not respond much to the eventual reduction in tax rates, and output and employment effects are modest. In fact, public debt reduction mostly crowds in private consumption. However, if wages are flexible, capital crowding in take place, wages are lower, employment is higher, and unemployment falls considerably.

On the transition path the effects of wage flexibility are different. A high degree of wage flexibility decreases the opportunities of the government to implement a tight fiscal policy. Raising wage taxes boosts wages on the transition path and lowers employment. Effects are particularly strong if the government pursues a 12-year plan for debt elimination. This induces huge welfare losses for current generations, up to seven percent of lifetime wealth. If leisure does not enter the objective function of the unions welfare losses are about half this size. If an excise tax is used to eliminate debt, current generations all lose to roughly the same extent, about 1 percent of lifetime wealth, while most future generations gain. In this case, a fairly even distribution of welfare across existing generations is achieved, irrespective of the amount of wage flexibility.

References

Ablett, J. (1996), "Generational Accounting, an Australian Perspective," *Review of Income and Wealth*, **42**, 91–105.

Auerbach, A.J., J. Gokhale, and L.J. Kotlikoff (1991), "Generational Accounts – A Meaningful Alternative to Deficit Accounting," NBER Working Paper No. 3589.

Auerbach, A.J., J. Gokhale, and L.J. Kotlikoff (1994), "Generational Accounting: A Meaningful Way to Evaluate Fiscal Policy," *Journal of Economic Perspectives*, **8**, 73–94.

Auerbach, A.J. and L.J. Kotlikoff (1987), *Dynamic Fiscal Policy*, Cambridge University Press.

Auerbach, A.J., L.J. Kotlikoff, R.P. Hagemann, and G. Nicoletti (1989), "The Economic Dynamics of an Ageing Population: The Case of Four OECD Countries," *OECD Economic Studies* no. 12, 97–130.

Barro, R.J. (1986), "U.S. Deficits since World War I," *Scandinavian Journal of Economics*, **88**, 195–222.

Barro, R.J. (1989), "The Ricardian Approach to Budget Deficits," *Journal of Economic Perspectives*, **3**, 37–54.

Bernheim, B.D. (1989), "A Neoclassical Perspective on Budget Deficits," *Journal of Economic Perspectives*, **3**, 55–72.

Blundell-Wignall, A., and F. Browne (1991), "Macroeconomic Consequences of Financial Liberalisation: a summary report," OECD Working Paper No. 98.

Boll, S., B. Raffelhüschen, and J. Walliser (1994), "Social Security and Intergenerational Redistribution: A Generational Accounting Perspective," *Public Choice*, **81**, 79–100.

Bovenberg, A.L. (1987), "The General Equilibrium Approach: Relevant for Public Policy?," in H.M. van de Kar and B.L. Wolfe, *The Relevance of Public Finance for Policy-Making*, Chicago: Wayne State University Press.

Bovenberg, A.L., D.P. Broer and E.W.M.T. Westerhout (1993), "Public Pensions and Declining Fertility in a Small Open Economy: an Intertemporal Equilibrium Approach," *Public Finance* (Supplement), **48**, pp. 43–59.

Breyer, F. and M. Straub (1993), "Welfare Effects of Unfunded Pension Systems When Labour Supply is Endogenous," *Journal of Public Economics*, **50**, 77–91.

Buiter, W.H. (1995), "Generational Accounts, Aggregate Saving and Intergenerational Distribution," *NBER Working Paper* No. 5087.

Buiter, W.H., G. Corsetti, and N. Roubini, "Maastricht's Fiscal Rules," *Economic Policy*, no. 16, 57–100.

Eckstein, Z., M. Eichenbaum and D. Peled (1985), "Uncertain Lifetimes and the Welfare Enhancing Properties of Annuity Markets and Social Security," *Journal of Public Economics*, **26**, 303–326.

Gelauff, G.M.M. and J.J. Graafland (1994), *Modelling Welfare State Reform*, North-Holland.

Goulder, L.H. and B. Eichengreen (1989), "Savings Promotion, Investment Promotion and International Competitiveness," in R. Feenstra (ed.), *Trade Policies for International Competitiveness*, Chicago.

Gordon, R.H. and H.R. Varian (1988), "Intergenerational Risk Sharing," *Journal of Public Economics*, **37**,185–202.

Hansen, L.P. and J.J. Heckman (1996), "The Empirical Foundations of Calibration," *Journal of Economic Perspectives*, **10**, 87–104.

Haveman, R. (1994), "Should Generational Accounts Replace Public Budgets and Deficits?," *Journal of Economic Perspectives*, **8**, 95–111.

Homburg, S. (1990), "The Efficiency of Unfunded Pension Schemes," *Journal of Institutional and Theoretical Economics*, December 1990, **146**, pp. 640–47.

Jensen, S.E.H., S.B. Nielsen, L.H. Pedersen and P.B. Sørensen (1994), "Labour Tax Reform, Employment and Intergenerational Distribution," *Scandinavian Journal of Economics*, **96**, 381–401.

Nelissen, J. (1987), "The Redistributive Impact of the General Old Age Pensions Act on Lifetime Income in the Netherlands," *European Economic Review*, **31**, 1419–1441.

Raffelhüschen, B. and A.E. Risa (1995), "Generational Accounting and Intergenerational Welfare," paper presented at the EEA meeting, Prague

Razin, A, and E. Sadka (1995), *Population Economics*, MIT Press.

Shoven, J.B. and J. Whalley (1992), *Applying General Equilibrium*, Cambridge University Press.
Sims, C. (1980), "Macroeconomics and Reality," *Econometrica*, **47**, 1267–1286.
Tabellini, G.E. (1991), "The Politics of Intergenerational Redistribution," *Journal of Political Economy*, **99**, 335–357.
Townley, P.G.C. and R.W. Boadway (1988), "Social Security and the Failure of Annuity Markets," *Journal of Public Economics*, **35**, 75–96.
United Nations (1994), *Long Range World Population Projections*.
Vérbon, H.A.A. (1988), *The Evolution of Public Pension Schemes*, Springer.

2 The Future of Public Pensions in the Seven Major Economies

Thierry Chauveau[1]
Rahim Loufir[2]
[1]University of Paris I and CEBI
[2]Research Department-OFCE

Abstract

We specify a computable general equilibrium model with overlapping generations allowing for variable life-expectancy, for studying the future of public pensions in the seven major economies. The main conclusions are: First, ageing of the population is a problem very similar from one developed country to another. Second, this problem is not so much worrying as is sometimes suggested and policies in which Pay-As-You-Go financing is maintained and the retirement age held constant are allowable. Third, there is no "one best social security policy". Fourth, there is a trade-off between, on the one hand, lower interest rates and taxes, higher investment and output, and so on, and, on the other hand, a higher standard of living of the retired. Fifth, these results hold under the assumption of closed economies as well as under the polar assumption of small open economies.

JEL Classification: D58, H55.
Keywords: Ageing, G7, life expectancy, overlapping generations, pensions, welfare.

2.1 Introduction

The tremendous development of the literature on pension economics is mainly due to the coming out, in developed countries, of financial problems of social old-age insurance systems. For an overview of this literature, see Fabel (1994)[1]. It is usually pointed out that, since public pension schemes broadly operate on a Pay-As-You-Go (hereafter PAYG) basis, these financial problems are associated

[1] This overview is coupled with an original analysis refering to retirement issues and focusing on the intra-generational effects of a variable retirement scheme.

Pension Policies and Public Debt in Dynamic CGE Models

with two phenomena: (i) an ageing population and (ii) the decrease of the average retirement age.

In this paper, some new evidence on the consequences of an ageing population on the "financial burden" of public pensions, in the seven major economies, is provided. Instead of using an econometric approach (see e.g. Heller, 1989) or a generational accounting one (see e.g. Van den Noord and Herd, 1993), a dynamic computable general equilibrium model with overlapping generations (hereafter CGEM-OG) is used, as in Auerbach and Kotlikoff (1987) or Auerbach, Kotlikoff, Hagemann and Nicoletti (1989). However, our approach is original since the model that has been built[2] rules out the well-known weakness of former CGEM-OG in which the simulated age structure (and total population) cannot not coincide with the actual (projected) ones. Indeed, this model allows for variable life expectancy.

Official demographic prospects are used and, whatever the country considered, the public pensions system is assumed to work on a PAYG basis; one must, therefore, remember that, for the two countries for which the public pension system is, at present, funded - Japan and the U.S.A. -, it is implicitly assumed that the reserves held by the Japanese and US funds will increase by the amount of their interest receipts during the period under review. Alternative assumptions could have been selected, allowing for a mix between funded and unfunded pensions systems. Such a point of view has been taken into account, for studying the French case by Chauveau and Loufir (1994b). For the sake of simplicity and in order to make the comparisons easily understandable, we assume, that, from 1995, all public pensions schemes work on a PAYG basis.

If the expenditures of a public pension system exactly balance its receipts, shifts in the demographic pattern will lead to an adjustment on either the expenditure side or on the revenue side (or on both sides) of the PAYG system. Indeed, two scenarios are, here, under review. Balancing the pension system may be reached in two opposite ways: in the first scenario, the instantaneous replacement rate[3] is held constant and this implies, in turn, that contributions increase to match current public expenditure. The second scenario, where the adjustment is made on the expenditure side, assumes a constant social contribution rate so that any demographic change is balanced by a change in the benefit level. Although none of these two basic scenarios is very likely to prevail, they must be considered as

[2] An earlier version of this model has been used in Chauveau and Loufir (1994b).

[3] For the exact definition of the instantaneous replacement rate see Section 4.

benchmarks, since more realistic policies [4] will usually combine a change in the contribution rate and in the level of per-head benefits [5].

Two antagonistic assumptions have been made, as far as the accounting framework is concerned: (a) each of the seven economies is assumed to be a closed economy or (b) there are six "small open economies dominated by the US economy". Perfect mobility of capital is assumed, i.e. the domestic interest rate of each of the six countries must equalise the "world" rate of interest which is identified to the US one.

For each of the seven countries (and under the two previous polar assumptions), main macroeconomic aggregates, intergenerational transfers, and welfare criteria are analysed. Of course, the two benchmark scenarios lead to substantially different redistribution of the burden between generations and the main conclusions are: (i) ageing of the population is a problem very similar from one developed country to another; (ii) this problem is not so much worrying as is sometimes suggested and policies where PAYG financing is maintained and the retirement age held constant are allowable; (iii) there is no "one best social security policy" since using different criteria (macroeconomic aggregates, actuarial fairness or welfare) will lead to different ranking of the two basic policies mentioned above (and consequently, any combination of these policies); (iv) on the contrary, there is a trade-off between, on the one hand, lowering interest rates, increasing investment and output, lowering taxes,... and, on the other hand, increasing the standard of living of the retired and (v) these results hold with under the assumption of closed economies as well as under the polar assumption of small open economies.

This paper is organised as follows: Section 2.2 summarises the study undertaken, in 1992, at the World Bank; it provides prospective demographic trends and contributes to a better understanding of the extent of the problems that lie ahead. It is also devoted to a brief review of the public pension systems in the countries under consideration. Section 2.3 gives a description of our new CGEM-OG, its calibration and the assumptions that have been made across countries. Section 2.4 shows, for the countries under review, the economic consequences and the welfare effects of the two above-mentioned basic institutional scenarios. Section 2.5 concludes.

---

[4] Of course, other policies could be undertaken but, since policies modifying the retirement rule are ruled out (see below), most of the remaining policies can be viewed as a combination of the two benchmarks; an exception is the partial funding of the PAYG system. Further details are given in Section 3.

[5] A fairly good approximation of the corresponding economic outcomes can be easily obtained by means of a linear combination of the outcomes of the baseline.

2.2 Demographic Trends and Institutional Aspects of Public Pension Systems in the Seven Major Economies

2.2.1 Demographic Trends in the Seven Major Economies

A consensus has almost been established, among the four major international institutions (IMF, OECD, United Nations, World Bank), about the evolution, in developed countries, of demographic variables and, consequently, on the size and the structure of the population in these economies[6]. Of course, demographic trends are very sensitive to key assumptions concerning the fertility rate, life expectancy and international migratory balance and noticeable differences between forecasts can be exhibited. However, whatever the study considered, the main conclusion is that a pronounced ageing of population appears to be ineluctable, entailing a significant increase, in the coming decades, of the so-called old-age dependency ratio (i.e. the number of elderly persons in proportion to the number of those in active age-groups).

For the sake of simplicity, we have, thus, used but one set of demographic projections; those prepared by the World Bank in 1992. They possess three interesting features:

- They allow for undertaking an international comparison of public pensions systems in the G7 using demographic trends derived from a common methodology. Consistency is, thus, reached.
- Their horizon is year 2150, where total population becomes stationary. Indeed, using Fair-Taylor (1983) algorithm implies that the horizon of the prospects should be long enough.
- The migratory balance is supposed to decrease gradually until it reaches and stabilises at zero. Of course, changes in net migration flows may alter drastically the demographic scenario; but this scenario is convenient as a benchmark.

The demographic projections by the World Bank are based on rather standard assumptions regarding fertility, mortality, and international migration. Fertility rates are assumed to move up, from year 2000, to the replacement rate by year

[6] For the UN projections see: *World Population Prospects: Estimates and Projections as Assessed in 1982,* UN, New York 1985. The assumptions and results of the OECD projections are described in *Ageing Populations: The Social Policy Implications,* OECD, Paris, 1988. The IMF estimations can be found in Heller, P.S., R.Hemming and P. Kohnert, *Aging and Social Expenditure in the Major Industrial Countries, 1980-2025,* IMF Occasional Paper n° 47, IMF, Washington, 1986. For the World Bank projections which have been used in this paper see *World Bank Development Report 1992,* World Bank, Washington.

2030. Mortality rates are based on recent trends in life expectancy until 2030 and assumed to remain constant hereafter. The international migration rates are extrapolated from past and present evolutions of migration trends and policies, and their net level is assumed to reach zero by year 2025. In the long run, the birth and death rates become constant, the net migration rate is held to zero, total population stabilises and the age structure becomes steady. Table 2.1 summarises the observed (from 1965 to 1990) and projected (from 1990 to 2160) evolution of the corresponding rate of growth of total population.

Table 2.1. Demographic Trends in the Seven Major Economies: 1965-2160. Annual average growth rate of population (%)

	1965-1980	1980-1990	1990-2000	2000-2030	2030-2060	2060-2160
Canada	1.3	1.0	0.8	0.4	0.0	0.0
France	0.7	0.5	0.4	0.2	-0.1	0.0
Germany	0.3	0.3	0.2	-0.1	-0.3	0.0
Italy	0.5	0.2	0.1	-0.2	-0.4	0.0
Japan	1.2	0.6	0.3	0.0	-0.3	0.0
U.K.	0.2	0.2	0.3	0.2	0.0	0.0
U.S.A.	1.0	1.0	0.8	0.5	0.1	0.0

Source: World Bank, 1992.

Table 2.2 shows the evolution, from 1990 to 2050, of total population and of the demographic structure in the seven major economies. Note that the population of Italy is projected to increase only marginally in the course of the present decade. After year 2000 it is projected to decline and may, by 2050, have fallen to some 50.4 million. As far as Germany and Japan are concerned, their populations are projected to peak respectively at around 81.5 million in 2005 and 130 million in 2010 and to decline marginally during the subsequent 40 years. The perspective of this decline contrasts sharply with the projections for Canada, France, the United States, and the United Kingdom whose populations are forecasted to increase throughout the next 60 years.

In the long run, demographic trends can be summarised as follows:

- in Canada and the U.S.A., total population stabilises at a relatively high level (20 to 30 % above the initial one) after having raised sharply at the beginning of the transition period.
- for a second group of countries including France and the United Kingdom, a similar phenomenon prevails but it is much less marked; after year 2050, total population stabilises at a level somewhat 10 % above the initial one.
- the remaining economies (Germany, Japan, Italy) are characterised by a final level of total population noticeably below the initial one (-10 % for the first two countries and -20 % for the last one).

Whatever the evolution of total population over the transition period (1990 to 2050), the share of 0-19 age-group in the population will decline by 1 to 6 percentage points and conversely the share of 60 and more age-group in the population will increase by 9 to 17 percentage points. The corollary of this phenomenon is a decrease of the share of 20-59 age group in total population in all these countries. At this point, three remarks can be made:

- In all the countries under consideration, ageing, defined as the increase of the share of elderly people (usually persons above 65 years of age) in total population, will increase considerably. This pronounced ageing will be accompanied by a steep increase of the so-called old-age dependency ratio i.e. the number of elderly persons in proportion to the number of those in active age-groups during the next 50 years. According to the projections of the World Bank (see Figure 2.2), there will be in year 2040:
  - 1.5 working-age individual for one retired in Canada whereas they were 3.7 in year 1990;
  - 1.4 working-age individual for one retired in France whereas they were 2.9 in year 1990;
  - 1.2 working-age individual for one retired in Germany whereas they were 2.9 in year 1990;
  - 1.1 working-age individual for one retired in Italy whereas they were 2.7 in year 1990;
  - 1.2 working-age individual for one retired in Japan whereas they were 3.2 in year 1990;
  - 1.7 working-age individual for one retired in the U.K. whereas they were 2.6 in year 1990;
  - 1.7 working-age individual for one retired in the U.S.A. whereas they were 3.3 in year 1990.
- The profiles of the so-called youth dependency ratios, i.e. the number of children in proportion to the number of those in active age-groups, are much flatter than the ones of the old-age dependency ratios and the long term equilibrium values of the former ratios are almost the same (see Figure 2.3). This is due to the assumed convergence of the fertility rates in these countries and the hypothesised zero-value of migratory balances at the end of the transition period.
- The youth dependency ratio is generally [7] U-shaped from year 1990 to year 2040; it, first, decreases due to the fall of the fertility rate and then increases, when this rate grows again; as far as the economic burden of the non-working generations is concerned, the evolution of the youth dependency ratio, thus, partially balances, at the beginning of the period, the effects of the one of the old-age dependency ratio; on the contrary, it, later, emphasises these effects

[7] This is the case for all countries but Germany and United Kingdom.

and has no more influence after year 2040 since the youth dependency ratio stabilises. These phenomena are somewhat marked but for Japan and Italy. Whatever the profile of the youth dependency ratio between 1990 and 2040, no real compensation can be expected, in the long run, between the evolutions of the two dependency ratios. Note that for the United Kingdom the youth dependency ratio is almost flat (i.e. has almost no influence, even between year 1990 and 2040 on the financial burden of the non-working generations) and that, for Germany, the youth dependency increases markedly from 1990 to 2040, since the fertility rate simultaneously increases (the present level is a minimum).

Table 2.2. Demographic Structure in the Seven Major Economies: 1990-2050. (Total population in million, others in percent of total population)

2.2.a. Canada

	1990	1995	2000	2005	2010	2020	2030	2040	2050
Total Population	26.5	27.9	29.2	30.3	31.2	32.7	33.8	34.0	33.7
Less than 20 years	29.0	28.2	27.3	26.2	25.3	23.7	23.3	23.1	23.2
Between 20 and 59 years	55.8	56.0	56.1	55.8	54.4	50.4	46.5	46.0	46.2
60 years and more	15.2	15.8	16.6	18.0	20.3	25.9	30.2	30.9	30.6

2.2.b. France

	1990	1995	2000	2005	2010	2020	2030	2040	2050
Total Population	56.4	57.7	58.8	59.8	60.7	62.0	63.0	63.1	62.5
Less than 20 years	27.6	26.2	25.6	24.9	24.1	23.2	22.9	22.9	23.1
Between 20 and 59 years	53.5	54.1	54.1	54.4	52.8	50.0	47.0	45.9	45.7
60 years and more	18.9	19.7	20.2	20.7	23.1	26.8	30.1	32.2	31.2

2.2.c. Germany

	1990	1995	2000	2005	2010	2020	2030	2040	2050
Total Population	79.5	80.5	81.1	81.5	81.3	80.4	79.1	77.2	74.4
Less than 20 years	22.1	22.0	22.3	21.9	21.3	20.4	21.3	21.8	22.4
Between 20 and 59 years	57.7	56.8	54.1	52.6	52.3	49.2	43.4	43.9	45.1
60 years and more	20.2	21.1	23.7	25.5	26.5	30.4	35.3	34.2	32.5

2.2.d. Italy

	1990	1995	2000	2005	2010	2020	2030	2040	2050
Total Population	57.7	57.9	58.0	57.9	57.6	56.2	54.7	52.8	50.4
Less than 20 years	24.1	21.3	19.8	19.4	19.3	19.0	19.3	20.4	21.2
Between 20 and 59 years	55.4	56.3	56.0	55.2	53.3	50.4	44.7	41.2	42.3
60 years and more	20.6	22.4	24.2	25.5	27.4	30.6	35.9	38.4	36.5

2.2.e. Japan

	1990	1995	2000	2005	2010	2020	2030	2040	2050
Total Population	123.5	125.7	127.6	129.2	130.0	129.0	126.3	122.7	119.7
Less than 20 years	26.5	23.4	21.6	20.9	20.7	20.6	20.6	10.6	22.0
Between 20 and 59 years	56.1	56.5	55.7	53.6	50.4	48.0	46.3	43.4	43.6
60 years and more	17.3	20.1	22.7	25.5	29.0	31.4	33.0	35.1	34.4

2.2.f. U.K.:

	1990	1995	2000	2005	2010	2020	2030	2040	2050
Total Population	57.4	58.3	59.1	59.7	60.3	61.5	62.7	62.9	62.8
Less than 20 years	25.7	25.5	25.4	25.7	25.1	23.7	23.7	23.6	23.5
Between 20 and 59 years	53.5	53.9	53.3	52.9	51.9	50.7	46.7	46.6	46.9
60 years and more	20.8	20.6	20.7	21.4	23.0	25.5	29.6	29.8	29.6

2.2.g. U.S.A.:

	1990	1995	2000	2005	2010	2020	2030	2040	2050
Total Population	250.0	261.9	272.8	282.5	291.3	307.5	319.3	323.6	324.1
Less than 20 years	29.5	29.0	28.5	27.5	26.5	24.9	24.4	23.9	23.8
Between 20 and 59 years	54.3	54.8	55.2	55.3	54.4	50.6	47.4	47.4	47.3
60 years and more	16.2	16.2	16.3	17.2	19.1	24.5	28.2	28.7	28.9

Source: World Bank, 1992.

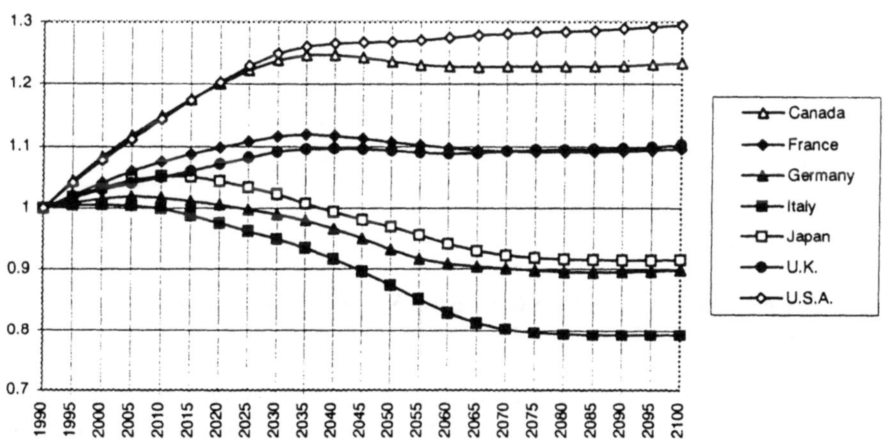

Fig. 2.1. Total Population (1990 = 1).

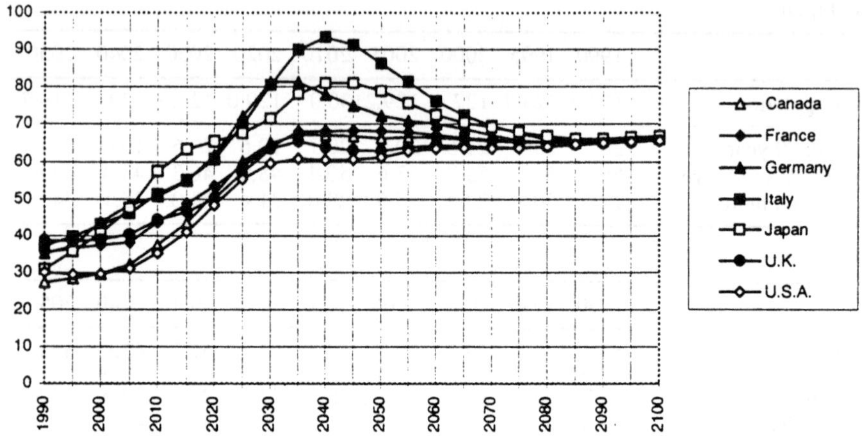

Fig. 2.2. Old Age Dependency Ratio (%).

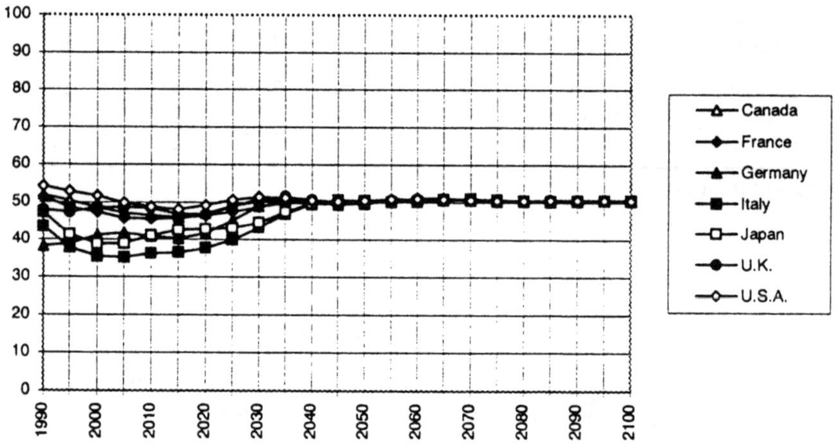

Fig. 2.3. Youth Dependency Ratio (%).

2.2.2 A Brief Overview of Public Pension Systems in the Seven Major Economies

We now turn to a brief description of the public pension systems in the seven major economies. Numerous and various public pension schemes coexist in these countries. They are financed either on a PAYG basis or by funds. The former mode of finance, adopted in Canada, France, Germany, Italy, and United Kingdom, ensures that, in any fiscal year, the current pension contributions of working population match the pension benefits given to the currently retired, whatever the value of their past contributions. The latter mode of finance, adopted in Japan and the United States, implies that expenditures and receipts have to balance over the life-span of the scheme. All members of the Fund are working and contributing. The retirement benefits are paid from contributions and interest earnings.

It is worth noting that, at present, in Japan, the main programme, called Koei-Nenkin-Hoken (KNH) scheme, operates on a PAYG basis since present contribution rates match current benefits while interest earnings are entirely used to accumulate further assets. It held assets of around 18 per cent of GDP at the end of 1990. Similarly, in the United States, at the end of 1990, the most important public scheme called Old-Age Survivors and Disability Insurance (OASDI) and the other public pension funds held respectively assets of around 4 per cent and 19 per cent of GDP. A detailed description of the pensions formulas and the financing of public pension systems in the countries under consideration [8] is beyond the scope of this paper. But a summary of the main features of the current schemes is given in Table 2.3. Despite these differences, almost uniform assumptions across countries will be made. Details are given in the next Section.

Table 2.3. A Summary of Pension Formula for General Old-Age Benefit Schemes in the Seven Major Economies in 1988

	Canada	France	Germany	Italy	Japan	U.K.	U.S.A.
Retirement Age:							
Statutory (M/F)	65/65	60/60	65/65	60/55	60/55	65/60	65/65
Average (M/F)	65.1/65.1	62.4	62.0/60.9	61.2	62.3/60.6	65.4/60.4	63.6/63.3
Minimum Contribution Period	10	10	5	15	25	1/4th of W.L.*	10
Contribution Period for Full Pension	40	37.5	40	40	40	50	35
Maximum Replacement Rate	25 %	50 %	60 %	80 %	30 %	20 %	41%
Indexation of Benefits on:	Prices	Wages	Wages	Prices and Wages	Prices and Wages	Prices	Prices

* W.L. means Working Life.
Source: OECD, 1988.

[8] For details, see *Reforming Public Pensions*, OECD, 1988.

2.3 Modelling the Seven Major Economies

2.3.1 The Model

Three agents are considered: households, firms, and a public sector.

2.3.1.1 Firms

A representative firm is assumed to operate on perfectly competitive markets. It produces a single good which can be consumed or invested. The production function is of the Cobb-Douglas type, with constant returns to scale. Technical progress is labour augmenting and its rate is constant. Productive capital depreciates at a constant annual rate. In equilibrium, the firm's profit is zero, because of perfect competition and constant returns to scale. One must notice that no adjustment costs are introduced although transition paths are considered; for a justification of this omission see earlier works (e.g. Auerbach and Kotlikoff, 1987). The program of the representative firm reads:

$$\underset{K_t,\, L_t}{MAX}\ \Pi_t$$

$$\Pi_t = Y_t - \omega_t L_t - c_t K_t$$

subject to:

$$Y_t = A_t K^{\epsilon}_t \left(\prod_{i=1}^{t} (1 + g_i) L_t \right)^{1-\varepsilon}$$

where Π_t, Y_t,ω_t, L_t, c_t, K_t and g_t are profit, output, real wage rate, labour, real cost of capital, capital, and technical progress rate at time t; A_t is a scaling constant, and e is the constant capital share. The gross investment is given by:

$$I_t = K_{t+1} - (1 - d_t) K_t$$

where d_t, and I_t are respectively the rate of depreciation of capital, and gross investment at time t.

The reasons for the choice of a Cobb-Douglas function have already been discussed (Chauveau and Loufir, 1993); they are briefly as follows: first, it is easier to compare our results to other authors' ones (Auerbach and Kotlikoff, 1987, Auerbach, Kotlikoff, Hagemann and Nicoletti, 1991; Steigum, 1993) since they all chose a function of the Cobb-Douglas type. Second, if macroeconometric studies, especially in France, exhibit very low estimates of the substitution elasticity of capital with respect to labour, panel data studies suggest that this elasticity is almost unitary. Third, the robustness of the results with respect to the change of the production function has been established (see Cazes, Chauveau, Le Cacheux and Loufir, 1994).

The cost of capital is the sum of the real interest rate and the rate of depreciation of capital and the cost of labour is the gross wage rate including social contributions i.e. the net wage multiplied by one plus the sum of the employer's social contributions rates (health and family rate, and pensions rate). Both factor prices are perfectly flexible. In equilibrium, the former equalises the marginal productivity of capital, and the latter the marginal productivity of labour.

2.3.1.2 Households

The household sector comprises two kinds of individuals: children, who are pooled in four age groups [9] (0-4, 5-9,...,15-19 years) and adults who are grouped among fourteen generations: eight for the working population (20-24, 25-29,..., 55-59 years) and six for the retired (60-64,...,85-89 years). Only adults take economic decisions so that our model actually comprises fourteen overlapping generations.

At each period, individuals belonging to the youngest generation of adults (generation n°1) enter the labour market; they become, at this very time, parents; they will rear their children during four periods (20 years) and work during eight periods (40 years); when they are 8 periods old (i.e. 60-64 year old), they will receive a bequest left by their parents (i.e.75-79 year old people) and they, simultaneously, retire.

At each period, children and adults may die: when a child dies, the expenditures of the representative adult who was in charge of his/her rearing are reduced, at the next period, by the corresponding amount; when an adult dies, two polar cases must be distinguished:

- if, at his death, he/she was bringing children up, then:
  - adults belonging to his/her generation are put in charge of his/her children; these children will, later, inherit their adoptive parents;
  - his/her wealth is given to the adoptive parents of his/her children; this is a compensation for the adults in charge of orphans.
- if he/she is no more breeding children then his/her wealth is given to the adults belonging to his/her generation. These last assumptions are equivalent to a fair insurance mechanism. The life cycle of an individual can be schematised as follows:

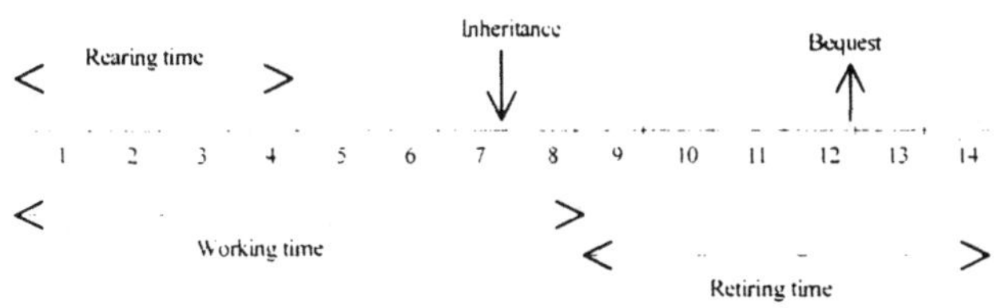

[9] Such a pooling has been done because taking into account periods of one year would have led to implementing a too large model.

Each representative grown-up individual entering the ath period of his life cycle at the beginning of period t determines the intertemporal profile of his/her consumption and leisure and the amount of the bequest he/she will leave according to the following program:

$$\underset{C_{j,t+j-a},\, l_{j,t-j-a},\, B_{12,t+12-a}}{\text{MAX}} \qquad E\,(Ua,\,t)$$

where lifetime utility function is:

$$E\left(U_{a,t}\right)=\frac{1}{1-\frac{1}{\gamma}}\sum_{j=a}^{14}\frac{s_{j,t+j-a}}{(1+\delta)^{j-a}}\left[C_{j,t+j-a}^{1-\frac{1}{\rho}}+\alpha_{j,t+j-a}\left(q_{j,t+j-a}l_{j,t+j-a}\right)^{1-\frac{1}{\rho}}\right]^{\frac{1-\frac{1}{\gamma}}{1-\frac{1}{\rho}}}$$

$$+\frac{1}{1-\frac{1}{\gamma}}\frac{\beta\, s_{12,t+12-a}}{(1+\delta)^{12-a}}B_{12,t+12-a}^{1-\frac{1}{\gamma}}$$

where $E[U_{a,t}]$ is expected intertemporal utility function of a representative grown-up individual entering the ath period of his life cycle at the beginning of period t, $C_{j,t+j-a}$, $a_{j,t+j-a}$, and $l_{j,t+j-a}$ are respectively consumption, leisure preference, and leisure in age-period j at time t+j-a, $B_{12,t+12-a}$ is bequest to offspring in age-period 12 at time $t+12-a$, $q_{j,t+j-a}$ is technical progress factor, γ is intertemporal elasticity of substitution, δ is time preference rate, ρ is intratemporal elasticity of substitution, β is bequest preference parameter and $s_{j,t+j-a}$ is the probability to survive such that:

$$s_{j,t+j-a}=\prod_{k=a}^{j}\left(1-\pi_{k,t+k-a}\right)$$

where $\pi_{k,t+k-a}$ is the probability of death before $t+k-a+1$ of a representative individual of generation j at $t+k-a$.

The intertemporal budget constraint reads:

$$CB_{a,t}=\sum_{j=a}^{14}\left[\prod_{s=a}^{j}\frac{s_{j,t+j-a}}{1+r_{t+s-a}\left(1-\bar{\tau}_{s,t+s-a}^{y}\right)}X_{j,t+j-a}\right]-\prod_{s=a}^{12}\frac{s_{12,t+12-a}}{1+r_{t+s-a}\left(1-\bar{\tau}_{s,t+s-a}^{y}\right)}B_{12,t+12-a}$$

$$+\prod_{s=a}^{8}\frac{s_{8,t+8-a}}{1+r_{t+s-a}\left(1-\bar{\tau}_{s,t+s-a}^{y}\right)}\frac{N_{12,t+8-a}}{N_{8,t+8-a}}\left(1-\tau_{t+8-a}^{b}\right)B_{12,t+8-a}+s_{a,t}A_{a,t}\left(1+r_t\left(1-\bar{\tau}_{a,t}^{y}\right)\right)=0$$

with:

$$X_{j,t+j-a}=\left(w_{t+j-a}e_{j,t+j-a}\left(1-l_{j,t+j-a}\right)\left(1-\theta_{t+j-a}^{s}\right)+PR_{j,t+j-a}\right)\left(1-\bar{\tau}_{j,t+j-a}^{y}\right)$$

$$+PA_{j,t+j-a}-C_{j,t+j-a}f_{j,t+j-a}\left(1+\tau_{t+j-a}^{c}\right)$$

where $CB_{a,t}$ is the difference between expected discounted earnings and expenses of a representative grown-up individual entering the ath period of his life cycle at the beginning of period t. $A_{a,t}$ is his/her wealth; $X_{j,t+j-a}$, $PR_{j,t+j-a}$, $PA_{j,t+j-a}$, $f_{j,t+j-a}$, $e_{j,t+j-a}$, and $\overline{\tau}^{y}_{j,t+j-a}$ are, respectively, pensions, family and health allowance benefits, "human capital" adjustment factor, equivalence scale, and average income tax rate in age-period j at time $t+j-a$. $N_{12,t+8-a}$ $(N_{8,t+8-a})$ is the number of adults belonging to generation 12 (8) in time period $t+12-a$ ($t+8-a$) and $B_{12,t+8-a}$ is bequest. r_{t+j-a} is real interest rate at $t+j-a$, τ^{b}_{t+j-a} is inheritance tax rate, τ^{c}_{t+j-a} is V.A.T. rate, θ^{s}_{t+j-a} is employee's contribution rate, θ^{ms}_{t+j-a} is employee's health and family contribution rate, and θ^{rs}_{t+j-a} is employee's pension contribution rate. Finally, the non-negativity of the labour supply constraint reads:

$$l_{j,t+j-a} < 1, j = 1,14 \text{ and } a = 1,14$$

The first order conditions characterising the behaviour of consumers are given in the appendix.

In earlier CGEM-OG models, everybody was assumed to die with certainty, at a given age. Hence demographic trends depended on but one parameter-the number of birth- and important discrepancies appeared, between simulated and actual or projected pyramid-shaped diagrams. Allowing for variable life-expectancy rules out this drawback which, in earlier studies lead to non negligible errors for macroeconomic aggregates, fairness ratios and social welfare (for a comparison of the results of the two kinds of models see e.g. Chauveau and Loufir (1994a))[10]. To sum up, the behaviour of households obey the lifecycle theory (Ando and Modigliani, 1963, Modigliani, 1986), augmented for a bequest motive, for children being taken into account and for demographic uncertainty (Yaari, 1965, Merton, 1981).

2.3.1.3 Public Sector

The public sector has three separate branches: the government, which levies taxes and provides collective goods or services; a public health and family allowance department and a pensions department; these two departments provide health or family allowances or pensions and levy social contributions on wage incomes at a proportional rate.

---

[10] Since actual and projected demographic pyramid-shaped diagrams take into account migratory movements, it does not always happen that the size of generation i is strictly less than the size of generation $i-1$; the requirement that probabilities should be less than one can thus be violated. To rule out this drawback, we have, for very few observations, slightly corrected the migratory balance.

The government expenditures (G_t) are the sum of three elements:
(i) general administration spending ($G1_t$) ;
(ii) spending on education ($G2_t$) .
(iii) subsidies ($TRANS_t$) given either to households or to the public pensions department;

We assume that the per adult amount of general administration spending discounted by the technical factor (1+g) is constant and, similarly, that spending on education again discounted by the technical factor is proportional to the number of children; transfers are assumed to be proportional to total output. Hence:

$$G_t = G1_t + G2_t + TRANS_t$$

with:

$$G1_t = g_0\ (1+g)^t\ POP_t$$
$$G2_t = g'_0\ (1+g)^t\ CHI_t$$
$$TRANS_t = g''_0\ Y_t$$

where POP_t stands for total population, CHI_t for total children and Y_t for total output.

There are three taxes: a VAT (T_t^c) which is proportional to households' consumption, an inheritance tax (T_t^b) proportional to bequests and an income tax (T_t^y). There is no public debt since the budget is balanced. The first two tax rates are exogenous and constant, whereas the third one (the income tax rate) is adjusted so that total tax revenues equal total spending. We thus write:

$$G_t = T_t = T_t^c + T_t^b + T_t^y$$

with:

$$T_t^c = \sum_{a=1}^{14} N_{a,t} \tau_t^c C_{a,t} f_{a,t}$$

$$T_t^b = N_{12,t} \tau_t^b B_{12,t}$$

$$T_t^y = \sum_{a=1}^{14} N_{a,t} \bar{\tau}_{a,t}^y \left(w_t e_{a,t} (1 - l_{a,t})(1 - \theta_t^s) + PR_{a,t} + r_t A_{a,t} \right)$$

The budget of the public health and family allowance department is also balanced; hence:

$$\sum_{a=1}^{8} N_{a,t} \left(\theta_t^{ms} + \theta_t^{me}\right) \left(w_t \, i_{a,t} \left(1 - l_{a,t}\right)\right) = \sum_{a=1}^{14} N_{a,t} \, PA_t$$

where $PA_{a,t}$ stands for per-head allowance, $i_{a,t}$ for instantaneous labour efficiency, θ_t^{ms} and θ_t^{me} for the employers' and employees' contribution rates.

Social contribution rates are exogenous and total outlays adjust to them. Note that health and family expenditure are assumed to be indexed on technical progress so that in steady-growth equilibrium, their amount is a constant fraction of national income; we, therefore, assume that the ratio of health expenditure to national income will not, in countries such as France and Italy, go on growing but will stabilise; such a phenomenon has already been observed in many other OECD countries. The distribution of the allowances among individuals has been modelled according to available panel data [11].

Pensions are assumed to be uniformly distributed among the retired population which is assumed to include all individuals over the legal retirement age. We assume a continuing PAYG financing: matching flows of pension contributions and pension expenditure on a year-by-year basis. Public pensions are indexed on the contemporaneous average net wage. Hence:

$$\sum_{a=1}^{8} N_{a,t} \left(\theta_t^{rs} + \theta_t^{re}\right) \left(w_t \, i_{a,t} \left(1 - l_{a,t}\right)\right) + \chi_t \, TRANS_t = \left(\sum_{a=1}^{14} N_{a,t}\right) PR_t$$

where PR_t stands for per-head pension benefit, χ_t for the proportion of public subsidies allowed to the public pensions department, θ_t^{rs} and θ_t^{re} for the employers' and employees' contribution rates. To ensure that annual budgets are balanced, two polar assumptions can be made:

- the rates of social contribution θ_t^{rs} and θ_t^{re} of the currently working population are endogenously determined, given a level of per-head pension benefit PR_t, by the budget constraint of the pensions department; for the sake of simplicity and with no loss of generality, we assume that employers' and employees' rates are, again, proportional.
- the rates of social contribution θ_t^{rs} and θ_t^{re} of the currently working population are exogenous (and constant) and the per-head pension benefit PR_t is endogenously determined by the previous accounting equation.

[11] Actually we have used French data (Mizrahi and Mizrahi, 1985).

To sum up, households get three kinds of subsidies from the Public Sector:
- health and family allowances from the corresponding department;
- lump-sum transfers from the government ($(1-\chi_t)$ $TRANS_t$) and
- pensions benefits from the pension department.

2.3.1.4 Main Assumptions

Finally, seven major assumptions have been made: (A1) Expectations are rational and, since macroeconomic uncertainty is ruled out, they are exact. (A2) Technical progress is exogenous and neutral with respect to the choice between consumption and leisure. (A3) There is an adjustment factor characterising the time path of individual earnings i.e the seniority age profile of compensation. (A4) Consumption of children is complementary to their parents'. (A5) The effective age of retirement coincides with the legal one. (A6) At each period only one generation gives a bequest to one's heirs. (A7) The fair insurance mechanism is compulsory. Assumptions (A1) to (A6) have already been discussed in earlier works (see e.g. Chauveau and Loufir, 1993). Just recall that

- Assumption A1 is a standard one as far as long term equilibria are looked at. A "forward-looking" simulation method allowing for forecasts being realised, must be used. We chose the well-known, Fair and Taylor's method (1983) [12]
- Assumption A2 implies that, in the utility function, the instantaneous rate of substitution between discounted consumption and leisure is constant. Hence leisure is, here, multiplied by a technical progress factor [13], unlike in most other studies. The reason for such an assumption is that omitting this factor in the utility function and assuming a significantly positive rate of technical progress leads to a quite unrealistic solution of the program of the representative household; indeed, the representative individual would work very little at the beginning of his life, and far too much before retiring, since he/she knows he/she will become more and more productive. In addition, an excessive growth of individual consumption would characterise the corresponding lifetime profile. On the contrary, assuming the individual's utility is specified as above, leads to realistic lifetime profiles of consumption, labour and leisure.
- Assumption A3 is, again, a standard one; for its discussion see e.g. Auerbach and Kotlikoff (1987).
- Panel data [14] clearly indicate that the share of children's consumption in total households', while growing with age [15], is independent of the household's

[12] By using Troll software.

[13] $qj = (1 + g)j$ with j = age of the adult.

[14] e.g. Glaude and Moutardier (1991) for France.

[15] e.g. Bloch and Glaude, (1983) for France.

income, thus suggesting that complementarity holds (Assumption A4). Therefore, children's consumption are not arguments of the utility function, but the cost of child rearing is explicitly taken into account in the budget constraint of adults with dependent children. Equivalence scales account for the fact that such a cost depends on the child's age. In the budget constraint, the *f*'s are equivalence scales, i.e. one plus an indicator of the "cost of child rearing" (the *s*'s). These equivalence scales are uniformly applied to the countries under consideration. Unfortunately, such a way of doing does not lead to perfectly realistic profiles of consumption, labour and leisure if variable leisure preference (${}_j$) during the rearing of the children (j=1,4) is not assumed. Consequently, we have, as in earlier works (Chauveau and Loufir, 1993, Cazes, Chauveau, Le Cacheux and Loufir, hereafter CCLL, 1994) supposed that α_j was decreasing with j.

- Since variable retirement schemes are beyond the scope of this study, we can identify, without loss of generality, the legal and the average age of retirement. There is a remaining problem due to the scattering of average ages among the seven major economies (see below: *Calibration*).
- Assumption 6 is but a technical assumption, made for the sake of simplicity: it allows for easy comparisons with earlier works using "standard CGEM-OG " in which no alternative assumption could reasonably be considered.
- Assumption 7 is obviously the simplest way of ruling out macroeconomic risk together with introducing variable life-expectancy.

2.3.2 Calibration

For each of the seven countries, the parameters are adjusted in such a way that simulated aggregates match those observed between 1985 and 1989. Table 2.4.a provides, for each country the values of these parameters together with the values of exogenous variables. As shown on this table, all the parameters and exogenous variables are identical except for three of them:

- the annual time preference rate (δ);
- the preference for bequest (β);
- the parameter in the Cobb Douglas function (ε).

Note that the range in which each of these parameters varies is *realistic and moderate.*

As far as households are concerned, δ lies between 0.5 % and 1.5 % per annum: this contrasts with AKHN's surprising one which varies between -5.5 % and +1 %. Similarly the preference for bequest β lies between 0.42 and 0.70 which corresponds to a very reasonable spread.

Concerning firms, all the parameters are equal but the capital income share coefficient ε. It is worth 0.25 except for the United States and Japan for which its value is 0.20 or 0.30. One may thus conclude that with a narrow range of very few parameters (only three), such kind of model may take into account broad differences between national saving rates (from 17.8 % in the USA to 29.6 % in Japan); indeed these three parameters are key parameters allowing the calculated national saving rate to match the observed national saving rate (see Table 2.4.b).

With regard to the Public Sector's parameters and exogenous variables, and the endogenous ratios and macroeconomic variables on the other hand, they are chosen in accordance with average historical values (OECD data between 1985 and 1989). The goodness of the fit can be appreciated from Tables 2.4.b.

Table 2.4. Calibration

2.4.a. Parameters and Exogenous Variables

Parameters and Exogenous Variables	Canada	France	Germany	Italy	Japan	U.K.	U.S.A.
Households							
Annual time preference rate (δ)	0.0125	0.0150	0.0100	0.0100	0.0050	0.0150	0.0150
Intertemporal elasticity (γ)	0.95	0.95	0.95	0.95	0.95	0.95	0.95
Intratemporal elasticity (ρ)	1.20	1.20	1.20	1.20	1.20	1.20	1.20
Preference for leisure (α)							
for individuals of 21 to 40	0.550	0.550	0.550	0.550	0.550	0.550	0.550
for individuals of 41 to 90	0.792	0.792	0.792	0.792	0.792	0.792	0.792
Preference for bequest (β)	0.465	0.450	0.700	0.600	0.625	0.600	0.420
Firms							
Annual depreciation rate (δ)	0.05	0.05	0.05	0.05	0.05	0.05	0.05
Annual productivity growth rate (γ)	0.02	0.02	0.02	0.02	0.02	0.02	0.02
Share of capital	0.25	0.25	0.25	0.25	0.30	0.25	0.20
Public Sector							
V.A.T. rate (τ^c)	0.085	0.140	0.101	0.085	0.020	0.097	0.036
Average tax rate (τ^y)	0.275	0.195	0.205	0.202	0.235	0.260	0.208
Bequest's tax rate (τ^b)	0.000	0.044	0.014	0.010	0.061	0.031	0.035
Social contribution rate (θ^m)	0.043	0.151	0.082	0.045	0.078	0.015	0.054
Pension contribution rate (θ^r)	0.022	0.157	0.123	0.132	0.052	0.080	0.063
Replacement rate (trp)	0.222	0.618	0.550	0.644	0.296	0.355	0.276

Table 2.4. (cont.)

2.4.b. Endogenous Variables.
Simulated Values (average 1990-1994).
Observed Values (average 1985-1989)

Endogenous Variables	Canada	France	Germany	Italy	Japan	U.K.	U.S.A.
Annual real interest rate (%)	5.08	5.07	4.58	5.23	4.23	5.26	4.61
	5.36	*5.56*	*4.92*	*5.92*	*4.36*	*4.76*	*5.26*
Capital/Output ratio	2.50	2.50	2.60	2.60	3.30	2.40	2.10
	n.a.	*n.a.*	*n.a.*	*n.a.*	*n.a.*	*n.a.*	*n.a.*
Saving (Investment) rate	22.54	18.97	20.84	20.66	29.59	18.66	17.78
	21.70	*18.83*	*20.74*	*20.42*	*29.95*	*18.04*	*16.95*
Consumption/Output ratio	58.67	61.20	59.44	63.18	61.24	62.10	64.61
	58.64	*60.95*	*58.51*	*62.67*	*60.38*	*62.08*	*65.12*
Public expenditure/	18.79	19.83	19.72	16.16	9.17	19.24	17.71
Output ratio	*19.66*	*20.22*	*20.75*	*16.91*	*9.67*	*19.88*	*17.93*
Total taxes/Output ratio	33.59	43.50	37.04	36.36	29.58	36.50	28.82
	34.30	*44.14*	*37.76*	*36.32*	*29.32*	*37.20*	*29.64*
Taxes/Output ratio	28.76	24.21	23.12	23.26	20.38	29.87	20.14
	29.62	*25.04*	*23.82*	*24.00*	*20.86*	*30.50*	*20.94*
Total social contributions/	4.83	19.30	13.92	13.10	9.20	6.61	8.68
Output ratio	*4.66*	*19.08*	*13.96*	*12.30*	*8.50*	*6.72*	*8.70*
Pensions/output ratio	4.23	12.14	11.77	14.81	5.56	9.42	5.91
	4.05	*11.96*	*10.41*	*13.96*	*4.76*	*9.67*	*5.94*
Bequests/Output ratio	6.41	6.69	6.84	6.28	7.48	6.80	5.89
	n.a.	*n.a.*	*n.a.*	*n.a.*	*n.a.*	*n.a.*	*n.a.*

n.a.: not available.
Sources: OECD, 1992a. and b.

2.4 Simulation Results

The interplay of an ageing population and a PAYG financed pension system may raise important issues for governments in the coming decades. Many policies may be considered, among which six may be viewed as benchmarks: (i) holding constant the replacement rate; (ii) holding constant the contribution rate; (iii) lengthening the minimum contribution period; (iv) switching the indexation of benefits from wages to prices; (v) increasing the legal retirement and (vi) giving incentives to people for postponing the date of their actual retirement. The last four policies are beyond the scope of this study. Note that leaving aside the third and the fourth ones implies no real loss of generality, since they aim but at decreasing the replacement rate; therefore, they can be viewed as a combination of the two first benchmark policies. The last two policies are not, here, taken into account for two reasons; first, their macroeconomic effects, when valuated using a CGEM-OG model, appear to be huge, but the likelihood of these policies is somewhat questionable (for a discussion of the French case see Chauveau and Loufir 1994a). Moreover, a partial equilibrium frame is generally used when the last policy is looked at, for the sake of tractability (see e.g. Fabel 1994). To sum up, only two basic schemes are, in this paper, considered: (i) holding constant the replacement rate and (ii) holding constant the social contribution rate.

For each of the seven countries under review (Canada, France, Germany, Italy, Japan, United Kingdom, USA), two dynamic simulations have, thus, been undertaken: they are referred to as CCR or CRR, where CCR (CRR) stands for "Constant Contribution Rate" ("Constant Replacement Rate"). In addition, since any "standard" social security policy may be viewed as being intermediate between these two benchmarks, the economic effects or the welfare consequences of any policy can be valued in a very simple way by making a linear combination of the corresponding results belonging to the two polar options [16].

Of course, the assumption about the social security policy to be undertaken has to be coupled with an assumption about the rhythm of technical progress: indeed, we limit ourselves to the usual assumption that the corresponding rate is constant at the level of 2 % per year. The sensitivity of the solutions to the rate of technical progress has already been studied, for the French case by Chauveau and Loufir (1994b) [17].

---

[16] If non-linearities appear to be important when simulating a baseline account, they play no prominent role when comparing a scenario from baseline; a linear approximation appears to be convenient.

[17] Other results, especially for the U.S.A., have also been obtained: they are very similar to the French ones. Note that the rate of technical progress is assumed to slowly increase (decrease) to reach the steady-growth value of 3 % (1 %).

Recall that two antagonistic assumptions have been made, as far as the accounting framework is concerned: (a) each of the seven economies is assumed to be a closed economy or (b) there are six "small open economies dominated by the US economy". Perfect mobility of capital is assumed, i.e. the domestic rate of interest of each of the six countries must equalise the "world" rate of interest which is identified to the US one. This last assumption is made for the sake of simplicity. Indeed, a rigorous general equilibrium analysis should take into account the feedback of capital movements on the US rate of interest, the values of which should be different from one case to the other. For the sake of simplicity [18], we have neglected such a discrepancy which happen to be moderate [19].

Also recall that, whatever the country considered, the public pensions system is assumed to work on a PAYG basis and that, for the two countries [20] for which the public pension system is funded, it is implicitly assumed that the reserves held by the Japanese and US funds will increase by the amount of their interest receipts during the period under review. Alternative assumptions could have been selected, allowing for a mix between funded and unfunded pensions systems. Such a point of view has been taken into account, for studying the French case by Chauveau and Loufir (1994a).

We, now, turn to an important caveat. In this paper, the phrase "replacement rate" may be misleading. Indeed, we use a rather unusual definition for this rate because of the following accounting equality :

$$PR_t = trp_t\left(\sum_{a=1}^{8} N_{a,t}\left\{w_t\, i_{a,t}\,(1-l_{a,t})\right\}\right)/\left(\sum_{a=9}^{14} N_{a,t}\right)$$

where trp_t is the "replacement rate" and should be understood as an "instantaneous" replacement rate. However, one must recall that the usual definition TRP_t of a replacement rate reads:

$$\underset{b=9,14}{PR_{b,t}} = TRP_t\left(\sum_{a=1}^{8} N_{a,t-b+a}\left\{w_{t-b+a}\, i_{a,t-b+a}\,(1-l_{a,t-b+a})\right\}\right)/\left(\sum_{a=1}^{8} N_{a,t-b+a}\right)$$

[18] Memory-space.

[19] The algebraic sum of capital movements between the U.S.A. and the other countries is very small, relative to American output.

[20] Japan and the U.S.A.

2.4.1 The Case of Closed Economies

A comment of the consequences of the demographic transition on the future of public pensions in the seven "closed" economies is, now, given, using alternatively two points of view: (i) a long-term analysis is, first, carried out, paying attention to the values taken, in each country and for each scenario, by many important variables (macroeconomic outcomes or social welfare) at the beginning of the "final state". Although a steady growth equilibrium value is reached for almost all variables as early as year 2070, or, even year 2060, we shall use year 2100 for our long-term comparisons since a steady demographic growth occurs, in Italy, not before the end of the next century. (ii) A short-term analysis is, next, undertaken, exhibiting the transition paths of those macroeconomic variables, from year 1990 to 2050. Note that, since most variables fluctuate very little after year 2050, it is useless to give a comment of their evolution between these two dates [21]. The results of both analysis are relative to output, prices, saving rates, pensions, taxes, actuarial fairness and welfare.

2.4.1.1 Output

The evolution of the demographic structure appears to be the key-variable which determines the profiles of economic aggregates: the reason for this is twofold: (i) the value of any per-capita aggregate highly depends on the value of the ratio Working Population / Total Population which fluctuates much; (ii) it also depends on the values of three other variables: capitalistic intensity (i.e. the ratio $k_t=K_t/L_t$), average efficiency of labour supply and average working hours. Obviously, the average efficiency of labour depends but on demographic structure and on technical progress. As far as the third variable is concerned, one must notice that its value depends on the values of the prices of the two factors of production (the wage rate and the real interest rate) [22] which, in their turn, depend on the value of capitalistic intensity. This last variable depends, again, on demographic variables although its fluctuations remain moderate (see below).

In the long run, the demographic transitions occurring in the seven major economies imply that discounted per-head outputs [23] will tend to decrease (see Table 2.5a.). The differences between the initial values and the long-term equilibrium values of per capita output are all the more important as the old-age dependency ratios increase more. The CCR option leads to higher outputs than the CRR one, since the interest rates are markedly lower (see below). However, this is not the only reason for a higher output; indeed, since wages are somewhat higher,

---

[21] Moreover, the longer the horizon of the projection, the more fragile the result.

[22] See the first order conditions of the program of the representative consumer.

[23] The discount factor will be, as usual, the technical factor $(1/(1+g))$.

people also work more and, consequently, the difference between the two polar options is quite important. Note that the unfavourable effects, on per-head output, of the demographic transition are both important and sensitive to the scenario under review.

Table 2.5. Per Head Output, Long-Run Values, Closed Economy

a. not including technical progress

1990=1	Canada	France	Germany	Italy	Japan	U.K.	U.S.A.
CRR: Final value, 2100	0.91	0.87	0.82	0.85	0.88	0.92	0.91
CCR: Final value, 2100	0.95	0.94	0.89	0.92	0.94	0.96	0.95

b. including technical progress

1990=1	Canada	France	Germany	Italy	Japan	U.K.	U.S.A.
CRR: Final value, 2100	8.00	7.71	7.25	7.52	7.73	8.10	8.03
CCR: Final value, 2100	8.42	8.33	7.84	8.17	8.26	8.48	8.40

The fluctuations of discounted per-head outputs (see Figures 2.4a. and b.) essentially depend on the evolution of the ratios Working Population / Total Population. The same could be said about per-head labour supplies which are closely related to these ratios. In addition, note that for some countries, the beginning of the period is somewhat favourable, due to the initial fall of the youth dependency ratio combined with the initial stability of old-age dependency ratio.

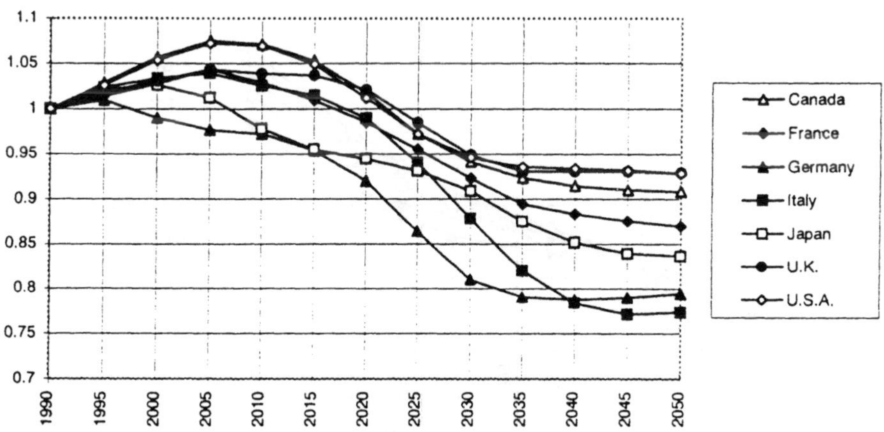

Fig. 2.4a. Per Head Output (not including technical progress, 1990 = 1), "Constant Replacement Rate" (CRR), Closed Economy.

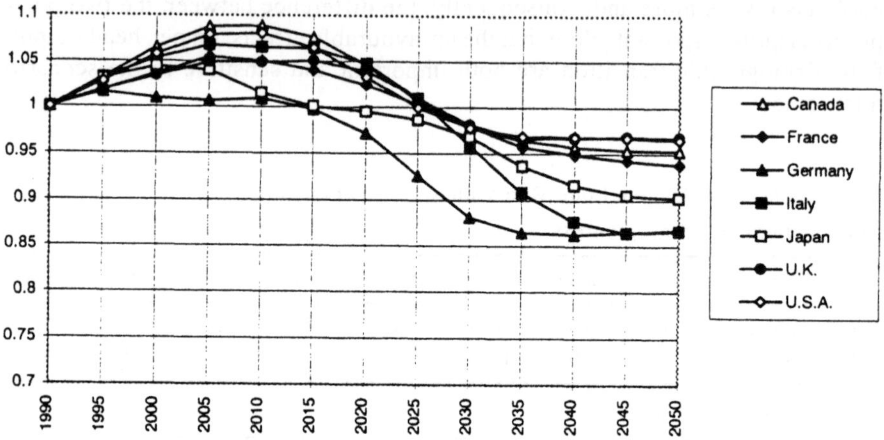

Fig. 2.4b. Per Head Output (not including technical progress, 1990 = 1), "Constant Contribution Rate" (CCR), Closed Economy.

The profiles of current per-head outputs (instead of discounted per-head outputs) are plotted on Figures 2.5.a and b. Since the rate of technical progress is not negligible, the paths of current outputs are always sloping upward. One must notice that, if the rate of technical progress were very low, a slump - i.e. a fall in current per-head output - could not be ruled out. However, such a contingency is unlikely to happen, since it requires very low values-almost zero values- for the rate of technical progress which are unrealistic.

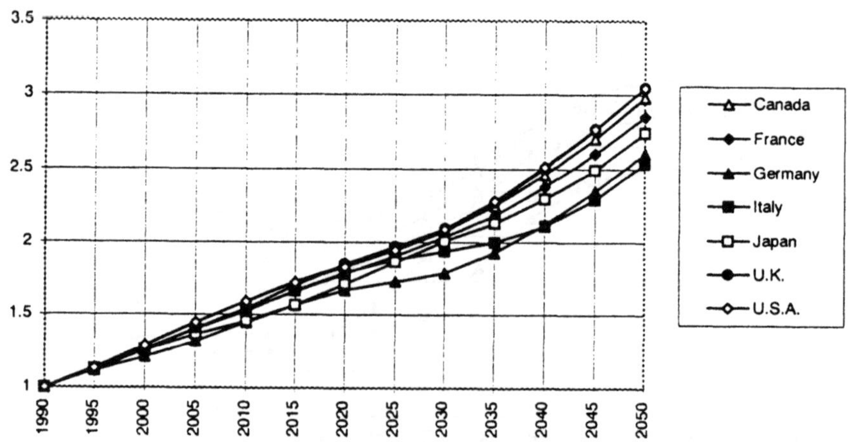

Fig. 2.5a. Per Head Output (1990 = 1), "Constant Replacement Rate" (CRR), Closed Economy.

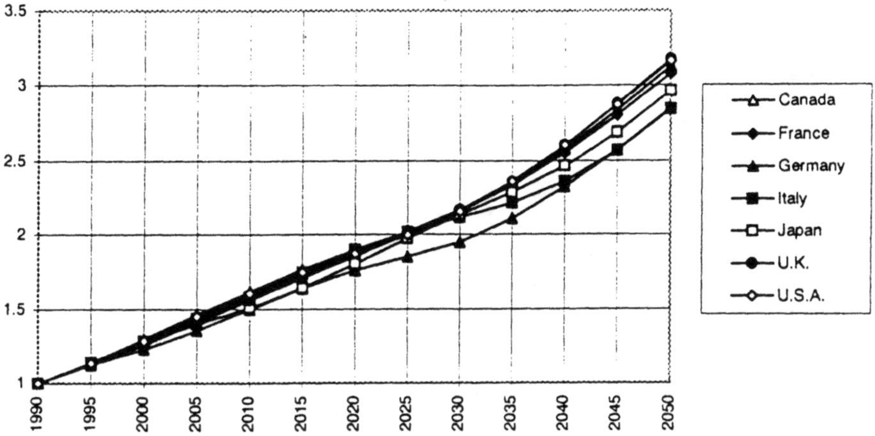

Fig. 2.5b. Per Head Output (1990 = 1), "Constant Contribution Rate" (CCR), Closed Economy.

2.4.1.2 Prices

During the demographic transition (1990-2100) real interest rates decrease more or less markedly, according to the country and the option considered. The CCR option leads to lower interest rates than the CRR one because households must, when the CCR option prevails, save much more than when the CRR does, since the benefits they will get during their retirement are much lower. This, in turn, tends to lower the rate of interest (see Table 2.6 and Figures 2.6.a and b). In the long run and if the U.S.A. are used as baseline, the differences are very small as far as Canada and Japan are considered; they are a little more important when Germany is looked at; they are quite substantial when France, Italy or the U.K. are under review.

Table 2.6. Real Interest Rate, Long-Run Values, Closed Economy

% per annum	Canada	France	Germany	Italy	Japan	U.K.	U.S.A.
CRR: Value in 1990	5.08	5.07	4.58	5.23	4.32	5.26	4.61
CCR: Value in 1990	5.12	5.10	4.60	5.25	4.38	5.28	4.63
CRR: Final value, 2100	3.68	4.72	4.02	4.76	3.12	4.28	3.41
CCR: Final value, 2100	3.03	3.84	3.10	3.55	2.46	3.72	2.70

Real interest rates, as well as real wages, fluctuate, from one country to another and from one option to the other, in a very similar manner. Indeed, capitalistic intensity can be shown to depend on the average efficiency of working population, since solving the equations characterising the equilibrium leads to a somewhat

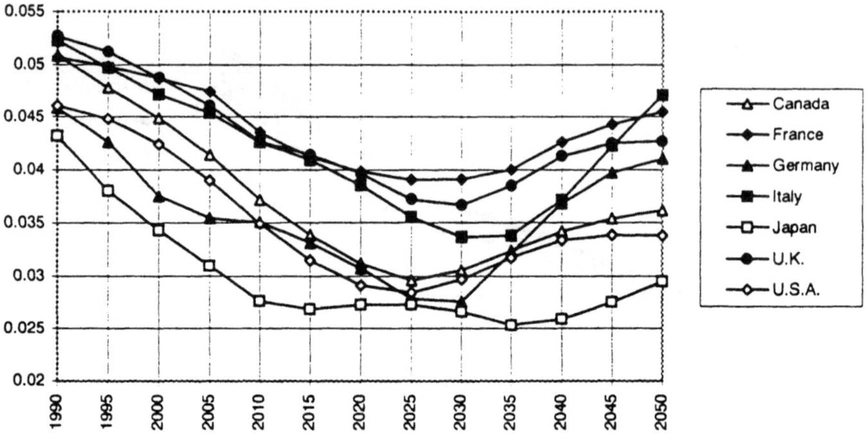

Fig. 2.6a. Real Interest Rate, "Constant Replacement Rate" (CRR), Closed Economy.

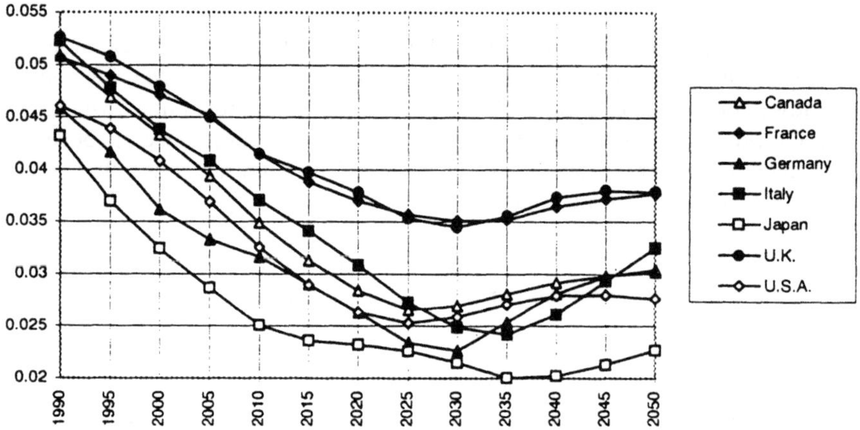

Fig. 2.6b. Real Interest Rate, "Constant Contribution Rate" (CCR), Closed Economy.

awkward expression of the k's in terms of the e's. Nevertheless, it is rather intuitive that a higher efficiency in labour will lead to a higher price of labour (i.e. an increase in the wage rate) and a lower price of capital (i.e. a decrease of the interest rate). The fluctuations of the wage rate (real interest rate) are moderate and parallel (opposite) to the ones of capitalistic intensity or of average efficiency of labour supply. This phenomenon is illustrated on Figures 6.a and b, where the profiles of real interest rates are plotted. The demographic transition does not affect all the countries identically: while the profiles of the interest rates in Canada, in Germany and in the U.S.A. lie in a tight range - the benchmark -, some gaps may become noticeable between, on the one hand, the rates in the remaining countries and, on the other, the rates of the benchmark. During the transition period (1990-2050), the British, the French and the Italian rates are markedly above the benchmark, while the Japanese one lies below. The German rate is, at the beginning of the period under review somewhat lower than the US one and, later, much higher.

2.4.1.3 Saving Rates

The life-cycle theory of saving assumes that people distribute their saving and consumption, over time and between themselves and their descendants, according to a system of preferences expressed in utility functions. According to this model, they save during their active lives to allow for a higher consumption during their retirement and to leave something to their descendants. A rise in the proportion of old people in the total population would therefore lead to a fall in households' overall saving rate and, consequently, in national saving rate. This phenomenon may be partially or totally offset by a decrease in the replacement rate which occurs when the CCR option is considered; indeed, holding constant the contribution rate when the old-age dependency ratio raises sharply, implies a steep decrease of the discounted per-head benefit which, in its turn, involves an increase of savings. Table 2.7 summarises the long run effects of the two polar policies.

Table 2.7. Saving (Investment) Rate, Long-Run Values, Closed Economy

%	Canada	France	Germany	Italy	Japan	U.K.	U.S.A.
CRR: Value in 1990	22.54	18.97	20.84	20.66	29.58	18.66	17.78
CCR: Value in 1990	23.40	19.75	22.02	22.24	31.40	19.00	18.42
CRR: Final value, 2100	19.57	17.19	18.81	18.43	25.52	18.03	16.24
CCR: Final value, 2100	21.41	19.20	21.26	20.93	27.92	19.47	18.02

The intertemporal profiles of the saving rates depend on those of the prices of the production factor; they are plotted on Figures 7a and b. They exhibit the following features:

- a slow increase till year 2005 or 2010 where it reaches its maximum value, except for Italy and Germany for which the profile is initially flat or eventually slightly decreasing;
- a substantial fall from year 2005 or 2010 to year 2030 or 2035 (or possibly 2040);
- a rise at the end of the period under review and, lastly, a stabilisation.

Note that, for Japan, the saving rate falls almost steadily, whatever the scenario considered.

Finally, recall that our model can explain huge differences among saving rates, with very few differences in the calibration process (see above Section 2.3.2.). In

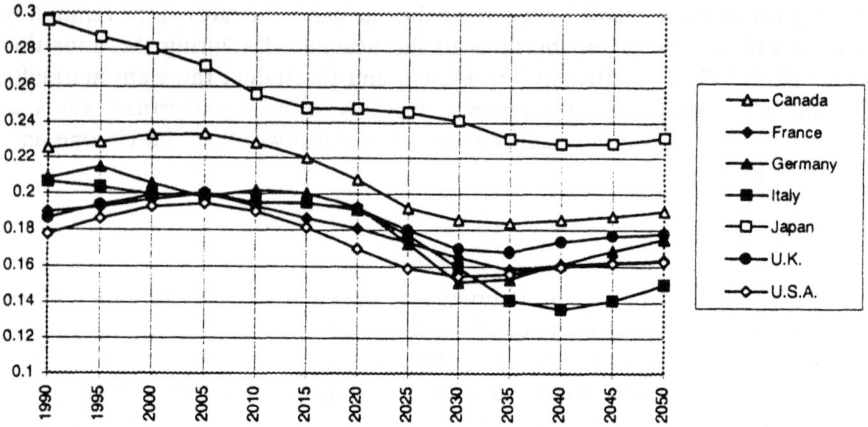

Fig. 2.7a. Investment (Saving) Rate, "Constant Replacement Rate" (CRR), Closed Economy.

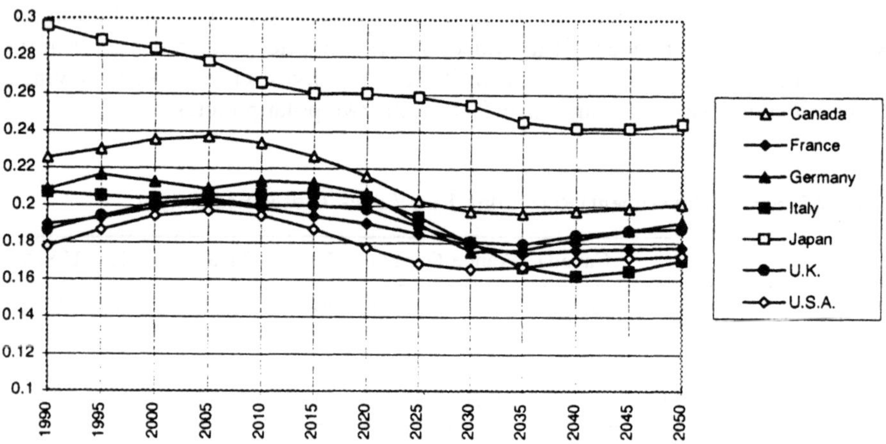

Fig. 2.7b. Investment (Saving) Rate, "Constant Contribution Rate" (CCR), Closed Economy.

addition, note that technical progress plays no role in the determination of the long-term equilibrium value of the saving rate. Only transitory distortions can be exhibited. These results are very intuitive since, in exogenous steady growth models, technical progress modifies but the rate of growth of aggregates (for details see Chauveau and Loufir 1994a).

2.4.1.4 Pensions

Pensions require a somewhat more detailed analysis.

Constant Replacement Rate

If the CRR option prevails, the increase of benefits induced by the increase in the total of the retired population must be compensated by an almost equivalent rise in pensions contributions, since public subsidies are quite moderate (see above). As these contributions are levied on wages, the profile of a contribution rate essentially depends on the evolution of two variables: (i) the old-age dependency ratio; (ii) the indexation of pensions on wages. Since we have assumed a perfect indexation of pensions on wages, the fluctuations of the pensions contribution rate (see Figure 2.8) are almost perfectly analogous to the ones of the old-age dependency ratio (see above Figure 2.2).

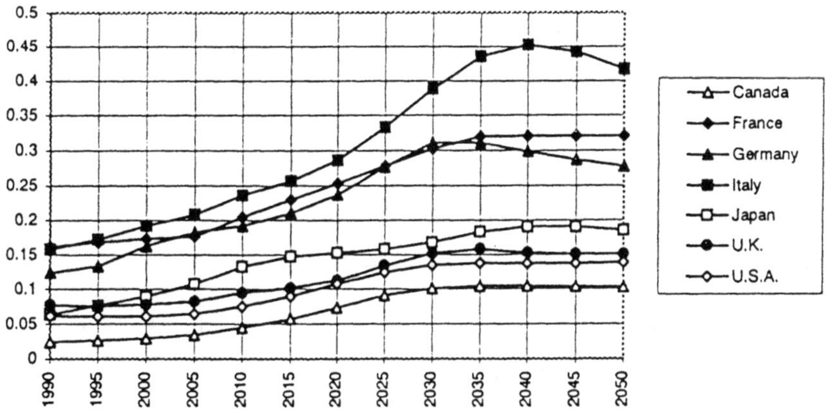

Fig. 2.8. Pensions Contribution Rate, "Constant Replacement Rate" (CRR), Closed Economy.

The long term effects of the demographic transition on the replacement rate are given in Table 2.8. The initial values of these rates are very low in Canada and Japan, moderate in the U.S.A. and in the U.K. and somewhat high in Germany Italy and France; these differences mainly reflect those in the size of the PAYG public pension system. One may notice that, whatever the country considered, contribution rates rise drastically; however, whereas the final values seem to be allowable for the U.S.A., Canada, Japan and the U.K., they are somewhat problematical for the other European countries, and especially for Italy and France.

Table 2.8. Pension Contribution Rate, Long-Run Values, Closed Economy

%	Canada	France	Germany	Italy	Japan	U.K.	U.S.A.
CRR: Value in 1990	2.43	16.17	12.42	15.78	6.44	7.76	6.22
CRR: Final value, 2100	10.29	31.12	25.33	31.50	15.57	15.76	14.88

Constant Contribution Rate

On the contrary, if the rate of contribution is held constant (see Table 2.9 and Figure 2.9), the replacement rate falls drastically as the contribution rate rises in the polar case. The cut in the replacement rate lies in the 60-80 % range, for all countries under review. Note that, at the very beginning of the transition period, the replacement rate is almost constant since the increase of total retired population is compensated by an equivalent increase of total working population.

Table 2.9. Replacement Rate, Long-Run Values, Closed Economy

%	Canada	France	Germany	Italy	Japan	U.K.	U.S.A.
CCR: Value in 1990	21.21	60.24	54.56	59.55	25.16	36.31	27.85
CCR: Final value, 2100	8.73	32.21	28.99	33.43	11.64	21.53	12.74

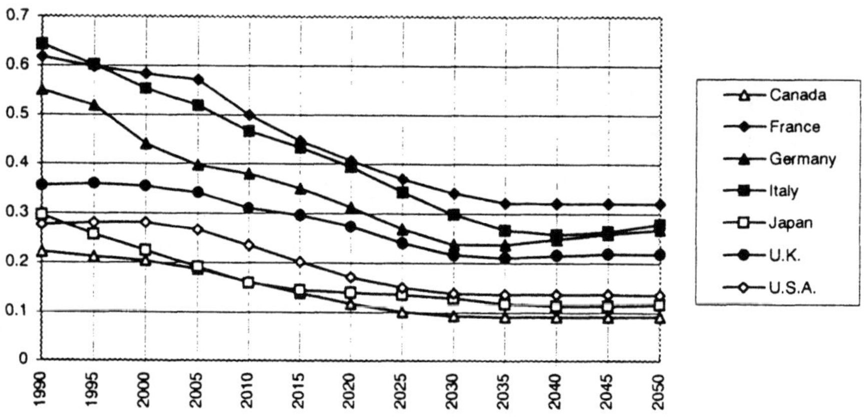

Fig. 2.9. Replacement Rate, "Constant Contribution Rate" (CCR), Closed Economy.

Discounted Per-Head Pension Benefits

A very important question must now be raised: if the rate of contribution is held constant, what will become of the level of per-head pension benefits? An elementary answer to this question is to underline that the retired are much better off in the CRR scenarios than in the corresponding CCR ones, mainly due to the differences, for the two scenarios considered, between the profiles of the replacement rate. However, a more detailed answer can be given, requiring that the way how per-head pension benefits are clearly defined.

If benefits are discounted with the technical factor (see Table 2.10a.), holding constant the contribution rate (CCR) induces a marked decrease of their level.

Such a decrease is more marked for Canada, Japan and the U.S.A. than for European countries and especially the United Kingdom. On the contrary, with the antagonistic scenario (CRR), the retired are, in Canada, Japan, the U.S.A. and the U.K., almost as well-off as they initially were. However, they are somewhat worse off in the remaining countries: Germany, France and Italy.

As a consequence, the spread between the long-term values of per-head pension benefits is wide for Canada (0.54) for the U.S.A. (0.47) and Japan (0.45) and less important for the U.K. (0.32), Germany (0.31), France (0.30) and Italy (0.27). Of course, this spread depends on the long-term values of three variables: the instantaneous replacement rate, the average discounted net wage and the old-age dependency ratio; indeed, the level of discounted per-head pensions is the product of these three variables.

Table 2.10. Per Head Pension, Long-Run Values, Closed Economy

a. not including technical progress

1990=1	Canada	France	Germany	Italy	Japan	U.K.	U.S.A.
CRR: Final value, 2100	1.01	0.89	0.90	0.89	0.98	0.98	0.98
CCR: Final value, 2100	0.47	0.59	0.59	0.62	0.53	0.66	0.51

b. including technical progress

1990=1	Canada	France	Germany	Italy	Japan	U.K.	U.S.A.
CRR: Final value, 2100	8.96	7.82	7.97	7.88	8.63	8.65	8.65
CCR: Final value, 2100	4.19	5.17	5.21	5.50	4.67	5.81	4.50

If replacement rates were held constant (CRR option), levels of discounted per-head pensions, for most countries, would first increase, due to the corresponding increase of wage rates. They would, next, decrease, more or less markedly and owing to the fall of contribution rates and, finally, either increase (if replacement rates would diminish more slowly and if wage rates would go on increasing) or just stabilise. If contribution rates (CCR option) were held constant, levels of per-head pensions would sharply fall, since replacement rates would decrease steeply.

Finally, note that a higher rate of technical progress leads to greater per-head pensions since technical progress influences the level of per-head pension benefits through the wage rate. Whatever the country considered, the long term effect of an increase of the rate of technical progress from 2 % to 3 % per year leads to a relative increase of the level of discounted per-head pensions of about 1 %. (see Chauveau and Loufir 1994a).

Current Per-Head Pension Benefits

When discounted benefits are considered, an implicit criterion is used for appraising the situation of the retired: their relative standard of living. Another point of view is to look at the evolution of the absolute level of their standard of living, i.e. to consider current benefits. Whereas the CRR option leads to an almost steadily increasing profile of the level of current per-head pension benefits, the CCR option induces some important inflexions of the profile of their level (see Table 2.10b. and Figures 2.10.a and b.).

In contrast with the results for current per-head output, a fall in the level of current per-head pension benefits can no more be ruled out, even with the CRR option, if the rate of technical progress is not high enough. Two "allowability rules" may, thus, be thought of:

(i) set that the level of per-head pensions should never be lower than its initial level (1990=1), or;

(ii) offset scenarios in which a decrease in the level of current per-head pensions may happen. Such a rule implies that the standard of living of the retired should always grow. The following tables show the floor-values of the rate of technical progress compatible with the two "allowability rules".

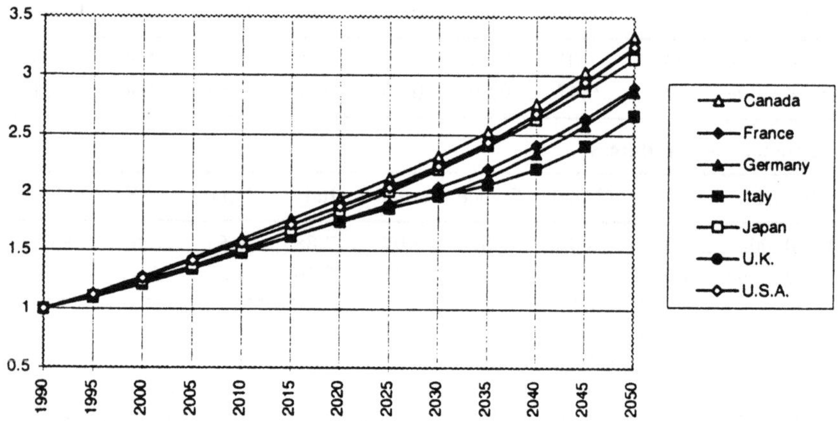

Fig. 2.10a. Per Head Pension (1990 = 0), "Constant Replacement Rate" (CRR), Closed Economy.

Table 2.11a. shows that both options are, for most countries, allowable if the rate of technical progress is, as usually thought, about 2 %. A major exception is Japan, for which the CCR option should be ruled out. Moreover, note that the CCR scenario is riskier than the CRR one since the floor-values of the rate of technical progress for the former option are much higher and much more likely than the corresponding ones for the latter. To sum up, if the first allowability rule is considered, the CCR option should be ruled out, undoubtedly, for Japan, and for the sake of safety, for Canada and Germany.

If the second rule were lay down, the CCR option should be ruled out for almost all countries (see Table 2.11b.) The cases of France and of the United Kingdom, for which the floor-value of technical progress is but slightly above 2 % remain

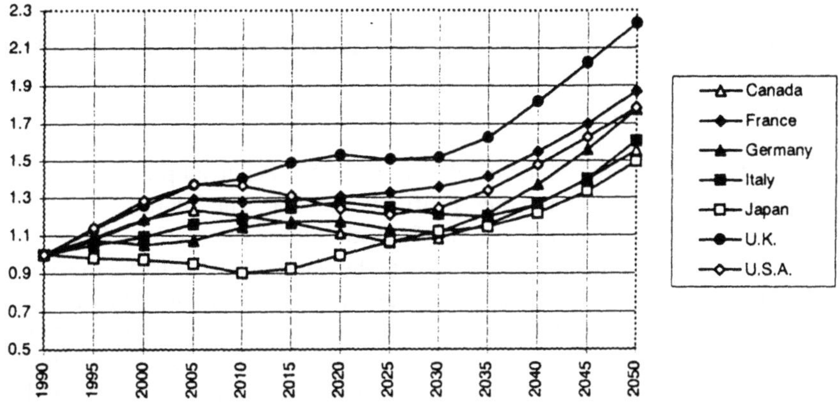

Fig. 2.10b. Per Head Pension (1990 = 0), "Constant Contribution Rate" (CCR), Closed Economy.

questionable. Actually, the latter rule is not very likely to be lay down, since it is too much binding; indeed, it would rule out all options which are not close enough to the CRR benchmark.

Table 2.11. Floor Values of the Rate of Technical Progress, Closed Economy

a. Rule n° 1

%	Canada	France	Germany	Italy	Japan	U.K.	U.S.A.
CRR	0.00	0.20	0.27	0.36	0.07	0.02	0.02
CCR	1.60	1.10	1.53	1.43	2.01	0.83	1.28

b. Rule n° 2

%	Canada	France	Germany	Italy	Japan	U.K.	U.S.A.
CRR	0.27	0.50	0.83	1.01	0.22	0.32	0.28
CCR	3.00	2.25	2.78	2.61	3.07	2.32	3.11

2.4.1.5 Taxes

We, now, turn to taxes. Two points of view will be alternatively used: we shall first take into account taxes levied by the government (i.e. strictly speaking taxes), and we shall, next, refer to total taxes, i.e. we shall consider taxes and social contributions as a whole.

Taxes Levied by the Government

Before considering the profile of the average income tax rate, recall that public expenditures (G) are the sum of three components: (i) general administration spending which is proportional to total population (per capita spending is held constant); (ii) spending on education which is proportional to the total of children and (iii) transfers which are proportional to output (Y). Per-head public expenditures are, thus, almost constant and their profile is very flat. The fluctuations of this ratio but depend on those of the ratio (total of Children/total Population). However, the ratio (G/Y) fluctuates much more since it is the quotient of the former ratio by the per-head output. Its fluctuations, which are opposite to the ones of per-head output must be compensated by those of taxes, and, essentially, of the average income tax since: (i) taxes are equal to expenditures;(ii) the other taxes (essentially VAT) are proportional to output and (iii) the basis on which income tax is levied is also approximately proportional to output.

The profile of the average income tax rate (see Figures 2.11a. and b.) is, thus, as follows: for most countries (USA, Canada, France, Italy and the UK) it first slowly decreases from year 1990 to a minimum value which is reached in year 2005 or 2010. It, then, rises somewhat sharply up to year 2035 or 2040 and later stabilises, near its long-term equilibrium value. Such an evolution is similar to the one of the ratio public expenditure /output; however, it is obviously more marked. As far as Japan and Germany are concerned, the average tax rate never decreases; it grows almost steadily in the former country whereas there is a sharp raise of the rate in the latter.

Finally, note that the profile of the average income tax rate is almost independent of the option considered; however its long-term equilibrium value (see Table 2.12) is somewhat sensitive to the scenario in review; it is, for all countries, higher for the first benchmark (CRR) than for the second one (CCR). Moreover, a higher (lower) rate of technical progress would allow for lower (higher) tax pressure.

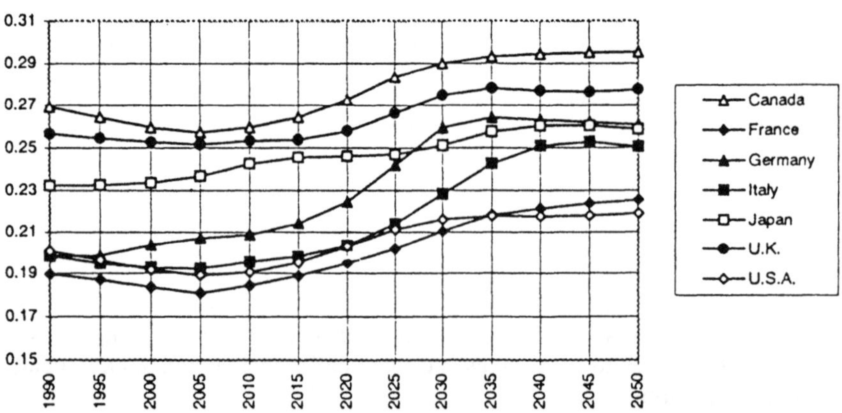

Fig. 2.11a. Average Tax Rate, "Constant Replacement Rate" (CRR), Closed Economy.

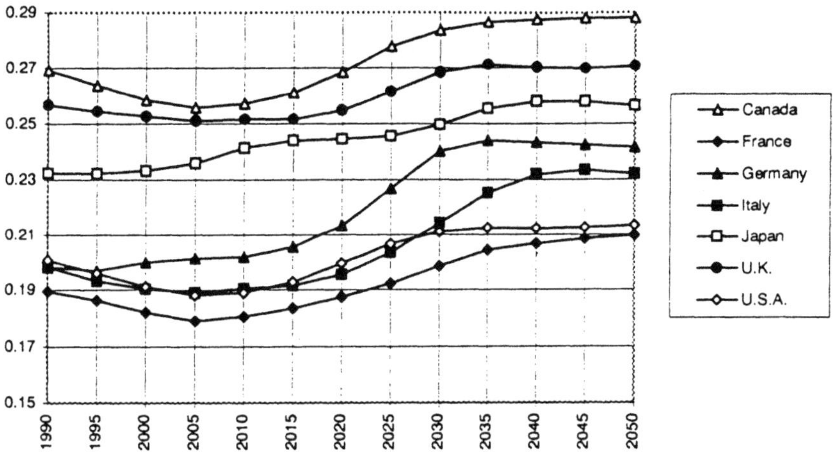

Fig. 2.11b. Average Tax Rate, "Constant Contribution Rate" (CCR), Closed Economy.

Table 2.12. Average Tax Rate, Long-Run Values, Closed Economy

%	Canada	France	Germany	Italy	Japan	U.K.	U.S.A.
Value in 1990	26.91	18.96	19.82	19.82	23.23	25.67	20.01
CRR: Final value, 2100	29.63	22.54	25.25	23.12	25.35	28.06	22.33
CCR: Final value, 2100	28.84	20.95	23.64	21.88	25.10	27.29	21.65

Total Taxes

It is also interesting to consider the ratio total taxes/output: total taxes are the sum of the taxes levied by the government and of the social contributions - pensions and health and family -; their profiles are plotted on Figures 2.12.a and b. Two cases must be distinguished:

(i) if a CRR option is considered total taxes appear to become a huge burden. This is due, essentially, to the profiles of pensions contribution rates which increase sharply after year 2005. Table 2.13 exhibits the long-term equilibrium values of total tax rates; France is undoubtedly the country for which this pressure is the strongest; it may be doubtful that French working population will tolerate such a pressure which increases from 43.5 % in year 1990 to 53.4 % at the end of the transition period; a somewhat similar phenomenon, although less pronounced, occurs in Italy and Germany and, to a less extent, in the United Kingdom; on the contrary the three remaining countries (Canada, Japan and the U.S.A.) appear to possess a marked margin.

(ii) with the CCR option, there is no problem of excessive tax pressure since the contribution rate is held constant. Finally, note that the previous results do not really depend on the rhythm of technical progress (see Chauveau and Loufir 1994a).

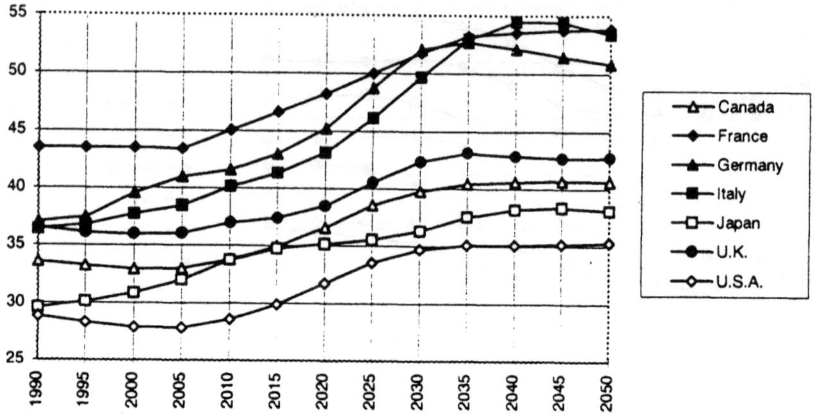

Fig. 2.12a. Total Taxes / Output (%), "Constant Replacement Rate" (CRR), Closed Economy.

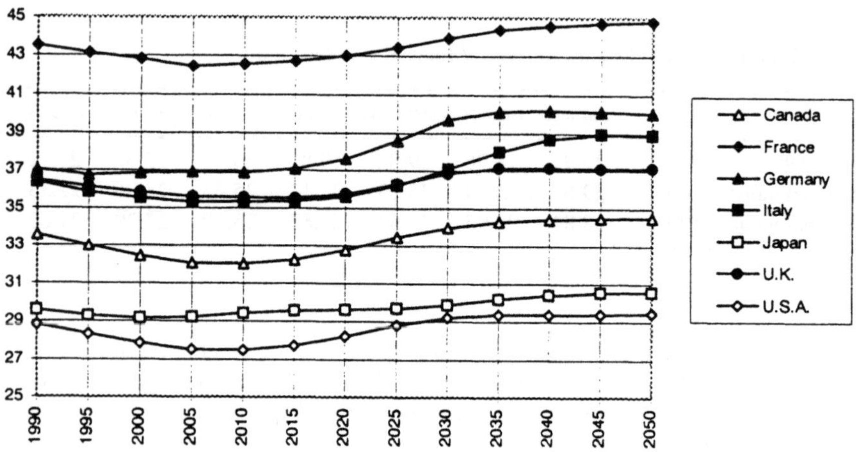

Fig. 2.12b. Total Taxes / Output (%), "Constant Contribution Rate" (CCR), Closed Economy.

Table 2.13. Total Taxes/Output Ratio, Long-Run Values, Closed Economy

%	Canada	France	Germany	Italy	Japan	U.K.	U.S.A.
Value in 1990	33.59	43.50	37.04	36.36	29.58	36.48	28.82
CRR: Final value, 2100	40.68	53.36	48.71	47.09	36.06	43.43	36.35
CCR: Final value, 2100	34.51	44.68	39.52	37.70	30.22	37.27	29.73

2.4.1.6 Actuarial Fairness

Up to now, social security policies have been valued with respect to per-head macroeconomic outcomes. We, now, analyse them from an actuarial fairness or social welfare point of view. Actuarial fairness is generally measured, for any individual or for any generation, by the ratio of the present value of lifetime benefits to the present value of lifetime contributions. A ratio equal to one corresponds to no intergenerational transfers. A ratio greater than one means a "positive" intergenerational transfer (from the "young" generations to the "old" ones). Symmetrically, a ratio less than one means a "negative" transfer. A "fair" system is reached when this ratio equals one. Of course the fairness of a system highly depends on the value of the interest rate since benefits are received much later than contributions are paid. When uncertainty is allowed for, expected benefits and expected contributions must be taken into account.

A first problem is to choose between two definitions of the fairness (or equity) ratio; (a) the numerator may refer to total pension benefits and the denominator may include contributions and public subsidies or (b) the numerator may take into account the difference between benefits and transfers and the denominator must include but contributions. From an empirical point of view, this does not really matter, since the values of the fairness ratio are almost independent of the chosen definition. It is also clear, from Table 2.14, that the long-term values of the fairness ratio are higher when the CCR option prevails than when the CRR one does. However the difference is moderate. In addition, as shown on Figures 2.13 a and b [24], the profiles of the fairness ratios are quite different according to the option under review: in CRR scenarios, these ratios decrease from a high initial value to a rather low minimum value; they, next, increase a little, steadily and slowly, since the minimum value is, for all countries, close to the corresponding long term equilibrium value. On the contrary CCR scenarios are characterised by a regular growth of fairness ratios, from an initial value which is markedly lower than the corresponding CRR value to a final value which is somewhat higher than the CRR long-term equilibrium value. Finally, note that the French ratios are low, due to the huge size of the social security system and high interest rates [25].

---

[24] Here, the dates on the X-axis refer to entries in the labour market.

[25] Since benefits are perceived later than contributions are paid, the higher the interest rate, the lower the fairness ratio and if the fairness ratio is less than unity, increasing both benefits and contributions leads to a lower ratio.

Table 2.14. Actuarial Fairness (Equity) Ratio, Long-Run Values, Closed Economy

	Canada	France	Germany	Italy	Japan	U.K.	U.S.A.
CRR: Value in 1990	1.33	0.83	0.92	0.86	1.13	0.93	1.28
CRR: Final value, 2100	0.79	0.57	0.71	0.66	0.90	0.67	0.79
CCR: Value in 1990	0.91	0.67	0.79	0.71	0.93	0.74	0.93
CCR: Final value, 2100	0.91	0.70	0.87	0.83	1.04	0.76	0.95

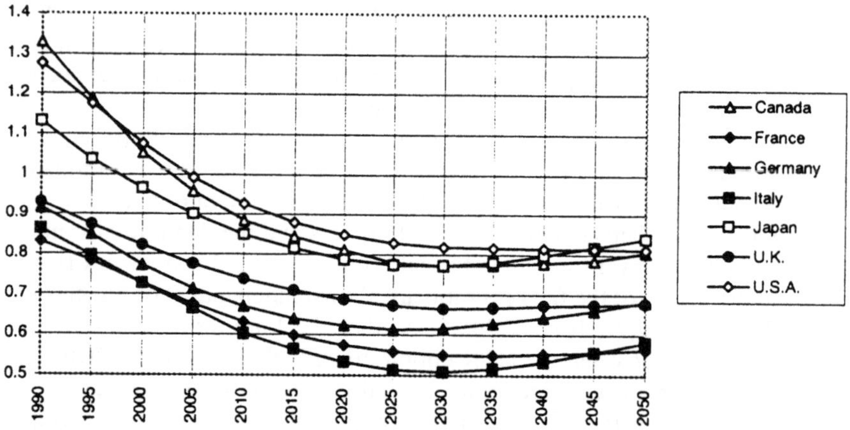

Fig. 2.13a. Actuarial Equity Ratio, "Constant Replacement Rate" (CRR), Closed Economy.

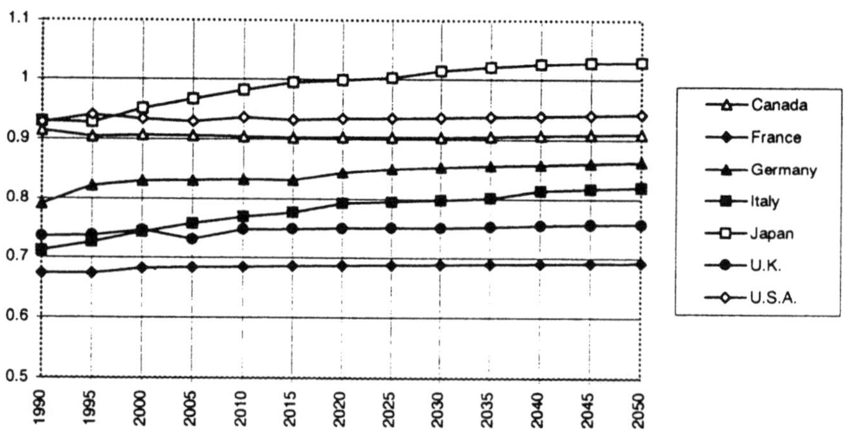

Fig. 2.13b. Actuarial Equity Ratio, "Constant Contribution Rate" (CCR), Closed Economy.

2.4.1.7 Social Welfare

Social security policies may also be appraised, by valuing the corresponding social welfare. Many definitions may be considered: according to Samuelson (1958,1959), one should consider the intertemporal utility of each generation; note that such a point of view is compatible with Pareto-efficiency. A preliminary remark must be made: many theoretical studies (see e.g. Breyer and Straub (1993)) point out that, with a standard overlapping-generations model, unfunded pension systems are Pareto-efficient unless one of the following assumption prevails:

(i) there is no utility attached to labour;
(ii) the contributions are levied in a lump sum fashion;
(iii) the benefits are actuarially fair, given the contributions.

In most empirical studies Pareto efficiency is reached since modifying the replacement rate or the contribution rate would lead to hurting some generation while improving the welfare; this is due to the fact that, in the first order conditions characterising the behaviour of households, the partial derivative of the per-head level of future pensions relative to current labour supply is but zero (see Appendix); indeed, in the real world, neither the contribution nor the replacement rate is fixed once for all, but, on the contrary, their value may be modified by the government at each period, whatever the "rights" accumulated by the generations who have, at the current date, already contributed. Contributions should, thus, be considered as lump-sum.

As shown on Figure 2.14 [26], and whatever the country considered, the generations entering the labour market, at the beginning of the period under review, are better off in the CRR scenario than in the CCR one. Later, an opposite configuration occurs, in which people are better off in the CCR scenario. However, it should be noticed that:

(i) the differences between utilities in the scenario CRR and the CCR one are very often negative and very few times positive: they are negative for all periods but one (year 1990) for Germany, France and Italy, but two (years 1990 and 1995) for Japan, but three (years 1990, 1995 and 2000) for Canada and the United Kingdom and but five (years 1990, 1995, 2000, 2005 and 2010) for the U.S.

(ii) the absolute values of these differences are much higher when the spreads are negative than when they are positive.

In the long run, individual welfare is greater in the CCR scenario than in the CRR one (see Table 2.15).

Therefore, if social welfare is defined as a linear combination of the elementary intertemporal utilities of each generation, it is higher in the CCR option than in the CRR one, unless very odd weights were chosen.

---

[26] Here, the dates on the X-axis refer to entries in the labour market.

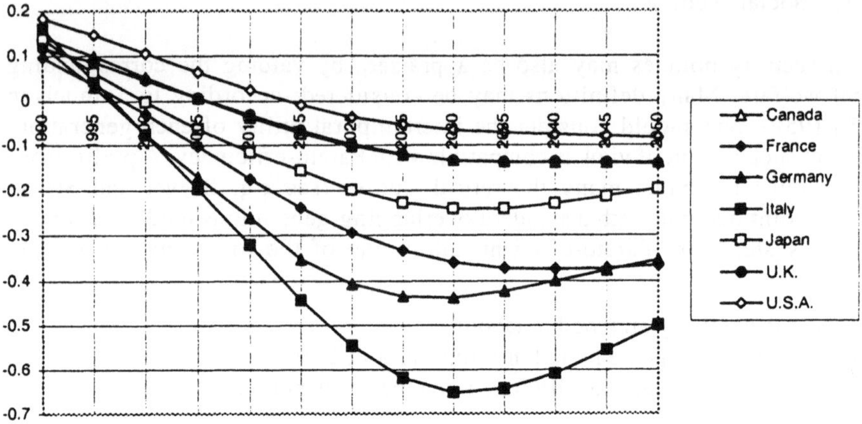

Fig. 2.14. Samuelson's Criterion, Deviations: CRR-CCR, Closed Economy.

Table 2.15. Samuelson's Criterion, Long-Run Values, Closed Economy

1990 = 0	Canada	France	Germany	Italy	Japan	U.K.	U.S.A.
CRR: Final value, 2100	0.091	0.079	0.079	0.073	0.073	0.072	0.087
CCR: Final value, 2100	0.093	0.081	0.081	0.076	0.074	0.073	0.088

Another way of doing is Lerner's (1959), for whom one should aggregate the instantaneous utilities of all living generations. The weights that are most often be used are either proportional to the size of each generation (this is Lerner's way of doing) or equal to one another (this is our point of view). Lerner's criterion is commonly used, for the sake of simplicity, by politicians. It is clear, from Figure 2.15, that, for the U.S.A., social welfare is greater in the CRR option than in the CCR one. An almost similar result is reached for Canada and the U.K.. On the contrary, no conclusion can be drawn, for the other countries. In the long run, social welfare is greater (or equal) in the CCR scenario than in the CRR one (see Table 2.16).

Table 2.16. Lerner's Criterion, Long-Run Values, Closed Economy

1990 = 0	Canada	France	Germany	Italy	Japan	U.K.	U.S.A.
CRR: Final value, 2100	0.091	0.100	0.098	0.100	0.102	0.102	0.101
CCR: Final value, 2100	0.093	0.102	0.099	0.102	0.104	0.103	0.101

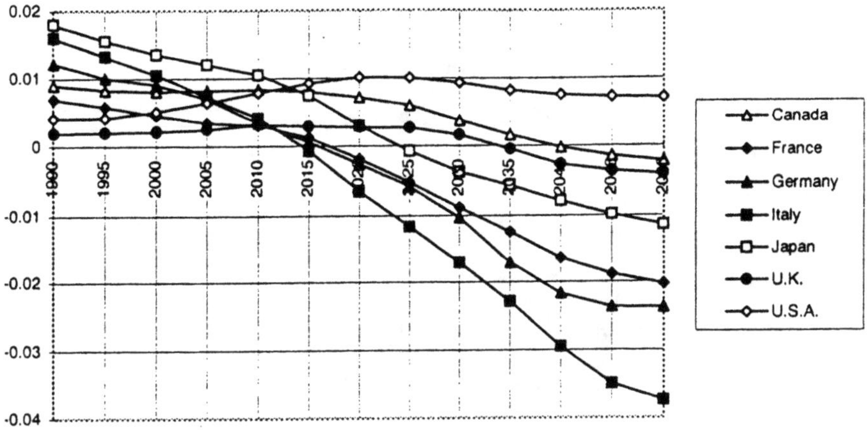

Fig. 2.15. Lerner's Criterion, Deviations: CRR-CCR, Closed Economy.

One could also consider the minimum of the instantaneous utility of a generation. This is Rawls' (1974) criterion. However, using this criterion leads, here, to some indeterminacy. To rule out this drawback, we, consider another criterion which we call dispersion criterion; it indicates whether the dispersion of the instantaneous utilities of all living generations is narrowing or not. Among all possible measures, we have selected the simplest, i.e. the difference between the highest instantaneous utility and the lowest. Note that the highest utility generally refers to a generation of retired whereas the lowest generally characterises a young working generation so that this criterion is a rough indicator of the difference of welfare between the retired and working population. Since maintaining the replacement rate benefits to the retired and injures the working population, the higher the replacement rate the higher should be the dispersion of social welfare.

Figure 2.16 exhibits the difference between dispersion social welfares calculated, for each of the seven countries under review, for the two basic scenarios. The better option corresponds to the minimum value of the dispersion criterion; hence, The CRR option clearly dominates the CCR one for three countries: Canada, Japan, the U.S.A. and the U.K. On the contrary, France is better off with the CCR option. The case of Italy is almost similar to the French one. For Germany, no clear-cut conclusion can be drawn.

In the long run, the better option is for France and Italy the CCR one. The opposite result holds for the remaining countries (see Table 2.17).

Table 2.17. Dispersion Criterion, Long-Run Values, Closed Economy

1990 = 1	Canada	France	Germany	Italy	Japan	U.K.	U.S.A.
CRR: Final value, 2100	0.831	0.684	0.829	0.631	0.549	0.719	0.827
CCR: Final value, 2100	0.873	0.671	0.841	0.593	0.585	0.751	0.873

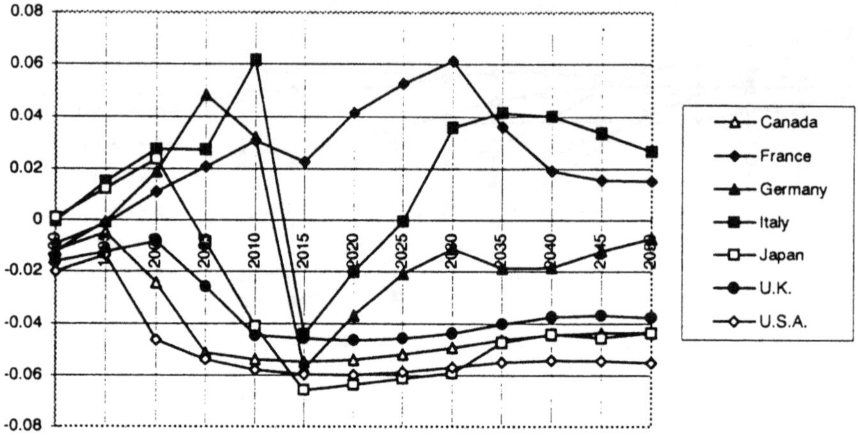

Fig. 2.16. Social Welfare: Dispersion Criterion, Deviations: CRR-CCR, Closed Economy.

2.4.2 The Case of Open Economies

We now examine how switching from the assumption of "closed economies" to the one of "open economies dominated by the US economy" may, or not, modify the preceding results. Recall, first, that with the latter assumption which implies perfect mobility of capital, the domestic interest rate equalises the rate of interest in the US economy. Simultaneously, the wage rate becomes exogenous, since the production function is a Cobb-Douglas one. The first order conditions of the program of the representative firm make both the wage rate and the real rate of interest depend but on capitalistic intensity. Therefore, fixing the value of the interest rate implies fixing the one of the wage rate. Actually, our small open economies are endowed with exogenous prices. Capital movements make the behaviours of economic agents and exogenous prices compatible.

The accounting framework used in this study is analogous to the one most often used in this kind of study (see e.g. Auerbach, Kotlikoff, Hagemann and Nicoletti, 1989). When economies are assumed to be closed, national wealth is equal to the domestic stock of capital. When economies are open, it is the sum of the value of the domestic stock of capital held by nationals and the net domestic wealth held by foreigners. If nationals hold more foreign capital than foreigners hold domestic capital, foreign wealth is negatively accounted; savings are no more equal to investment but they equalise the difference between domestic investment and capital movements positively accounted when they are inflows.

Two further remarks must be made:

- The six small open economies comprise three groups of countries: (i) three European countries (France, Italy and the United Kingdom) the interest rates of which are, under the assumption of closed economies, markedly above the American rate, during almost the whole period under review; (ii) two countries (Canada and Germany) the interest rate of which is, under the same assumption, very close to the US one; (iii) one country (Japan) the corresponding rate of which is below the one in the United States. Therefore, simulations made under the assumption of open economies lead to results significantly different only for countries belonging to the first and the last groups of countries. For the sake of simplicity, we shall limit our comments to those two groups of countries and, as far as the first one is concerned, we shall but look at one of the three countries, France.
- If simulations had been run, with an endogenous US rate of interest, the results would not have been very different since the effect of opening American frontiers to Japanese investment would have almost compensated their opening to European borrowing.

2.4.2.1 Investment and Savings

The main effect of opening the frontiers to capital movements is a fall (rise) of the investment rate according to the fact that the US rate of interest is lower (higher) than the one prevailing in the small economy considered, as shown in Table 2.18. Indeed, a decrease (increase) of the domestic interest rate implies a rise (fall) of domestic investment which implies capital inflows (outflows) and, later, a rise (fall) of the domestic saving rate. The highest jump is, in France, from 17.19 to 20.36 %. The most important fall is, in Japan, from 25.52 to 24.41 %. All these figures refer to a CRR scenario (see Tables 2.7 and 2.18).

The differences between the two options (CCR and CRR) are the same (see Figures 2.17a. and b.) as those relative to the case of closed economies but for France and Italy. In these two economies, the fall of the investment rate is smaller, in the long run, than the one prevailing under the antagonistic assumption of closed economy. The reason is that the difference between the rate of interest in one of these two economies and the US one is smaller, when the CCR option prevails (e.g. 1.15 % for France), than when the CRR option is taken into account (e.g. 1.31 % for France).

Table 2.18. Investment Rate, Long-Run Values, Small Open Economy

%	Canada	France	Germany	Italy	Japan	U.K.	U.S.A.
CRR: Final value, 2100	20.29	20.36	20.39	20.36	24.41	20.29	16.24
CCR: Final value, 2100	22.53	22.62	22.63	22.62	27.10	22.54	18.02

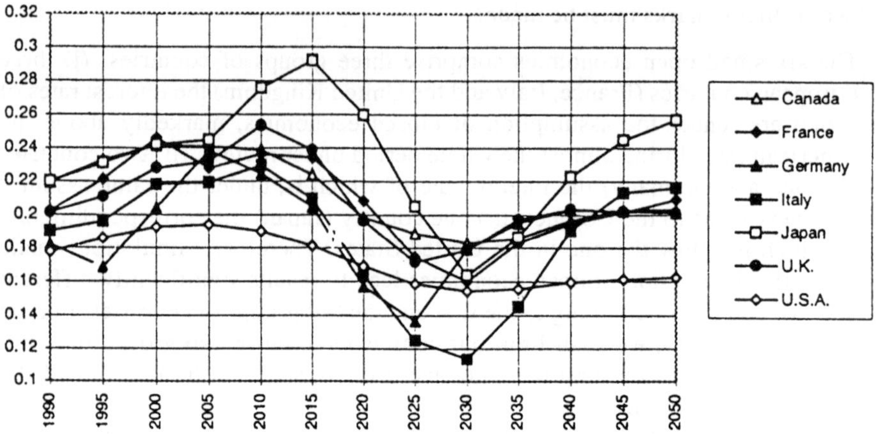

Fig. 2.17a. Investment Rate, "Constant Replacement Rate" (CRR), Open Economy

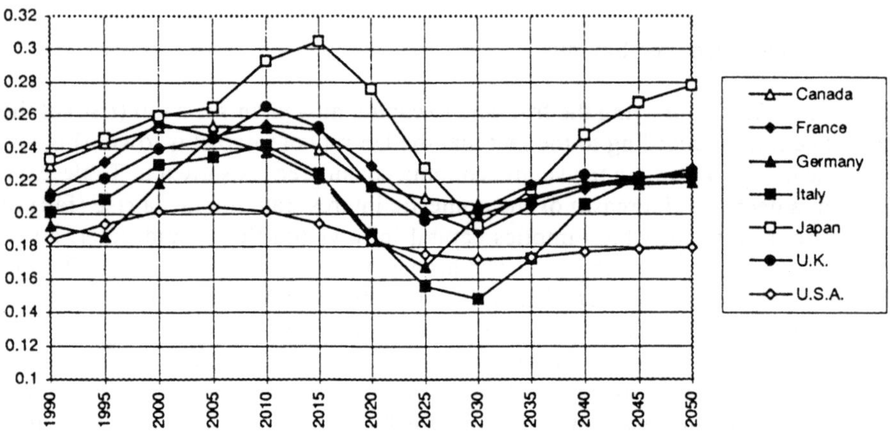

Fig. 2.17b. Investment Rate, "Constant Contribution Rate" (CCR), Open Economy

2.4.2.2 Per-head Output

The evolution of the demographic structure appears to be, again, the key-variable which determines the profiles of economic aggregates. Hence, as far as output is concerned, differences between the two benchmark scenarios are moderate. However, in the long run, significant spreads can be exhibited for France, (+3.9 % for CRR and +4 % for CCR), Japan (-3.4 % for CRR and -3.6 % for CCR), for the United Kingdom (+2.0 % for CRR and +3.3 % for CCR) and Canada (-1.5 % for CRR and -1.2 % for CCR). Of course, a rise (fall) of the domestic interest rate induces a decrease (increase) of output.

The profiles of current per-head outputs (instead of discounted per-head outputs) are plotted on Figures 2.18.a and b. They are, again sloping upward and a demographic slump is, once more, very unlikely to happen.

Table 2.19. Per Head Output, Long-Run Values, Small Open Economy

1990=1	Canada	France	Germany	Italy	Japan	U.K.	U.S.A.
CRR: Final value, 2100	7.88	8.01	7.23	7.58	7.47	8.26	8.03
CCR: Final value, 2100	8.32	8.70	7.78	8.13	7.97	8.76	8.40

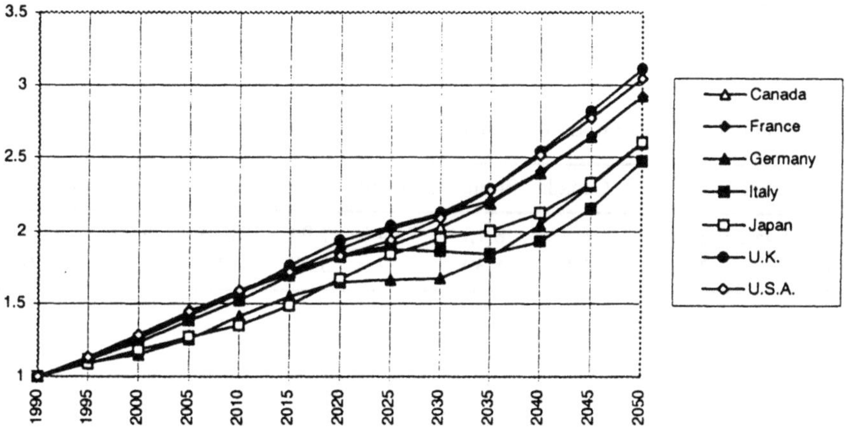

Fig. 2.18a. Per Head Output (1990 = 1), "Constant Replacement Rate" (CRR), Open Economy

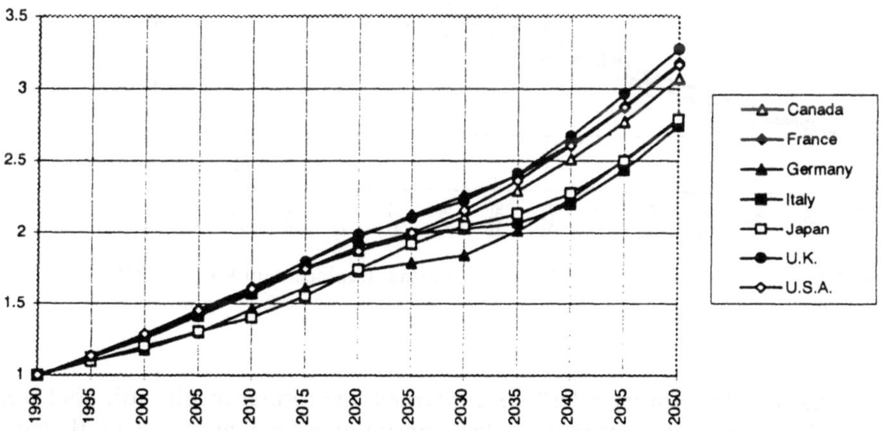

Fig. 2.18b. Per Head Output (1990 = 1), "Constant Contribution Rate" (CRR), Open Economy

2.4.2.3 Pensions

One must first notice that, whatever the option under review, switching from the closed economies assumption to the antagonistic one changes neither the long run values of replacement rates nor the ones of contribution rates. The same remark prevails for the corresponding profiles. The reason is that they are, by definition, but linked to the demographic variables (see above).

However, the level of per-head pensions is -slightly- modified. Although, in most countries, opening the economy leads to a similar spread of per-head pension levels between the two options (see Table 2.20), the CCR scenario is characterised by numerous inflexions of the corresponding profiles (see Figures 2.19a. and b.). For Japan, the level of per head-pensions is lower than the initial one from 1995 to 2020 and for all the remaining economies but France, it happens to fall during several periods.

Table 2.20. Per Head Pension, Long-Run Values, Small Open Economy

1990=1	Canada	France	Germany	Italy	Japan	U.K.	U.S.A.
CRR: Final value, 2100	8.83	8.13	7.94	7.94	8.33	8.22	8.65
CCR: Final value, 2100	4.14	5.39	5.17	5.48	4.50	6.00	4.50

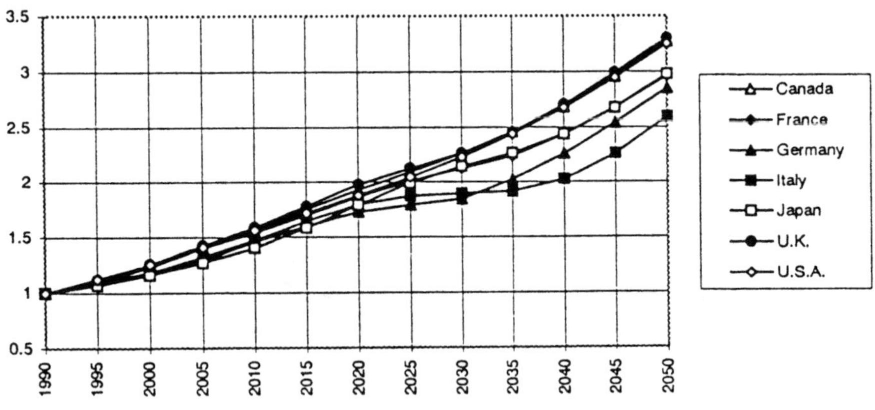

Fig. 2.19a. Per Head Pension (1900 = 1), "Constant Replacement Rate" (CRR), Open Economy

As far as "allowability rules" are concerned, the former results still hold (see Table 2.21) These rules seem to be less constraining for France and a little more for Germany and Italy.

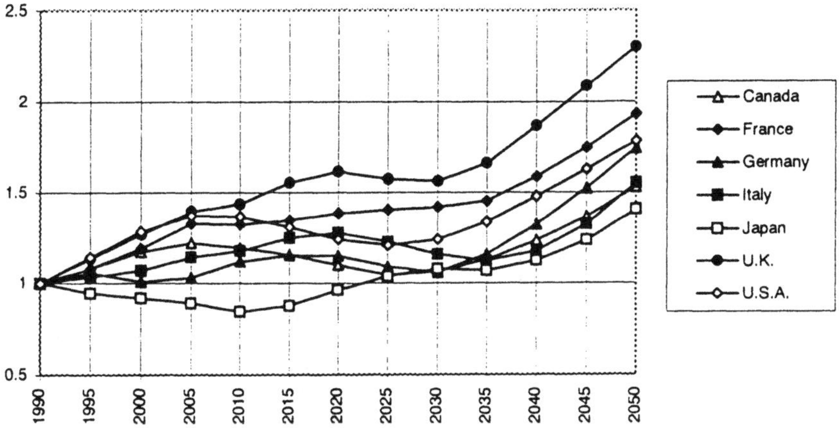

Fig. 2.19b. Per Head Pension (1900 = 1), "Constant Contribution Rate" (CCR), Open Economy

Table 2.21. Floor Values of the Rate of Technical Progress, Small Open Economy

a. Rule n° 1

%	Canada	France	Germany	Italy	Japan	U.K.	U.S.A.
CRR	0.00	0.18	0.40	0.52	0.35	0.00	0.02
CCR	1.64	1.04	1.65	1.56	2.31	0.77	1.28

b. Rule n° 2

%	Canada	France	Germany	Italy	Japan	U.K.	U.S.A.
CRR	0.37	0.95	1.40	1.79	0.88	0.71	0.28
CCR	3.08	2.12	3.16	3.17	3.18	2.52	3.11

2.4.2.4 Taxes

The profiles and the long run values of average income taxes are very close to the former ones (see Table 2.22). However, the spread between the value with a CRR scenario and the one under the opposite one CRC is somewhat greater under the assumption of open economies; the case for France is the most marked. Since there are very small differences between the values of taxes and contribution rates from one assumption to the other, the long run values and profiles of total tax pressure are, again, close (see Table 2.23 and Figures 2.20a. and b.).

Table 2.22. Average Tax Rate, Long-Run Values, Small Open Economy

%	Canada	France	Germany	Italy	Japan	U.K.	U.S.A.
Value in 1990	26.91	18.96	19.82	19.82	23.23	25.67	20.01
CRR: Final value, 2100	28.77	23.39	26.60	24.84	24.42	28.37	22.33
CCR: Final value, 2100	27.95	20.43	23.87	21.72	24.56	27.27	21.70

Table 2.23. Total Taxes/Output Ratio, Long-Run Values, Small Open Economy

%	Canada	France	Germany	Italy	Japan	U.K.	U.S.A.
Value in 1990	33.59	43.50	37.04	36.36	29.58	36.48	28.82
CRR: Final value, 2100	41.04	52.47	48.82	46.97	36.44	43.04	36.35
CCR: Final value, 2100	34.74	43.79	39.67	37.78	30.57	36.63	29.73

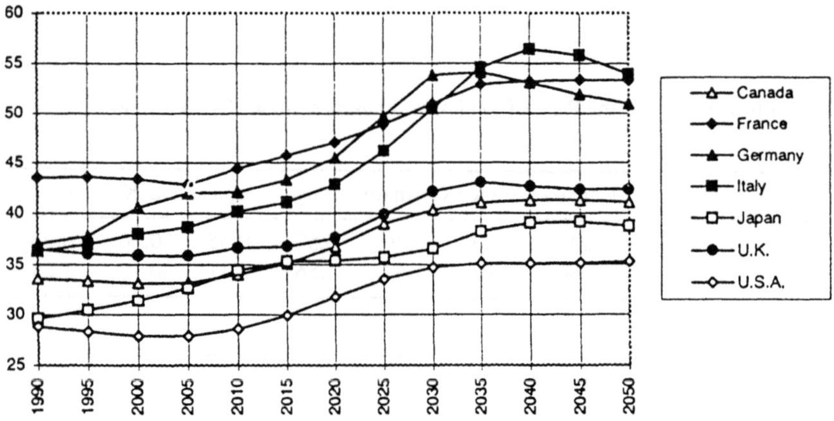

Fig. 2.20a. Total Taxes / Output (%), "Constant Replacement Rate" (CRR), Open Economy

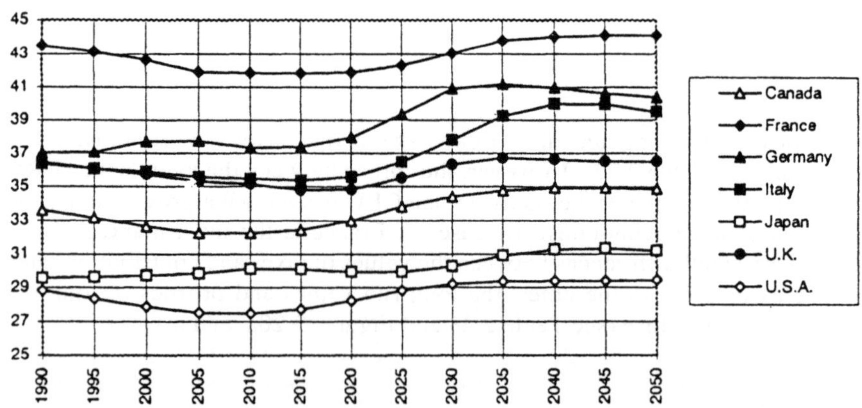

Fig. 2.20b. Total Taxes / Output (%), "Constant Contribution Rate" (CCR), Open Economy

2.4.2.5 Actuarial Fairness

Ceteris paribus, when the fairness ratio is greater (less) than unity, a rise (fall) of the interest rate induces a decrease (increase) of this ratio. The differences between its values in a "closed economy" account and in an "open economy" one highly depend on those of the interest rates (and to a less extent on the levels of pensions and contributions). As shown on Table 2.24, in the long run, French ratios rise sharply whereas the Japanese ones fall. Under the new assumption, the intertemporal profiles of fairness ratios are very similar in the CRR option to the former ones, but much less flat in the CCR scenario (see Figures 2.21a. and b.).

Table 2.24. Actuarial Fairness (Equity) Ratio, Long-Run Values, Small Open Economy

	Canada	France	Germany	Italy	Japan	U.K.	U.S.A.
CRR: Value in 1990	1.35	1.01	0.93	0.85	1.00	1.08	1.28
CRR: Final value, 2100	0.86	0.80	0.81	0.78	0.82	0.82	0.79
CCR: Value in 1990	0.94	0.84	0.77	0.66	0.80	0.90	0.93
CCR: Final value, 2100	1.00	0.93	0.96	0.94	0.98	0.96	0.95

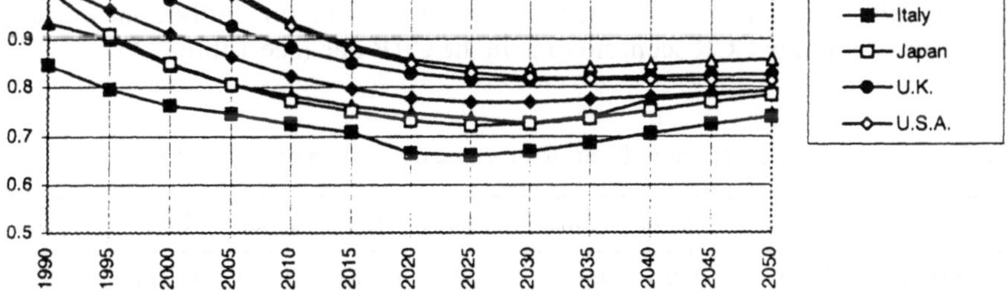

Fig. 2.21a. Actuarial Equity Ratio, "Constant Replacement Rate" (CRR), Open Economy

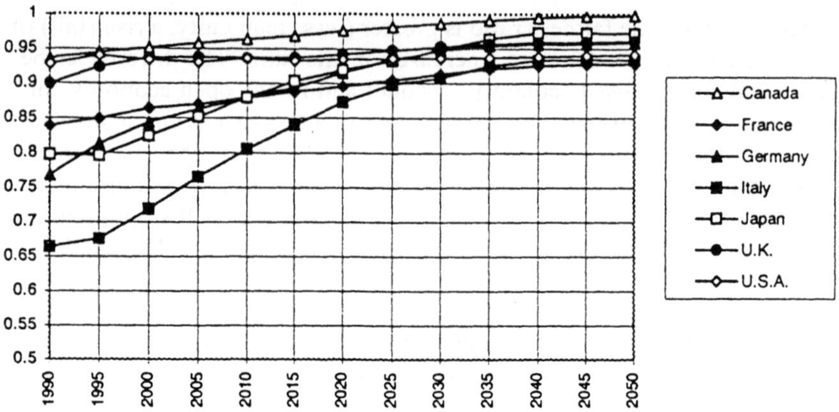

Fig. 2.21b. Actuarial Equity Ratio, "Constant Contribution Rate" (CCR), Open Economy

2.4.2.6 Social Welfare

For similar reasons, switching from the "closed economies" assumption to the "open economies " one does not much modify the results relative to social welfare.

If the spread between intertemporal utilities were plotted, one could, again, notice that the corresponding profiles are U-shaped; most of the generations are worse off with the CRR scenario except for the first ones. The generations entering the labour market in years 2020-2050 are much penalised. It can be, again, stated that, if social welfare is defined as a linear combination of the elementary intertemporal utilities of each generation, it is higher in the CCR option than in the CRR one, unless very odd weights were chosen. In the long run, individual welfare is, again, greater in the CCR scenario than in the CRR one (see Table 2.25).

Table 2.25. Samuelson's Criterion, Long-Run Values, Small Open Economy

1990 = 0	Canada	France	Germany	Italy	Japan	U.K.	U.S.A.
CRR: Final value, 2100	0.081	0.078	0.078	0.073	0.073	0.071	0.087
CCR: Final value, 2100	0.083	0.082	0.081	0.076	0.074	0.074	0.088

The new results, using Lerner's criterion, are very close to the former ones. the U.S. are, again, the one country for which a clear-cut conclusion can be drowned in favour of the CRR option. In the long run, social welfare is, again, greater (or equal) in the CCR scenario than in the CRR one (see Table 2.26).

Table 2.26. Lerner's Criterion, Long-Run Values, Small Open Economy

1990 = 0	Canada	France	Germany	Italy	Japan	U.K.	U.S.A.
CRR: Final value, 2100	0.103	0.099	0.098	0.100	0.105	0.102	0.101
CCR: Final value, 2100	0.103	0.102	0.101	0.104	0.107	0.102	0.101

On the contrary using our dispersion criterion leads to some new results: Figure 2.22 exhibits the difference between dispersion social welfares calculated, for each of the 7 countries under review, for the two basic scenarios. Again, the better option corresponds to the minimum value of the dispersion criterion; One can notice that now, the CRR option clearly dominates the CCR one for the following countries: Canada, France, the U.S.A. and the U.K. On the contrary, Japan is better off with the CCR option. The results, thus, switch, as far as France or Japan are considered. The cases of Italy and of Germany remain similar to the preceding ones. In the long run, the better option is, now, for Japan and Italy, the CCR one. The opposite result holds for the remaining countries (see Table 2.27).

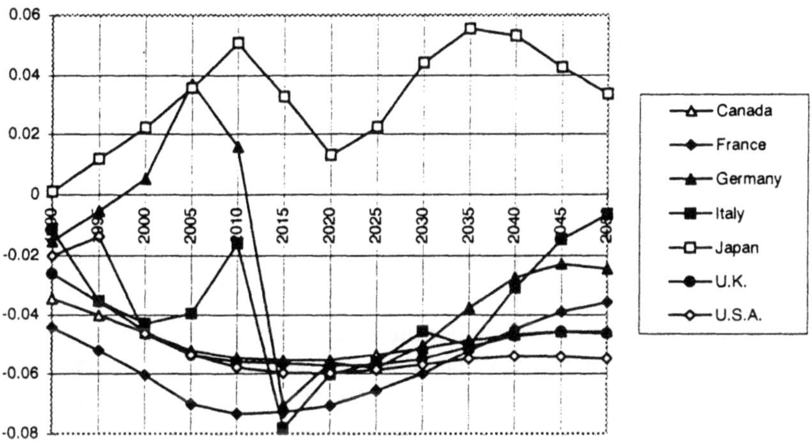

Fig. 2.22. Social Welfare: Dispersion Criterion, Deviations: CRR-CCR, Open Economy.

Table 2.27. Dispersion Criterion, Long-Run Values, Small Open Economy

1990 = 1	Canada	France	Germany	Italy	Japan	U.K.	U.S.A.
CRR: Final value, 2100	0.988	0.948	0.846	0.645	0.549	0.854	0.827
CCR: Final value, 2100	1.010	0.945	0.883	0.680	0.537	0.883	0.873

2.5 Conclusion

A few conclusions can be drawn from this study:

- Ageing of the population is a problem very similar from one developed country to another, inducing a sharp increase of the old-age dependency ratio.
- This problem is not so much worrying as it is sometimes suggested; indeed, the huge increase of the old-age dependency ratio will have but two macroeconomic consequences: (i) a more or less marked slowdown of growth and (ii) a more or less marked fall of the relative standard of living of the retired. There is no one best policy since there is a trade-off between, on the one hand, lower contribution rates, tax pressure and interest rates, lower per-head pensions, higher investment and output, and, on the other hand, higher contribution rates, tax pressure, hence interest rates, higher per-head pensions, lower investment and output. Such a trade-off can be summarised by ranking the two benchmark policies, according to eight criteria, as shown in Table 2.28. It appears that:
  - per head output is always higher with the CCR option than with the CRR one;
  - per head pensions are always lower with the CCR option than with the CRR one;
  - total taxes are always higher with the CCR option than with the CRR one;
  - there is no clear-cut conclusion, when actuarial fairness is considered;
  - using welfare criteria leads to somewhat ambiguous results; Samuelson's criterion is in favour of the CCR option; Lerner's one is in favour of the CRR one for the U.S. The CRR option outclasses the CCR one, according to the dispersion criterion, for most countries except France and Italy for which the CCR option dominates the CRR one;
- The first allowability rule is not checked, with the CCR option, in Japan. The second one is never strictly checked, whatever the option considered; however it is almost, in France and in the U.K, with the CCR option.

All these results, but two, prevail under the assumption of "closed economies" as well as the opposite assumption of "small open economies": note that the CRR (CCR) option outclasses the CCR (CRR) one, according to the dispersion criterion, when France (Japan) is considered as an open economy. Nevertheless, for countries in which the domestic real rate of interest is higher than the American one, opening leads to better macroeconomic outcomes and higher actuarial fairness. It is the case for France and the United Kingdom; the opposite situation characterises Japan.

- There are two major reasons for ruling out a policy: (i) scenarios close to the CCR one should be ruled out because they induce or might induce a fall in the absolute standard of living of the retired; this is the case for Japan, and, to a lesser extent, for Canada and Germany. In these countries, a decrease of the absolute level of the standard of living induced by a fall of the rate of technical progress is likely to occur. (ii) CRR option should be ruled out if total tax pressure appears to be unbearable. This is the case for countries such as France, Germany and Italy because of an increasing absolute standard of living of the retired.

To sum up, policies close to the CCR scenario should be undertaken in France and Italy; on the contrary, policies close to the CRR benchmark should be implemented in Japan, Canada, the U.S.A. and the U.K. Note that, for Japan and the U.S.A., this last conclusion holds all the more that reserves of the public pension funds can be used to lower the contributions of working population.

Table 2.28. Synthetic Ranking of the Benchmark Scenarios

a. Closed Economies

	Canada	France	Germany	Italy	Japan	U.K.	U.S.A.
Per Head Output	CCR	CCR	CCR	CCR	CCR	CCR	CCR
Per Head Pension	CRR	CRR	CRR	CRR	CRR	CRR	CRR
Total Taxes/Output	CCR	CCR	CCR	CCR	CCR	CCR	CCR
Actuarial Equity	–	–	–	–	–	–	–
Individual Welfare (Samuelson)	CCR	CCR	CCR	CCR	CCR	CCR	CCR
Social Welfare (Lerner)	(CRR)	–	–	–	–	–	CRR
Social Welfare (Lerner-Rawls)	CRR	CCR	(CRR)	(CCR)	(CRR)	CRR	CRR
Rules on Technical Progress	CRR	CRR	CRR	CRR	CRR	CRR	CRR

b. Small Open Economies

	Canada	France	Germany	Italy	Japan	U.K.	U.S.A.
Per Head Output	CCR	CCR	CCR	CCR	CCR	CCR	CCR
Per Head Pension	CRR	CRR	CRR	CRR	CRR	CRR	CRR
Total Taxes/Output	CCR	CCR	CCR	CCR	CCR	CCR	CCR
Actuarial Equity	–	–	–	–	–	–	–
Individual Welfare (Samuelson)	CCR	CCR	CCR	CCR	CCR	CCR	CCR
Social Welfare (Lerner)	(CRR)	–	–	–	–	–	CRR
Social Welfare (Lerner-Rawls)	CRR	CRR	(CRR)	(CRR)	CCR	CRR	CRR
Rules on Technical Progress	CRR	CRR	CRR	CRR	any	CRR	CRR

CRR means CRR > CCR;
CCR means CRR < CCR;
– means that it is impossible to rank CRR and CCR;
any: means that no scenario is acceptable;
parentheses denote that the scenario over-rank the other.

Two other conclusions can be drawn: differences of interest rates appear to be, in the long run, moderate, inducing limited capital movements; this is an ex-post rationale for working with "closed" economies. Finally the use of a new CGEM-OG has allowed for a much better calibration than in earlier standard models.

References

Ando A. and Modigliani F., 1963: "The 'life cycle' hypothesis of saving: aggregate implications and tests", *American Economic Review 53.*

Auerbach A.J. and L.J. Kotlikoff, 1987: *Dynamic Fiscal Policy*, Cambridge, Cambridge University Press.

Auerbach A.J., L.J. Kotlikoff, R.P. Hagemann and G. Nicoletti, 1989: "Conséquences du vieillissement démographique pour l'évolution de l'économie: une étude sur le cas de quatre pays de l'OCDE", *Revue Economique de l'OCDE*, n° 12, pp. 111-147.

Breyer F. and M. Straub, 1993: "Welfare Effects of Unfunded Pension Systems when Labor Supply is Endogenous", *Journal of Public Economics*, 50, n°1, january.

Bloch L. and M. Glaude, 1983: "Une approche du coût de l'enfance", *Economie et Statistique*, n° 155, mai.

Cazes S., T. Chauveau, J. Le Cacheux and R. Loufir, 1994: "Public Pensions in an Overlapping-Generations Model of the French Economy", *Keio Economic Studies*, Vol. XXXI, n° 1.

Chauveau T. and R. Loufir, 1993: "Demographic Transition and Social Security Policies in France: a welfare analysis", *OFCE Working Paper*, n° 94-2, mai. Forthcoming in *Applied Stochastic Models and Data Analysis Review.*

Chauveau T. and R. Loufir, 1994a: "Croissance et évolution des retraites: les enseignements d'un nouveau modèle à générations imbriquées", Published in *"Mélanges en l'honneur d'E. Andréani"* P.Artus et F.Legros eds, *Armand Colin, 1995,* Paris.

Chauveau T. and R. Loufir, 1994b: "L'avenir du système de retraite français: les enseignements d'un modèle à générations imbriquées", *Revue économique*, mai.

Fabel O., 1994: *The Economics of Pensions and Variable Retirement Schemes*, Wiley Pub.

Fair R.C. and J.B. Taylor (1983): "Solution and Maximum Likelihood Estimation of Dynamic Rational Expectations Models", *Econometrica*, vol. 51, pp.1169-85.

Glaude M. and M. Moutardier (1991): "Une évaluation du côut direct de l'enfant de 1979 à 1989", *Document de Travail de l'INSEE,* G , n°9108.

Heller P., 1989: "Aging, Savings, and Pensions in the Group of Seven Countries: 1980-2025", *IMF Working Paper*, n° 89/13.

R.Hemming and P. Kohnert, "Aging and Social Expenditure in the Major Industrial Countries, *1980-2025" IMF Occasional Paper* n° 47, IMF, Washington, 1986

Lerner A.P., 1959: "Consumption-loan, interest and money", *Journal of Political Economy*, n° 67.

Merton R.C.,1981: "On the Microeconomic Theory of Investment under Uncertainty", in *Handbook of Mathematical Economics*, vol. 2, K.J. Arrow and M.D. Intriligator eds., North-Holland, Amsterdam.

Mizrahi A. and A. Mizhari, 1985: *Débours et dépenses médicales selon l'âge et le sexe - France 1970-1980,* Credes, Paris.

Modigliani F., 1986: "Cycle de vie, épargne individuelle et richesse des nations", conférence Nobel, *Revue française d'économie*, vol. I, n° 2.

OECD, 1988a. *Reforming Public Pensions,*OECD, Paris.

OECD, 1988b. *Ageing Populations: The Social Policy Implications,* OECD, Paris.

OECD, 1992a. *National accounts, 1978-1990,* OECD, Paris.

OECD, 1992b. *Revenue Statistics, 1965-1991,* OECD, Paris.

Rawls J., 1974: "Some reasons for the maximin criterion", *American Economic Review,* 64.

Samuelson P.A., 1958: "An exact consumption-loan model of interest with or without the social contrivance of money", *Journal of Political Economy*, 66(6).

Samuelson P.A., 1959: "Reply to A.P. Lerner: consumption-loan, interest and money", *Journal of Political Economy*, 67.
Steigum E., 1993: "Accounting for Long-Run Effects of Fiscal Policy By Means of Computable Overlapping Generations Models", *in Macroeconomic Modelling and Policy Implications*, S. Honkapohja and M. Ingberg Editors, Elsevier Science Publishers B.V.
United Nations 1985. *World Population Prospects: Estimates and Projections as Assessed in 1982*, U.N., New York 1985.
Van den Noord P. and R. Herd, 1993: "Pensions Liabilities in the Seven Major Economies", *OECD Working Paper*, n° 142.
World Bank 1992: *World Bank Development Report 1992*, World Bank, Washington.
Yaari M.F.,1965: "Uncertain Lifetime, Life-Insurance and the Theory of the Consumer", *Review of Economic Studies*", vol 32, pp. 137-160.

Appendix

First Order Conditions of the Consumer's Program

The Lagrange equation reads:

$$\boldsymbol{L} = E\left(U_{a,t}\right) + \lambda_{a,t} CB_{a,t} + \sum_{j=a}^{14} \varsigma_{j,t+j-a}\left(1 - l_{j,t+j-a}\right) \qquad j = 1{,}14 \; and \; a = 1{,}14$$

where $\lambda_{a,t}$ is the multiplier of the intertemporal budget constraint, and $\varsigma_{j,t+j-a}$ is the multiplier of the non-negativity of the labour supply constraint. It follows:

A) First order condition with respect to $C_{j,t+j-a}$:

$$\frac{\partial \boldsymbol{L}}{\partial C_{j,t+j-a}} = \frac{\partial E\left(U_{a,t}\right)}{\partial C_{j,t+j-a}} + \lambda_{a,t}\left[\frac{\partial CB_{a,t}}{\partial C_{j,t+j-a}} + \sum_{s=j+1}^{14} \frac{\partial CB_{a,t}}{\partial \tau^{-y}_{s,t+s-a}} \frac{\partial \tau^{-y}_{s,t+s-a}}{\partial C_{j,t+j-a}}\right] = 0$$

or:

$$\frac{\partial \boldsymbol{L}}{\partial C_{j,t+j-a}} = \frac{s_{j,t+j-a}}{(1+\delta)^{j-a}} C_{j,t+j-a}^{-\frac{1}{\rho}} \left[C_{j,t+j-a}^{1-\frac{1}{\rho}} + \alpha_{j,t+j-a}\left(q_{j,t+j-a} l_{j,t+j-a}\right)^{1-\frac{1}{\rho}} \right]^{\frac{\frac{1}{\rho}-\frac{1}{\gamma}}{1-\frac{1}{\rho}}}$$

$$-\lambda_{a,t} \prod_{s=a+1}^{j} \frac{1}{1+r_{t+s-a}\left(1-\tau^{-y}_{s,t+s-a}\right)} \prod_{s=j+1}^{14} \frac{1+r_{t+s-a}\left(1-\tau^{y}_{s,t+s-a}\right)}{1+r_{t+s-a}\left(1-\tau^{-y}_{s,t+s-a}\right)} s_{j,t+j-a} f_{j,t+j-a}\left(1+\tau^{c}_{t+j-a}\right) = 0$$

B) First order condition with respect to $l_{j,t+j-a}$:

$$\frac{\partial \mathcal{L}}{\partial l_{j,t+j-a}} = \frac{\partial E(U_{a,t})}{\partial l_{j,t+j-a}} + \lambda_{a,t}\left[\frac{\partial CB_{a,t}}{\partial l_{j,t+j-a}} + \sum_{s=j+1}^{14} \frac{\partial CB_{a,t}}{\partial \bar{\tau}^{y}_{s,t+s-a}} \frac{\partial \bar{\tau}^{y}_{s,t+s-a}}{\partial l_{j,t+j-a}}\right] - \varsigma_{j,t+j-a} = 0$$

or:

$$\frac{\partial \mathcal{L}}{\partial l_{j,t+j-a}} = \frac{s_{j,t+j-a}}{(1+\delta)^{j-a}} \alpha_{j,t+j-a} q_{j,t+j-a} (q_{j,t+j-a} l_{j,t+j-a})^{-\frac{1}{\rho}}$$

$$\left[C_{j,t+j-a}^{1-\frac{1}{\rho}} + \alpha_{j,t+j-a} (q_{j,t+j-a} l_{j,t+j-a})^{1-\frac{1}{\rho}} \right]^{\frac{\frac{1}{\rho}-\frac{1}{\gamma}}{1-\frac{1}{\rho}}}$$

$$-\lambda_{a,t} \prod_{s=a+1}^{j} \frac{1}{1+r_{t+s-a}(1-\bar{\tau}^{y}_{s,t+s-a})} \prod_{s=j+1}^{14} \frac{1+r_{t+s-a}(1-\tau^{y}_{s,t+s-a})}{1+r_{t+s-a}(1-\bar{\tau}^{y}_{s,t+s-a})}$$

$$s_{j,t+j-a}\left(w_{t+j-a} e_{j,t+j-a} (1-\theta^{s}_{t+j-a})(1-\bar{\tau}^{y}_{j,t+j-a})\right) - \varsigma_{j,t+j-a} = 0$$

with:

$$\varsigma_{j,t+j-a} = \lambda_{a,t} \prod_{s=a+1}^{j} \frac{1}{1+r_{t+s-a}(1-\bar{\tau}^{y}_{s,t+s-a})} \prod_{s=j+1}^{14} \frac{1+r_{t+s-a}(1-\tau^{y}_{s,t+s-a})}{1+r_{t+s-a}(1-\bar{\tau}^{y}_{s,t+s-a})} s_{j,t+j-a} \mu_{j,t+j-a}$$

Two groups of behavioural equations are then derived from the previous first order conditions. The first group concerns the working population (generations j = 1,8):

$$C_{j,t+j-a} = C_{j-1,t+j-a-1}\left(\frac{f_{j-1,t+j-a-1}}{f_{j,t+j-a}} \frac{1+r_{t+j-a}(1-\tau^{y}_{j,t+j-a})}{1+\delta}\right)^{\gamma} \left(\frac{\Omega_{j,t+j-a}}{\Omega_{j-1,t+j-a-1}}\right)^{\frac{\gamma-\rho}{\rho-1}}$$

with:

$$\Omega_{j,t+j-a} = 1 + \alpha^{\rho}_{j,t+j-a} f^{\rho-1}_{j,t+j-a} \left(\frac{w_{t+j-a} e_{j,t+j-a}(1-\theta^{s}_{t+j-a})(1-\tau^{y}_{j,t+j-a}) + \mu_{j,t+j-a}}{q_{j,t+j-a}(1+\tau^{c}_{t+j-a})}\right)^{1-\rho}$$

and:

$$l_{j,t+j-a} = C_{j,t+j-a} \frac{\alpha^{\rho}_{j,t+j-a} f^{\rho}_{j,t+j-a}}{q_{j,t+j-a}} \left(\frac{q_{j,t+j-a}(1+\tau^{c}_{t+j-a})}{w_{t+j-a} e_{j,t+j-a}(1-\theta^{s}_{t+j-a})(1-\tau^{y}_{j,t+j-a}) + \mu_{j,t+j-a}}\right)^{\rho}$$

The second group concerns the retired (generations j = 9,14):

$$\left(\frac{C_{j,t+j-a}}{C_{j-1,t+j-a-1}}\right)^{-\frac{1}{\rho}}\left(\frac{C_{j,t+j-a}^{1-\frac{1}{\rho}}+\alpha_{j,t+j-a}q_{j,t+j-a}^{1-\frac{1}{\rho}}}{C_{j-1,t+j-a-1}^{1-\frac{1}{\rho}}+\alpha_{j,t+j-a}q_{j-1,t+j-a-1}^{1-\frac{1}{\rho}}}\right)^{\left(\frac{\gamma-\rho}{\rho-1}\right)\frac{1}{\gamma}}=\frac{1+\delta}{1+r_{t+j-a}(1-\tau^{y}_{j,t+j-a})}$$

and:

$$l_{j,t+j-a}=1$$

C) First order condition with respect to $B_{12,t+12-a}$

$$\frac{\partial \mathbf{L}}{\partial B_{12,t+12-a}}=\frac{\partial E(U_{a,t})}{\partial B_{12,t+12-a}}+\lambda_{a,t}\frac{\partial CB_{a,t}}{\partial B_{12,t+12-a}}=0$$

Combining the previous condition with the first order condition for consumption of the twelfth generation yields:

$$B_{12,t+12-a}=\left(\beta\,(1+\tau^{c}_{t+12-a})\right)^{\gamma}C_{12,t+12-a}^{\frac{\gamma}{\rho}}\left(C_{12,t+12-a}^{1-\frac{1}{\rho}}+\alpha_{12,t+12-a}q_{12,t+12-a}^{1-\frac{1}{\rho}}\right)^{\frac{\rho-\gamma}{\rho-1}}$$

3 Pension Systems in Europe: A General Equilibrium Study

Turalay Kenc*
Birkbeck College, London
William Perraudin*
Birkbeck College, London and CEPR

Abstract

Demographic and fiscal pressures make pension reform in Europe an important issue. The need for reform represents an opportunity for countries to reconsider the design of their pension systems and reduce the distortions they induce in labour and savings markets. This paper examines the economic effects of public pension systems in the four largest European economies using a general equilibrium simulation model with overlapping generations. We focus particularly on the aggregate effects of microeconomic distortions introduced by pension systems. To organize the analysis, we consider what would happen if the different governments harmonized their respective pension systems, moving to a system with parameters equal to the average of those for individual countries.

JEL Classification numbers: H55, J26, J65.
Keywords: Pensions, International Comparisons, Overlapping Generations, Simulation Models.

3.1 Introduction

3.1.1 The Pension Reform Debate

The prospect of a substantial ageing of the population in most industrial economies (see Bös and von Weiszäcker (1989) and OECD (1988)) has stimulated

* Our research was financed in part by a grant from the Leverhulme Foundation. Correspondence should be addressed to the authors at the Department of Economics, Birkbeck College, University of London, 7–15 Gresse Street, London, W1P 1PA, United Kingdom, (Tel.: 44-171-6316404, Fax: 44-171-6316416, Email: WPERRAUDIN or TKENC@ECON.BBK.AC.UK).

Pension Policies and Public Debt in Dynamic CGE Models

widespread debate among civil servants and academics about the appropriate policy response. The views expressed range from calls for substantial cutbacks in public pension provision (for example, Kessler (1995)) to optimistic suggestions that the burden of financing the larger pension benefit bill will be much less onerous than claimed (for example, see Cutler, Poterba, Scheiner, and Summers (1990) or Chauveau and Loufir (1995)).

In part, the conclusions follow from the methodologies adopted by different researchers. Those like Hageman and Nicoletti (1989) who follow a generational accounting approach, calculating the first round effects of the demographic shock on different cohorts, tend to take a pessimistic view. The authors of studies based on general equilibrium simulation models which allow for capital deepening and other second round effects operating through factor prices are generally more sanguine. Cutler, Poterba, Scheiner, and Summers (1990) actually argue that the optimal response to the demographic shock in the United States is an increase in consumption by the current generation.

Sensible policies probably lie somewhere between these two positions. General equilibrium effects such as capital deepening and real wages rises are indeed likely to lessen the burden for the cohorts that suffer most from the baby-boom and bust according to the generational accounting studies. But, the magnitude of the fiscal effects of the demographic shock, especially in European countries such as Germany and Sweden, dictate a cautious response by policy-makers correctly dubious of the precision of model-based analyses. This cautious response must necessarily involve some attempt to rein back the scale of public pension provision.

Given this background, an important objective of research is to shed light on the distortionary impact of pension systems. If cuts are to be effected, they should clearly be well-designed. It is probably fair to say that the architects of most social security systems paid little attention to the economic distortions they induce. The purpose of this paper is to study different European pension systems and their economic effects from a comparative perspective. In so doing, we hope to uncover general lessons about pension system design while also supplying results that have practical relevance for policy-makers in the countries considered.

3.1.2 General Equilibrium Analysis

Different countries have pension systems that vary substantially in their detailed regulations and in the over all 'scale' or 'generosity' of the transfers involved. Few attempts have been made to quantify the implications of this heterogeneity. For example, the normal presumption must be that substantial, unfunded pension provisions discourage savings. Just how serious are the effects and what if any are the sacrifices they imply in capital accumulation, real output and welfare? Furthermore, how much do commonly-observed public pension regulations such as averaging periods and retirement dates affect welfare and economic behaviour at a macro-economic level? Kenc and Perraudin (1995) examine microeconomic implications of detailed pension regulations but it is interesting and important to ask whether their results continue to hold if one aggregates across generations and allows for general equilibrium feedbacks.

In this paper, we address these questions using an overlapping generations simulation model. The countries we study are Germany, France, Italy and the United Kingdom. Building on past work by Auerbach and Kotlikoff (1987) and Perraudin and Pujol (1991), we formulate an overlapping generations model of an open economy in which terms of trade are variable and the supply of savings from the rest of the world is imperfectly elastic. Two domestic industries employ labour and capital to produce respectively an exportable and a non-traded good and adjust their capital stocks over time making optimal allowance for adjustment costs. Using parameters appropriate to our four countries, we simulate the effects of a harmonization of pension arrangements. This 'harmonization' should be viewed as a useful way of organizing our investigation of the heterogeneity implicit in current systems rather than as a policy that is likely to be implemented.

3.1.3 Related Research

Pension systems in the four European countries we study differ in a variety of ways. The most important 'dimensions of variation' are (i) the retirement age, (ii) the replacement ratio (i.e., the ratio of eligible wages to benefit entitlements), (iii) the level of contributions (typically some fraction of labour income), (iv) the averaging period (i.e., the period of the working life in which labour income counts towards the benefit entitlement calculation), (v) whether or not labour supply is restricted or indeed prohibited after pension benefit payments commence. These rules may have substantial effects on savings and labour supply incentives by altering the timing of income over the life cycle and by changing the after-tax real wage.

Much of the literature on the distortionary impact of pensions has concentrated on their implications for labour supply. The crucial question is how much do the rules of a given pension system link benefits and contributions? In the limit, if an agent's benefit is independent of the level of contributions, the latter become equivalent to a distortionary wage tax. On the other hand, if benefits provide actuarially fair recompense for contributions, then pension contributions introduce no distortion whatsoever. Recently, a theoretical literature has developed that examines the welfare effects of abolishing an unfunded pension scheme (see Homburg (1990) and Breyer and Straub (1993)). The results in these papers turn crucially on whether contributions are actuarially fair and whether they are linked to benefits.

Relatively few papers have applied general equilibrium simulation models of the kind we use here to examine the labour supply effects of pension systems. The closest study is that by Broer, Westerhout, and Bovenberg (1994) which employs an overlapping generations model of a small open economy to look at different reforms of a Pay-as-You-Go (PAYG) system closely resembling that of the

Netherlands. The welfare impact of the policy changes considered (cutting benefits, subjecting retirement benefits to PAYG contributions or taxing the income on the funded element in the pension scheme) turn on how they influence the existing labour market distortion. Craig and Batina (1991) also employ an overlapping generations model to study social security and labour supply. Their focus is much more on family choices between male and female labour supply, however.

Lastly, it should be mentioned that the impact of unfunded pension schemes on savings has been the subject of an extensive literature. As is well known, the impact of intergenerational transfers on savings depends on households' bequest behaviour. Since there is little to choose at a theoretical level between different ways of modelling bequests, it then becomes an empirical question to what degree unfunded pensions depress savings. The consensus view that has emerged from the empirical literature (see Feldstein (1974, Kotlikoff (1979b), Feldstein and Pellechio (1979), Barro and MacDonald (1979), Diamond and Hausman (1984)) is that increasing pension wealth reduces savings but at a rate rather less than dollar-for-dollar.

3.1.4 Structure of the Paper

Section 3.2 describes the public pension systems operating in the four European countries. We concentrate on differences between the various systems that are likely to have the greatest impact on household behaviour. Section 3.3 of the paper sets out the model, describing in detail our assumptions about household and firm behaviour and the parameterisation we employ. Section 3.4 describes our simulation results. Section 3.5 concludes the paper. Appendices provide a more detailed description of the model and more information about our parameterisation.

3.2 Pension Systems Heterogeneity

In this section, we summarize the main differences that we shall analyze in our simulations. Each country has a basic statutory pension arrangement plus supplementary pension plans. The latter are either organized as occupational or as private pension schemes (on the latter, see Foster (1994) and OECD (1992)). Private pension plans are difficult to analyze since they often form part of complicated implicit labour contracts. In this study, we shall limit attention to public schemes.

3.2.1 Comparing Pension Regulations

Tables 3.1 and 3.2 summarize the main regulations of the four pension schemes we study. The most important regulations for our purposes are: (i) the retirement age, (ii) the averaging period, (iii) accrual rates, and (iv) contributions rates. Other important aspects of schemes that we shall not investigate in the present study are indexation provisions and benefit rules for spouses.

1. Retirement Age

Of the four countries in our sample, Germany and France apply the same retirement age to both men and women, while the UK and Italy do not. France and Italy are unusual among industrialised countries in having basic retirement ages for men of 60 rather than 65. In Italy, it is currently planned that retirement ages will gradually rise to 65 and 60 for men and women respectively by 2002. If agents choose to retire early or late, in Germany, their benefits are adjusted for the change in the actuarial value of their pension. The UK adjusts benefits for late but not for early retirement. Italy is unusual in that no adjustment is made to benefit levels for different retirement dates.

2. Averaging Period

The most complex aspect of pension schemes we analyze here is the formula used in calculating pension benefits. In all countries we examine, state pension benefits depend on labour income in the period before retirement. The usual approach consists of designating some portion of an agent's working life, for example, the last five years as in Italy or the entire working career as in Germany or the UK. Pension benefits are, broadly-speaking, proportional to average wage income in the designated period. This dependence can generate a complicated profile for effective marginal tax rates over the life cycle since the discounted value of additional future benefits that an agent receives if he supplies an extra unit of labour is equivalent to a deferred negative tax. The impact of such negative taxes depends on how far one is from retirement and on whether or not the current year is included in the averaging period.

3. Accrual Rates

A crucial parameter for determining the 'generosity' of a pension scheme is the accrual rate. The accrual rate equals the percentage of average wage income in the averaging period by which pension benefits increase for each additional year of contributions to the scheme. The variation in accrual rates across countries is great, ranging from 2 % for Italy to 0.4 % in the UK. The latter is so low partly because the UK has a flat-rate pension scheme in addition to its State Earnings Related Scheme (SERPS) and partly because the over all level of UK benefits is low.

4. Contribution Rates

The contribution rates for pensions are summarized in the upper part of Table 3.1. The data given there, which are based on OECD estimates, show great variation across countries both in marginal and average rates. The total average rate is 11 % in the UK, while in France and the Italy, it is 34 % and 26 %, respectively. In most countries, the majority of total contributions is levied on employers.

3.3 The Model

The model developed in this paper is similar to the overlapping generations model employed by Auerbach and Kotlikoff in their studies of the United States economy and builds on the open economy model of Perraudin and Pujol (1991). The Perraudin and Pujol model generalized Auerbach-Kotlikoff by introducing a demand curve for exports, a supply curve for savings from the rest of the world and export- and non-tradeable-producing domestic industries. The model described here generalizes the Perraudin-Pujol framework by introducing bequests, labour-endowment-augmenting technological change and a growing population. Furthermore, the solution algorithms employed are new to this study.

3.3.1 Household Behaviour

The model of households follows the life-cycle approach. Aggregate consumption, saving and labour supply are derived from the intertemporal optimising behaviour of forward-looking individual age cohorts. Each cohort has an economic life of 55 years, becoming active at age 21 and dying at 75. To limit the computational burden, we assume that a time period equals five years. Hence, in any given period, 11 cohorts of different ages are economically active. We suppose that the population increases over time at a constant rate.

Household utility functions are assumed to be time-separable, nested Constant Elasticity of Substitution (CES) functions of consumption, leisure and bequests. Leisure endowments are normalised to unity. The lifetime utility, U, of a household is:

$$U \equiv \frac{1}{1-1/\alpha} \sum_{t=1}^{n} \frac{1}{(1+\delta)^{t-1}} u_t^{1-1/\alpha} + \frac{\alpha_B}{1-1/\alpha} \frac{b_n^{1-1/\alpha}}{(1+\delta)^n} \tag{1}$$

Here, $n = 11$ is the last period of life while b_n is a bequest made at the start of the household's n^{th} period. u_t is a utility index which depends on leisure l_t and consumption of goods 1, 2, and 3, denoted c_{1t}, c_{2t}, and c_{3t},in the following way:

$$u_t \equiv [c_t^{1-1/\rho} + \alpha_L l_t^{1-1/\rho}]^{1/[1-1/\rho]} \tag{2}$$

$$c_t \equiv [c_{1t}^{1-1/\rho_1} + \alpha_T c_{0t}^{1-1/\rho_1}]^{1/[1-1/\rho_1]} \tag{3}$$

$$c_{0t} \equiv [c_{2t}^{1-1/\rho_2} + \alpha_X c_{3t}^{1-1/\rho_2}]^{1/[1-1/\rho_2]} \tag{4}$$

α, ρ, ρ_1, and ρ_2 are respectively the elasticities of substitution between utility in different periods, leisure and consumption, tradeables and nontradeables, and imports and exportables. α_L, α_T, α_X and α_B are the utility intensity (or expenditure share) parameters for leisure, tradeables, exports and bequests.

We assume that all households retire at the start of some given period. It might be preferable to allow households to select different retirement ages but the fiscal incentives for retirement at the statutory age are so great in most countries that it is simplest to impose this from the outset. We suppose that households' marginal labour productivities vary over the life cycle. Within each group, productivity and therefore wages are assumed to increase initially, peaking at period 4 and declining slightly thereafter.

Taxation and transfers affect household behaviour through their influence on income and prices. Lump-sum transfers have a direct impact on income, VAT affects consumer prices, and direct taxation (including social security contributions) influence interest rates and wages. Households maximize utility subject to an intertemporal wealth constraint. Let W be the household's total lifetime wealth. Then if r_t is the interest rate at t and τ_r is the tax rate on household interest income, the lifetime wealth constraint is:

$$W = \frac{b_n}{\prod_{t=2}^{n} [1+(1-\tau_r)r_t]} + \sum_{t=1}^{n} \frac{(1+\tau_v)p_t c_t}{\prod_{s=2}^{t} [1+(1-\tau_r)r_s]} \tag{5}$$

where τ_υ is the rate of value added tax and p_t is a price index defined in the Appendix which involves parameters of the utility function.

Total lifetime wealth (W) equals the sum of human wealth (W_h), pension wealth (W_p), and anticipated future bequests (W_b). Let τ_i for i = x, w, r, d, g, v denote the rates of employee social security contributions, wage income tax, interest income tax, dividend income tax, capital gains and value added tax, respectively. z_t denotes lump-sum transfer received from the government. w_t is the wage rate, and e_t is the "effective labour input". Human wealth inclusive of lump sum transfer-payments can then be written as:

$$\textit{Human wealth} \equiv W_h = \sum_{t=1}^{n} \frac{(1-\tau_x-\tau_w)w_t e_t(1-l_t)+z_t}{\prod_{s=2}^{t} [1+(1-\tau_r)r_s]} \tag{6}$$

Let us define the parameters of the pension system as follows. γ_{ac} is the accrual factor, n_r is the retirement age, $\overline{n}$ is the number of years worked to qualify for the maximum level of old age pension benefit, $\overline{w}$ is the average weighted wage rate calculated by taking into account wage income and working hours during the period specified for this purpose by the pension authorities, and λ is the factor used to index pension income towages. Then, social security wealth may be written as:

$$\textit{Pension wealth} \equiv W_p = \gamma_{ac} \sum_{t=n_r}^{n} \frac{\overline{n}\,\overline{w}^{\lambda} w_t^{1-\lambda}}{\prod_{s=2}^{t} [1+(1-\tau_r)r_s]} \tag{7}$$

Finally, if b_{rt} is bequests received in period t, anticipated future bequests may be written as:

$$\textit{Bequest wealth} \equiv W_b = \sum_{t=1}^{n} \frac{b_{rt}}{\prod_{s=2}^{t} [1+(1-\tau_r)r_s]} \tag{8}$$

We assume in our simulations that bequests are made in the last period of life. Households have offspring in the first period of adult life (i.e., when 20 to 25 years old) and hence children receive bequests between the ages of 50 and 55 years.

If there were no further constraints, solving the dynamic programming problem for a given household would be easy and indeed we would be able to derive closed form consumption and leisure demands. However, we shall assume that the household is not allowed to supply labour after the retirement age, n_r. One may think of this as reducing the shadow wage just enough that the household wishes to supply zero labour in its last few periods. Since the shadow wage is not obtainable in closed form, neither are the associated consumption and leisure demands, however. We must therefore solve the household's programme numerically. More details are provided in the Appendix.

3.3.2 Firm Behaviour

We suppose that the economy contains two domestic industries labelled 1 and 3 which produce non-tradeable and tradeable goods respectively in a perfectly competitive manner. Each sector is made up of exactly similar firms which possess a constant returns-to-scale CES production function which depends on capital,[1] K_t, and labour, L_t. Scaling up variables, the production function for the industry as a whole is:

$$F_t(K_t, L_t) \equiv \bar{\varepsilon}\,[\varepsilon_0 K_t^{1-(1/\varepsilon)} + (1-\varepsilon_0)\,L_t^{1-(1/\varepsilon)}]^{1/[1-(1/\varepsilon)]} \tag{9}$$

In each period, producers decide on cost minimising intensities of labour given the current stock of capital. They alter the stock of capital through investment so as to maximize the value of firms' equity. Optimal investment involves balancing the costs of new capital (acquisition and installation costs) against the higher future revenues made possible by a larger capital stock. If firms invest in this way and adjustment costs are convex, the capital stock will follow a smooth transition path. In equilibrium, it must be the case that dividends and capital gains equal the required return:

$$(1-\tau_d)\,D_t + (1-\tau_g)\,(V_{t+1} - VN_t - V_t) = (1-\tau_r)\,r_{t+1}\,V_t \tag{10}$$

where V is the equity value of the firm, D is dividends, VN, the proceeds from share issues, and τ_d, τ_r, and τ_g are the tax rates on dividend and interest income, and the accrual-equivalent capital gains tax rate, respectively.

[1] Capital is, in fact, a composite good made up of fixed shares of the domestic and imported goods.

Ruling out bubbles, we can write this as

$$V_t = \sum_{v=t}^{\infty} \frac{[\frac{1-\tau_d}{1-\tau_g} D_v - V N_v]}{\prod_{s=t+1}^{v} [1 + (1-\tau_r) r_s/(1-\tau_g)]} \tag{11}$$

To solve the firms' programming problems, we must make assumptions concerning their financial behaviour. In particular, we shall suppose (i) that firms pay dividends equal to a constant fraction of after-tax profits net of depreciation; (ii) that they issue debt to maintain a constant debt-capital ratio; and (iii) that they issue new shares as the marginal source of finance. This financial behaviour is consistent with the assumptions behind the "old view" of capital taxation. The adjustment cost function is assumed to be convex in the ratio of investment (I) to the capital stock. We also assume that the installation costs of capital are internal to the firm. Such behaviour gives rise to a ''q'' investment function.

3.3.3 The Government

The government performs various functions in the model including exhaustive expenditure on goods, the operation of a system of transfers, the levying of taxes and the issuance of debt. Our approach also implicitly assumes that the government owns the firms and consequently receives their profits in the form of dividends. The government faces an intertemporal budget constraint which, for given public expenditures G_t and tax receipts T_t, can be written as:

$$\sum_{t=0}^{\infty} \frac{T_t}{\prod_{s=1}^{t} (1+r_s)} = \sum_{t=0}^{\infty} \frac{G_t}{\prod_{s=1}^{t} (1+r_s)} + B_1^G \tag{12}$$

The fact that government expenditure on goods does not contribute to households' utility or to firms' production means that any cut in public expenditure allows an uncompensated tax cut and therefore increased welfare. The model is therefore inappropriate for studying such questions as the optimal design of expenditure programs.The level of government debt, B_1^G, primarily affects the distribution of wealth across different generations. Since we do not incorporate a social welfare function capable of evaluating such distributions, the model is ill-equipped to study questions of optimal debt levels. We therefore concentrate in the analysis on policies that can improve social welfare for given levels of public expenditure and given steady state debt.

3.3.4 Open Economy Aspects of the Model

Our model departs in several respects from the commonly-adopted 'small country' approach. In describing industrial economies, it appears quite unrealistic to assume that they can sell unlimited quantities of their exports at constant prices. In modeling international capital flows, the assumption that interest rates are independent of the level of debt is hard to justify. The stylised facts of international capital markets suggest that the supply of world savings is imperfectly elastic for all but the smallest countries.

We therefore adopt the following assumptions.

1. Demand for the export good (which is also consumed by domestic households and used as an input to capital by firms) is assumed to equal a constant elasticity function, $X_3 = X_0 P_0^{\omega}$, where X_3 and P_3 are export quantities and their foreign currency prices respectively.

2. The net stock supply of savings from the rest of the world depends positively on the gross interest rate according to the equation: $W_{ROW} = \overline{K}\, sign(r_t - \overline{r})\,(|r_t - \overline{r}|)^{\omega^*}$. When $\overline{K} = \infty$, the interest rate is internationally given and the small country assumption holds for capital markets. (If $\omega = \infty$ then the same is true of the goods market.) When $\overline{K} = 0$, the autarky case, the interest rate adjusts to give current account equilibrium with constant capital flows between the domestic economy and the rest of the world.

3. The imported good, which is consumed by households and used by firms in their constant coefficient production of capital, has a price, P_2, which is exogenously fixed in terms of foreign currency.

3.4 Simulations

3.4.1 Summary of the Provisions to be Simulated

In this section, we describe the simulations we performed in order to assess the economic effects of differences between the pension systems of our four countries. Table 3.5 provides a summary of the four different aspects of the pension systems on which we focus. As one may see, the range of contribution rates is very substantial. At the lower end of the scale, the UK and Germany have total contribution rates of 18 % and 36.4 % respectively. France and Italy, on the other hand, have rates of 60.9 % and 59.1 %. The UK rate is so low because we suppose that households have contracted out of the state supplementary pension scheme and hence only receive the basic state pension. (State Earnings Related Pensions or SERPS are described in Section 3.6.1.5 in the Appendix.) This is consistent with our approach of restricting attention to public pension schemes.

The cost side of the different pension schemes is summed up by the replacement ratios and retirement ages. The French state pension scheme actually has a lower replacement rate than the German system but the extra five years of the retirement period in France more than offsets the relative saving. Once again, the UK figures are strikingly ungenerous in the level of benefit provision but pensioners would have substantial private pension incomes. Lastly, Table 3.5 shows the averaging periods for our four national pension systems. The UK and German systems use the entire working life as the averaging period while the Italian and French schemes involve averaging over ten and fifteen year periods. The fact that the Italian scheme is extremely generous in its provisions makes the relatively short averaging period especially troublesome since the fluctuations it implies for effective labour income taxes are quite considerable.

3.4.2 The Baseline Parameters

To assess the magnitude of the differences between our four pension systems, we simulated the dynamic path that the economy of each country would have followed if pension systems were harmonized. By harmonization, we mean that the contribution and replacement rates are set equal to the average of the rates for the four individual countries, that the entire working career be adopted as the averaging period, and that the retirement age be set equal to the German and UK figure of 65 years. Studying this kind of harmonization is a way of organising the analysis and we do not regard it as a likely or necessarily advisable policy.

Figures 3.1, 3.2 and 3.3 summarize the dynamic paths followed by the four economies after the surprise announcement of the harmonization. The paths shown are deviations from a balanced growth path in which no changes are implemented in the pension system. The model is simulated here under a set of baseline parameters summarized in Tables 3.3 and 3.4 and justified in Subsection 3.6.3 of the Appendix. The most notable features of this parameterisation are that we assume capital mobility with an interest elasticity of world savings, ω^*, of 5. The crucial parameters ρ, the consumption-leisure elasticity of substitution, and ε_1 and ε_3, the elasticities of substitution in production between capital and labour for the industries producing goods 1 and 3, are set to 1.10, 0.92, and 0.71 respectively. Lastly, the profile of labour productivity over the life cycle (before taking account of technological progress) which is based on Kotlikoff and Gokhale (1992) is relatively steeply declining in the latter part of the household's working life. In the sensitivity analysis performed below, we shall explore how our results are affected when these assumptions are altered.

3.4.3 Baseline Simulations

Each panel in Figures 3.1 to 3.3 shows the percentage change in the path followed by a given variable in the four different economies following the simultaneous announcement and implementation of the pension reform. Percentage changes are measured as deviations from the balanced growth path the economy would have followed in the absence of harmonization. Figure 3.1 shows the paths followed by aggregate consumption and labour supply. The striking initial impact of the changes is a sharp rise in labour supply in France and Italy where harmonization involves a cutback in benefits and contributions and a move over to averaging based on the entire working life, and a major fall in UK labour supply. Labour supply in Germany also falls but by a much smaller amount. It is noticeable that labour supply more or less adjusts immediately to the new steady state levels which for the French and UK cases are respectively 7.4 % higher and 10.7 % lower than the levels prior to reform.

It is interesting to note that the labour supply response in Germany is much less than that in the UK, the other country for which harmonization involves an expansion in pension provision. Since the main initial impact of the reform in through labour supply, as we shall see below, other economic variables change much less in Germany than in the UK. This finding is partly due to the obvious fact that the expansion in pension provision entailed by harmonization is less substantial for Germany than it is for the UK. However, a second important reason is that the wage taxes are lower in Germany, leading to a much lower labour supply elasticity. Recall that we assume throughout that all utility function parameters except the subjective discount rate are identical across countries. Representative households in different countries can still have radically different labour supply elasticities, however, if different tax rates mean they are more or less far along their labour supply curves.

Aggregate consumption levels in each country move in the same direction as labour supply. Adjustment to the new steady state levels occur more gradually for consumption than for labour supply, however. In the UK, for example, forty years pass before aggregate most of the change in consumption has taken place. Eighty years after the shock, almost all of the adjustment has occured. French and UK consumption change most, ending 9.2 % higher and 14.3 % lower, respectively. Italian consumption increases by 4.8 % in the long run while in Germany, consumption suffers a minor fall of 0.7 %.

Figure 3.2 shows the price response to the shock. Wages jump immediately most of the way to their new steady state levels. Italian and UK change very substantially, increasing and decreasing by plus and minus 16 % after 40 years. Other prices adjust less smoothly. For example, the decline in UK labour supply accompanied by little initial change in consumption generates a real appreciation (implying a decline in the exchange rate). The stronger domestic currency implies a fall in the domestic price of the UK export good. In the longer run, the decline in domestic consumption means that the relative price of the nontraded good falls in relation to that of the exportable, i.e., P_3 rises.

Figure 3.3 shows the impact of the shocks on capital and investment in the two industries. In each country, the industries producing the non-traded good 1 and the exportable good 3 are affected symmetrically, investment in both cases immediately jumping most of the way to the new steady state level. The dynamics of investment are dictated by the convex investment cost function: $CK(I_t, K_{t-1}) \equiv \xi(I_t/K_{t-1} - \kappa)^2/(I_t/K_{t-1})/2$. The values of the parameters κ and ξ we assumed are similar to those chosen by Summers (1981). The magnitude of the impact on long-run capital implied by the pension reform is substantial, with capital in France and the UK, for example, changing by 9.5 % and -13.9 %, respectively. These figures are broadly in line with the results of previous studies of the effects of unfunded public pension systems. Kotlikoff (1979a) and Auerbach and Kotlikoff (1987) suggest that unfunded schemes on the scale developed in many industrial countries by the 1980s in the long run reduce the capital stock by 20 to 30 %.

Returning to Figure 3.1, we report the utility changes (in absolute utility units) of successive generations. The zero generation is the cohort that has one period (five years) to live when the policy change occurs. As one may see, in each country there is a conflict of interest between old people about to die when the pension system is changed, on the one hand, and the very young and those born subsequently, on the other. Cuts in the extent of the scheme like those that take place in Italy and France harm the old but in the long run produce significant welfare gains. The contrary occurs in the UK. In Germany, where labour supply elasticities are relatively low and hence macroeconomic responses rather different from those in the UK, all generations lose slightly by the change.

Another way to appreciate the impact of the policy changes is to compare the leisure and consumption paths of *individual households* facing the factor prices and possessing the endowments that apply on the initial and terminal balanced growth paths. Figure 3.4 presents such a comparison. The upper panels of the figure show labour supply and consumption profiles over the life cycle on each countries' initial balanced growth path. The lower panels contain plots of the change over the life cycle between the two paths. As one may see, the microeconomic responses to the policy change mirror directly the changes in macroeconomic magnitudes already marked upon.

3.4.4 Components of the Reform

Table 3.6 presents an analysis of the steady state implications of the various components of the harmonization reform. Each block of numbers in the table represents the percentage changes in a series of variables consequent upon some degree of harmonization of the different countries' pension systems. Figures are adjusted for population and technological change and should be thought of as per capita and for given productive possibilities. Most of the simulations in the Table are calculated assuming trade flows and capital mobility. In the lowest part of the Table, we consider the effects of harmonization without capital mobility.

3.4.4.1 Contribution and Replacement Rate Harmonization

In the upper three blocks, we examine the effects of harmonizing the contribution and replacement rates. As one may observe, there are two major effects of the contribution rate changes on household behaviour. First, the increases in the German and UK effective labour income tax rates and the decreases in French and Italian effective tax rates produce significant impacts on labour supply. Second, decreasing the contribution rate, given our assumption of balanced government budget, alters the timing of tax payments over the life cycle in that households pay less to the government when they are young. The effect in France and Italy, for example, is to boost saving.

The main impact of the replacement rate harmonization is on saving. Germany and Italy experience a decrease in replacement rates and, as one might expect, this induces a rise in saving. One might expect in addition to find an effect on labour supply. Since changing the replacement rate affects the effective tax rate on labour income during the averaging period. (The gain in discounted future benefits that a household obtains from supplying additional units of labour is equivalent to a decrease in taxes.) However, such effects appear to be negligible.

The net effect of the replacement and contribution rate changes is shown in the third block of numbers in Table 3.6. Labour supply and savings in the UK are severely reduced by the harmonization. The UK capital stock declines by 13.9 %. Contrary effects may be observed in France and Italy where capital stock rises by 4.0 % and 4.8 %, respectively. Although for some countries our simulations yield substantial effects, the numbers are consistent with earlier simulation model analyses of the effects of unfunded pension schemes by Kotlikoff (1979a) and Auerbach and Kotlikoff (1987), for example.

3.4.4.2 Retirement Age and Averaging Period Harmonizations

Harmonizing the retirement ages involves simply increasing the Italian and French retirement ages to 65 from the level of 60 assumed in the baseline simulation. Although the number of years worked increases by more than 10 %, aggregate labour supply rises by much less since (i) there will be some diminution in labour supply for those in the pre-60 age group when the retirement constraint is partially relaxed, (ii) productivity falls with age for an individual household and (iii) productivity increases with each successive generation. The latter effect means that on a balanced growth path, the extra five years at the end of the working life contributes relatively little. Hence, the over all increase in the labour supply is 2.0 % and 1.3 % for Italy and France respectively. Other aggregates rise broadly in line with this boost to labour input, in that output and capital in the two countries expand by around 2-3 %.

The last component of the pension harmonization is that of the averaging period. We suppose that France and Italy adopt career-long averaging rather than their current approach based on rather shorter averaging periods. (From Table 3.2, note that Italian averaging is based on the last five years and French on the ten best years of wage earnings.) Increasing the averaging period has two effects. First, it reduces the distortions associated with the substantial fluctuations in effective labour income taxes implied by short averaging periods. Second, it changes the level of the wage base used for calculating pension entitlements, i.e., there is an effect analogous to a change in the replacement rate. Since the productivity and hence wage profile over the working life for a given worker is hump-shaped, extending the averaging period in the Italian case resembles an increase in the replacement ratio, whereas the French extension is like a reduction. The net effect for Italy and France, respectively, is a 5.2 % fall and a 1.6 % rise in the aggregate capital stock.

3.4.4.3 Summary Results With and Without Capital Mobility

The last two blocks of figures in Table 3.6 show the effect of the entire package of harmonization measures with and without capital mobility. The dominating factor is the harmonization of the contribution rate that produces substantial increases in savings and labour supply in Italy and France and corresponding declines in Germany and the UK. In the absence of capital mobility, interest rate changes are somewhat greater, as one might expect, although the difference is not great. The large interest rate declines in Italy and France boost demand for capital and induce substitution away from labour.

3.4.5 Sensitivity Analysis

Apart from the degree of capital mobility discussed above, the three aspects of parametrisation most likely to influence the results are (i) the elasticity of intertemporal substitution, α, (ii) the elasticity of substitution between consumption and leisure, ρ, and (iii) the degree of 'humpedness' of the wage-earnings profile, and (iv) the beqest preference parameter, α_B. We performed a series of simulations to explore the sensitivity of our findings to these three aspects. The results are reported in Table 3.7.

Raising the elasticity of intertemporal substitution, α, does no alter the qualitative impact of harmonization on aggregate variables although the effects are slightly dampened. For example, the absolute magnitude of aggregate consumption changes for Italy, France and the UK are around 0.5 percentage points less when α is increased from 0.9 to 1.2.

Changing the consumption-leisure substitution elasticity, ρ, altered the results very much as expected in that a rise in ρ from 1.1 to 1.4 increased the impact of harmonization on labour supply in Germany, France, Italy and the UK from -0.9 %, 7.4 %, 3.8 % and -10.7 % in the baseline to -1.1 %, 8.9 %, 4.5 % and -13.5 %. The impact of harmonization on other variables was changed commensurately.

Tilting the wage-earnings profile so that the decline from the peak level of productivity is smaller than that implied by the work of Kotlikoff and Gokhale (1992) has only a slight effect on the percentage changes in savings, for France and Italy in particulat. French and Italian labour supply changes were also somewhat different. Lastly, changing the bequest intensity parameter, α_B, has almost no effect on the simulations.

3.5 Conclusion

This paper uses overlapping generations models to examine the impact of important provisions of pension systems in the four largest European economies. To organize our analysis, we focus on a notional harmonization of the four systems, with contribution and replacement rates being replaced by the corresponding averages and with the retirement ages and averaging periods in France and Italy being set to those prevailing in the UK and Germany.

The magnitudes of the effects of this harmonization on real output, labour supply, consumption and investment is quite striking. Our calculations suggest that in the long run, France, for example, would enjoy a rise in output of 8.4 % with the long-run capital stock and labour supply being 9.5 % and 7.4 % higher. The UK which relies much less on unfunded PAYG state pensions would suffer a 12.3 % decline in output in the long-run if it adopted our 'average' system with its much greater level of state pension provision.

Our findings suggest that the current pressure on state pension systems through population ageing should be seen as an important opportunity to reform European pensions. Some economies are already suffering severe distortions in their savings and labour markets through the operation of badly designed pension systems. Our results provide a metric for the costs of bad design.

3.6 Appendix

3.6.1 The Model

In this section, we supply more details of our overlapping generations model. We discuss the utility and profit maximization problems facing households and firms respectively.

3.6.1.1 Household Sector

This Appendix provides a derivation of the principal behavioural equations of the model. The dynamic programme of each individual household may be stated compactly as that of choosing consumption, leisure and bequests, $c_{j1}, c_{j2}, \dots, c_{jn}$, for $j = 1, 2, 3$; $l_1, l_2, \dots, l_n$, and b_n, to maximize:

$$U \equiv \frac{1}{1-1/\alpha} \sum_{t=1}^{n} \frac{1}{(1+\delta)^{t-1}} u_t^{1-1/\alpha} + \frac{\alpha_B}{1-1/\alpha} \frac{b_n^{1-1/\alpha}}{(1+\delta)^n} \tag{13}$$

where

$$u_t \equiv [c_t^{1-1/\rho} + \alpha_L l_t^{1-1/\rho}]^{1/[1-1/\rho]} \tag{14}$$

$$c_t \equiv [c_{1t}^{1-1/\rho_1} + \alpha_T c_{0t}^{1-1/\rho_1}]^{1/[1-1/\rho_1]} \tag{15}$$

$$c_{0t} \equiv [c_{2t}^{1-1/\rho_2} + \alpha_X c_{3t}^{1-1/\rho_2}]^{1/[1-1/\rho_2]} \tag{16}$$

subject to the retirement constraints:

$$l_t = 1 \qquad t = n_r, \ldots 11 \tag{17}$$

and the lifetime wealth constraint:

$$\frac{b_n}{\prod_{t=2}^{n}[1+(1-\tau_r)r_s]} + \sum_{t=1}^{n}\frac{(1+\tau_v)p_t c_t}{\prod_{s=2}^{t}[1+(1-\tau_r)r_s]} = \tag{18}$$

$$\sum_{t=1}^{n}\frac{(1-\tau_x-\tau_w)w_t e_t(1-l_t)+z_t}{\prod_{s=2}^{t}[1+(1-\tau_r)r_s]} + \gamma_{ac}\sum_{v=n_r}^{n}\frac{\overline{n}\,\overline{w}^{\lambda}w_t^{1-\lambda}}{\prod_{s=2}^{t}[1+(1-\tau_r)r_s]} +$$

$$\sum_{t=1}^{n}\frac{b_{rt}}{\prod_{s=2}^{t}[1+(1-\tau_r)r_s]}$$

Here, the right hand side is the sum of human, pension and bequest wealth, and the price indices p_t^u and p_t are defined as:

$$p_t^u = [p_t^{1-\rho} + \alpha_L^{\rho}((1-\tau_w-\tau_x)w_t e_t + \mu_t)^{1-\rho}]^{\frac{1}{1-\rho}} \tag{19}$$

$$p_t = [((1+\tau_\upsilon)p_{1t})^{1-\rho_1} + \alpha_T^{\rho_1} p_{0t}^{1-\rho_1}]^{\frac{1}{1-\rho_1}} \tag{20}$$

$$p_{0t} = [((1+\tau_\upsilon)p_{2t})^{1-\rho_2} + \alpha_X^{\rho_2} p_{3t}^{1-\rho_2}]^{\frac{1}{1-\rho_2}} \tag{21}$$

Here, the homothetic specification of the subutility function makes it possible to interpret the normalised expenditure function as a price index p_t^u of total consumption, where μ_t in equation (19) is the Lagrange multiplier associated with retirement.

If the levels of full consumption, u, and retirement Lagrange multiplier μ_t are known, then it is easy to obtain optimal consumption and leisure in closed form as:

$$c_t = (p_t^u)^{\rho} u_t/(p_t)^{\rho} \tag{22}$$

$$l_t = (p_t^u)^{\rho} u_t/((1-\tau_w-\tau_x)w_t e_t + \mu_t)^{\rho} \tag{23}$$

To find optimal full consumption and bequests requires the solution of an intertemporal maximisation problem which has first order conditions:

$$u_t = \Omega^{-\alpha}\left[\frac{\prod_{s=2}^{t}[1+(1-\tau_r)r_s]}{(1+\delta)^{t-1}}\right]^{\alpha}(p_t^u)^{-\alpha} \tag{24}$$

$$\frac{1}{(1+\delta)^{n-1}}\alpha_B b_n^{-\frac{1}{\alpha}} = \Omega\prod_{s=2}^{n}[1+(1-\tau_r)r_s] \tag{25}$$

where Ω is the Lagrange multiplier associated with the intertemporal wealth constraint.

Further steps to obtain expressions for full consumption and bequest can be summarised as follows. We modify the intertemporal wealth constraint so as to comprise full consumption and full time endowments. Substituting the first order condition for full consumption into the modified intertemporal wealth constraint gives rise to a useful expression for Ω. Inserting this (i.e., Ω) into the first order conditions yields desired expressions for full consumption and bequest. However, forcing cohorts to retire at certain periods cannot be defined analytically. We apply a numerical procedure to determine retirement decisions.

3.6.1.2 Firm Sector

The economy we examine has two production sectors producing goods nontraded and tradeable using capital K and labour L inputs. Each industry consists of identical firms with C.E.S. production functions of the form:

$$F_t(K_t, L_t) \equiv \bar{\varepsilon}\left[\varepsilon_0 K_t^{1-\frac{1}{\varepsilon}} + (1-\varepsilon_0) L_t^{1-\frac{1}{\varepsilon}}\right]^{\frac{1}{(1-\frac{1}{\varepsilon})}} \tag{26}$$

Firms face convex costs of adjusting their capital inputs:

$$CK(I_t, K_t) \equiv \frac{\xi}{2}\frac{[I_t/K_t - \kappa]^2}{I_t/K_t} \tag{27}$$

where I stands for investment at period t. κ and ξ are parameters.

We postulate that managers of firms maximise the equity value of the firm (V). This equity value can be expressed as the discounted value of after-tax dividends D net of share issues VN:

$$V_t = \sum_{s=t}^{\infty} \frac{\left[\frac{1-\tau_d}{1-\tau_g} D_s - VN_s\right]}{\prod_{v=t+1}^{s}[1+(1-\tau_r)\, r_v/(1-\tau_g)]} \tag{28}$$

subject to capital accumulation

$$K_{s+1} = (1-d)\, K_s + I_s \tag{29}$$

In the above equations, τ_d is the dividend tax rate, τ_g is the capital gains tax rate, d denotes the rate of capital depreciation, r is the interest rate, τ_r represents the tax rate applied to interest income.

In order to obtain an explicit expression for $D_s - VN_s$, we use a series of definitions. The first is the cash flow identity that equates sources and uses of funds:

$$R_s + BN_s + VN_s = r_s B_{s-1} + D_s + IE_s + T_s \tag{30}$$

This identity states that firms use earnings before taxes and interest payments R and funds from borrowing BN and share issues VN to pay interest payments $r_s B_{s-1}$

to bondholders on accumulated debt B_{s-1}, dividends D_s to shareholders, investment expending IE_s and taxes to government T_s. The second expression defines R_s earnings before taxes and interest payments:

$$R_s = [\, p_s F (K_s, L_s)] - (1 - \tau_L) \, w_s \, L_s \,] \tag{31}$$

where w_s is the wage rate and τ_L is the employer contribution rate. The third definition is dividend rule

$$D_s = \bar{a} [\, (1 - \tau_c) (R_s + r_s B_{s-1}) + \tau_c A_s - d \, P_{Ks} K_s \,] \tag{32}$$

This definition states that firms pay dividends equal to a constant fraction, $\bar{a}$, of after-tax profits and interest payments net of economic depreciation. Here, τ_c stands for the corporation tax rate and A is the value of currently allowable capital depreciation allowances. The fourth definition is given by

$$B_{s-1} = \bar{b} \, P_{Ks-1} \, K_s \tag{33}$$

It states that firms maintain debt as a fraction, $\bar{b}$, of the value of their capital $P_{Ks-1} K_s$ with P_K the replacement price of capital goods. The rule defines firms' borrowing policy

$$B N_t = \bar{b} [\, P_{Kt} K_t - P_{Kt-1} K_{t-1} \,] \tag{34}$$

The value of investment expenditure IE_s is defined as:

$$I E_s = (1 - \tau_k) \, P_{Ks} \, I_t \tag{35}$$

where τ_k is the investment tax credit rate. Finally, we define firms' corporation tax liabilities as:

$$T_t = [\, R_t - r_t B_{t-1} \,] (1 - \tau_c) - \tau_c A_t \tag{36}$$

Using these definitions one can find the following expression for the market (equity) value of the firm:

$$V_t = \sum_{s=t}^{\infty} \{ (1 - \omega) (1 - \tau_c) [\, A_s - r_s \bar{b} \, P_{Ks} K_{s-1} \,] - \bar{b} [\, P_{Ks} K_s - P_{Ks} K_{s-1} \,] +$$
$$\omega [(1 - d) P_{Ks} K_s - P_{Ks-1} K_s] + (1 - \tau_k - (1 - \omega A_s^N)) \, P_{Ks} I_s \,\} \, \Gamma (s) + A_t^E$$

where $(1 - \omega) = \bar{a} \dfrac{1 - \tau_d}{1 - \tau_g} - \bar{a} + 1$ and $\Gamma (s) = \prod_{v=t+1}^{s} [1 + (1 - \tau_r) \, r_v / (1 - \tau_g)]$ is the discounting operator. To obtain the above expression we made two assumptions: (1) The present value of depreciation allowances can be split into the present value of allowances on current A_t^E and future investments A^N. (2) Adjustment costs to investing are internal to firms and thus subtracted from production to obtain net product level.

Hence we write the Lagrangian as:

$$L_t = \sum_{s=t}^{\infty} \{(1-\omega)(1-\tau_c)[A_s - r_s \bar{b} P_{K\,s-1} K_s] - \bar{b}[P_{K\,s} K_s - P_{K\,s-1} K_s] + \quad (37)$$

$$\omega[(1-d) P_{K\,s} K_s - P_{K\,s-1} K_s] + (1 - \tau_k - (1 - \omega A^N)) P_{K\,s} I_s \} \Gamma(s) + A_t^E -$$

$$\sum_{s=t}^{\infty} q_s [K_s - (1-d) K_s - I_s] \Gamma(s)$$

The first order conditions for optimal labour input, investment in period s are given by $\partial L_s / \partial L_s = 0$, $\partial L_s / \partial I_s = 0$ and $\partial L_s / \partial K_s = 0$, or

$$\frac{\partial F_t(K_t, L_t)}{\partial L_s} = (1 - \tau_L) w_t \quad (38)$$

$$(1 - \tau_k - (1 - \omega A^N)) P_{K\,t} + (1 - \omega)(1 - \tau_c) P_s \left(CK + CK' \frac{I_s}{K_s}\right) = q_s \quad (39)$$

$$\{ (1-\omega)(1-\tau_c)\left[\frac{\partial A_{s+1}}{\partial K_s} + P_{s+1} CK' \left(\frac{I_s}{K_s}\right)^2\right] - (1-\omega)(1-\tau_c) r_{s+1} \bar{b} P_s + \quad (40)$$

$$(\bar{b} - \omega)[(1-d) P_{K\,s+1} - P_{K\,s}] \} \Gamma(s+1) q = \Gamma(s) - (1-d) q_{s+1} \Gamma(s+1)$$

3.6.2 Four European Pension Systems

3.6.2.1 Basic and Supplementary Schemes

In this section, we briefly sketch the public pension systems of the four European countries in our sample.

3.6.2.2 Germany

The German retirement income system has been significantly reformed in recent years, most notably by the State Pension Reform Act of 1992. The changes were precipitated by the costs of absorbing the population of the former GDR into the social security system, and demographic developments that imply rapidly increasing dependency ratios in decades to come. The main aim of the reforms has been to reduce the incentives for early retirement contained in the existing social security system. Prior to January 1992, a number of categories of workers could retire early (between 60 and 63 years old) on full pension. After that date, early retirement on full pension has been limited to the disabled with 35 years or more of social security contributions. Other workers wishing to retire early face benefit cuts.

An unusual feature of the German system is that contributions, except for a particular of employer contributions, are not tax deductible. In practice, this means that all contributions are made by employers. Pension benefit entitlements are based on a points system which approximates to career-average revalued wages. Supplementary pensions in Germany are voluntary but nevertheless cover around 65 % of the work force. Supplementary pension arrangements and the state pension scheme are integrated in that supplementary plans commonly provide benefits equal to 0.3 to 0.5 per cent of final earnings up to the social security contribution ceiling, plus 1.2 to 1.5 per cent of final earnings in excess of the social security contribution ceiling.

3.6.2.3 France

The French social security and supplementary pensions are relatively generous. After 37.5 years of contributions, recipients receive 50 % of average, revalued covered earnings, where the averaging is based on the best ten years of earnings. A series of mandatory supplemental plans agreed through collective bargaining have been gradually extended by government decree to cover almost all employees. The generosity of the French system was significantly increased in 1983 when pensions paid by both the social security system and the other main schemes became payable from the age of 60.

An interesting characteristic of both social security and additional mandatory schemes in France is that they are rigidly Pay-As-You-Go (PAYG). Given the claims on the system in a particular year, contribution rates are adjusted so that the net receipts and expenditures match. A retired individual's social security benefit entitlement is calculated using the formula given above while his income from the supplemental schemes depends on accumulated 'points' that reflect his and his employer's contributions through his working life. The supplementary pension for an average worker after 37.5 years' contributions is 20 per cent of career average pay.

3.6.2.4 Italy

Italian pensions are extremely generous and substantially increase employers' labour costs. In 1993, total contribution rates for an average blue-collar worker and his employer were 46.55 % (of which 27.27 % was pension contributions) plus a 4.6 % contribution for the health service. The economic crisis of 1992 has finally precipitated serious attempts at reform of the system. Intended changes include (i) a move from 5 to 10 year averaging in benefit entitlement calculations, (ii) a gradual increase in the retirement age from 60 and 55 for men and women respectively to 65 and 60, (iii) an increase in the minimum number of contributory years required of social security retirement pension recipients, (iv) price rather than wage indexing of pension benefits. As partial compensation for these very substantial changes, some accrual rates will be adjusted up.

Given the lavish levels of provision afforded by the Italian social security system, there has been little or no demand for supplementary schemes. For relatively low paid individuals, accrual rates of 2 % and a maximum number of contributory years of 40 imply a replacement ratio of 80 % applied to final covered earnings. For higher income tranches, accrual rates fall to an eventual minimum of 1 %. Early retirement is fairly easy to obtain and benefits are not reduced in this case. On the other hand, those who retire late receive increased benefits.

3.6.2.5 United Kingdom

The United Kingdom pension system is quite complex, comprising a flat-rate element plus a State Earnings Related Pension Scheme (SERPS) from which individuals may contract out if they are members of an alternative, private scheme. The basic flat-rate pension delivers pension benefits equal to 20 % of average earnings. SERPS benefits amount to 25 % of average revalued covered earnings in the best 20 years of the contribution period. However, a gradual reduction in SERPS benefits was announced in 1988. In particular, benefits as a fraction of covered earnings will be reduced from 25 % to 20 % starting in the year 2000. Total employee and employer contributions, including those on for the flat-rate pension, for someone enrolled in SERPS and on moderate income, amount to 9.0 % and 10.4 % respectively.

Supplementary schemes are widespread in the UK. Of those in supplementary, private pensions, 97 % have contracted out of SERPS. Employees who contract out and their employers pay reduced contribution rates to the flat-rate pension scheme. The rebate for contracting out is 2 % for employees and 3.8 % for employers. Most plans are defined benefit in nature although defined contribution plans are increasingly becoming popular. Tax privileges are accorded only if benefits are less than around 2/3 of final earnings. For defined benefit plans, the cap on pensions is provided by the rule that total contributions be less than 17.5 % of earnings.

The United Kingdom regulates supplementary pension schemes quite strictly. The intention of this regulation is that participants to supplementary schemes receive given target levels of pension income. Thus, the minimum pension income is set equal to the SERPS pension. In practice, this constraint does not bind as most occupational schemes have more generous provision, commonly according payments equal to 1/60th or 1/80th of final earnings for each year of membership. If the fraction is 1/80th, pensioners often receive a tax free lump sum payment at retirement equal to 1.5 times final salary in addition.

3.6.3 Sources for Parameterisation

3.6.3.1 Tax Rates

Wherever feasible, we employ average and marginal income tax rates for married couples with two children. Wage income tax rates come from the *OECD Eco-*

nomic Outlook of June 1993, and two other OECD publications: the *Tax/Benefit Position of Production Workers* (1992b), and *Revenue Statistics of OECD Member Countries*, (1991a). Average and marginal social security contribution rates also come from *Revenue Statistics of OECD Member Countries*, while marginal rates are taken from again from the above *OECD Economic Outlook and the Tax/Benefit Position of Production Workers*. The savings tax rates we employ are for taxes on interest income and are drawn from the OECD study *Taxing Profits in a Global economy: Domestic and International Issues*, (1991b). Finally, VAT rates are taken from the series *OECD Economic Surveys* of individual member countries.

3.6.3.2 Pension Schemes

The treatment of retirement age we assume is based on Foster (1994), while replacement ratio parameters come from the EC Commission publicationem *Old Age Replacement Ratios, Volume I: Relations Between Pensions and Income from Employment at the Moment*, (1993). Some aspects of minimum pension provisions come from Van Den Noord and Herd (1993) and Foster (1994). Averaging period details are taken from Foster (1994), as are contribution periods for full pensions and maximum replacement ratios. Accrual factors come from Foster (1994), supplemented with information from Van Den Noord and Herd (1993) in the case of Germany and France. Replacement ratios for unemployment are taken from the *OECD Economic Outlook*, 53, June 1993.

Tables 3.2 to 3.4 describe features of the different types of public pension regimes in the countries in our sample. These include retirement age, whether benefits are lump-sum payments or other, earnings-related pension elements such as averaging period, contribution period and accrual factor, maximum replacement ratio, and indexation. Values for parameters describing pension systems across European countries can be found in 'Employee benefits in Europe and USA', edited by H. Foster (1994), for EU countries EUROSTAT, 'Old age replacement ratios' volume I. We take male retirement age as standard retirement age.

3.6.3.3 Household Parameters

We supposed that utility and production function parameters are the same across countries. This approach was justified, first, by our aim of isolating the impact of the pension system and tax parameters and, second, by the fact that even though these parameters probably do differ across our four countries, the knowledge we have of these differences is sketchy. A summary of all the parameters used in the simulations is provided in Tables 3.1-3.4. In making our selection, we drew on the large number of empirical studies that estimate utility function parameters.

Estimated values for the intertemporal elasticity of substitution are commonly either in a low range of 0.2 to 0.4 (see Hall (1988): US time series data, Bayoumi (1990): UK time series data and Patterson and Pesaran (1992): US and UK quarterly time series data) or in a high range of 1.0 to 1.3 (see Lawrance (1991): US panel data and Mankiw, Rotemberg and Summers (1985): US quarterly time series). We take a value of 0.9 as an average of these estimated values.

Of the other utility function parameters, we set the consumption-leisure elasticity of substitution at 1.1 respectively. For a reasonable value of the consumption-leisure parameter, this yields an uncompensated wage elasticity of labour supply of 0.2 which seems a sensible figure for the combined labour supply of a husband and wife couple. Such a value may be justified by the various studies surveyed in Hum and Simpson (1994).

The bequest preference parameter and the bequest substitution elasticity are hard to establish. Our chosen values of 0.5 and 0.9 respectively imply reasonable ratios of bequests to peak savings and seem broadly consistent with the levels estimated by Kotlikoff and Summers (1981).

The wage-age profile we used is hump-shaped in accordance with the findings of Kotlikoff and Gokhale (1992), Davies (1992) and Gottschalk and Joyce (1992). Kotlikoff and Gokhale (1992) argue that productivity peaks at around age 45 and declines thereafter. Productivity at age 65 is less one-third of the peak. Davies (1992) and Gottschalk and Joyce (1992) both using cross-country data find that the ratios of mean earnings for 40-49-year-old men to mean earnings for 25-29-year-old men are in the range 1.08 to 1.30. Lastly, the subjective discount rate, δ, and the consumption-leisure parameter, α_0, were determined in the model calibration.

3.6.3.4 Firm Parameters

Estimates of the elasticity of substitution between labour and capital range between 0.45 and 0.9. For instance, Boskin (1978), Feldstein (1982) and Artus (1984) found 0.45, 0.9 and 0.50 values using U.S. annual time series, respectively. Artus (1984) also obtained an estimate of 0.85 for Canada. As for European countries, Törmä, Rutherford and Vaittinen (1995) made an attempt to estimate the Finnish production function parameters in traded and nontraded industries. Their estimates are in the range of U.S. and Canadian ones and are 0.915 and 0.703 for traded and nontraded industries, respectively. In our simulations, we use these Finnish values because they are more likely to be relevant for the European countries we are studying and because their estimates relate to traded and non-traded industries as in our model.

The adjustment cost parameters are important determinants of the economy's dynamics following shocks. Recall that the convex investment cost function is: $CK(I_t, K_{t-1}) \equiv \xi(I_t/K_{t-1} - \kappa)^2/(I_t/K_{t-1})/2$. We select values of the parameters κ and ξ similar to those chosen Summers (1981).

3.6.3.5 Rest of the World Parameters

The rest of the world elasticities of export demand and savigs supply, ω and ω^*, were set at the levels used by Perraudin and Pujol (1991), namely -1.2 and 5. The constant in the savings supply function was chosen in such a way that a 1 % deviation from world interest rates elicited a change in world savings supply equal to 10 % of GDP.

Table 3.1. Tax and Contribution Parameters.

Parameter	Germany	France	Italy	UK	Average
Contribution Rates					
a) public schemes[a]					
1) average employee	10.9	11.0	5.5	4.9	8.1
2) marginal employee	18.2	17.1	9.0	7.6	13.0
3) average employer	12.9	23.1	20.4	6.3	15.7
4) marginal employer	18.2	43.8	50.1	10.4	30.6
5) total average (1)+(3)	23.8	34.1	25.9	11.2	23.8
6) total marginal (2)+(4)	36.4	60.9	59.1	18.0	43.6
b) supplementary schemes[b]					
7) employee	0.0	2.0		6.5	2.1
8) employer	15.0	3.0		10.0	7.0
Wage Tax[c]					
9) average rate	8.7	1.0	14.2	15.4	9.8
10) marginal rate	17.6	6.7	23.7	25.0	18.3
Contribution plus Tax Rates					
11) average (5)+(9)	32.5	34.1	40.1	26.6	33.3
12) marginal (6)+(10)	54.0	67.8	82.8	43.0	61.9
Other Taxes					
13) Savings tax rate[d]	39.1	4.5	12.5	24.0	20.0
14) VAT rate	14.0	18.6	12.6	17.5	15.7

[a] Marginal contributions rates are OECD calculations for production worker with two children for the year 1991. Average social security contributions are defined as the ratio of contributions relative to compensation and are taken from OECD (1992b).

[b] A negligible percentage of Italian pensioners possess private, supplementary pensions so we omit such pensions in the relevant simulations for these countries.

[c] OECD calculations for production worker with two children for the year 1991.

[d] Defined as marginal tax rate on interest income

Source: OECD (1992b), OECD (1991a) and OECD (1991b).

Table 3.2. Public Pension Schemes.

	Germany	France	Italy	UK
Retirement age (M/W)	65/65 (normal)	60/60 (minimum)	60/55[a] (normal)	65/60[b] (normal)
Early retirement provisions (M/W)	63/60: 0.3% benefit cut for each month	55: 35% benefit cut	No	No
Late retirement provisions (M/W)	67: 0.5% benefit rise for each month	No	No	70/65: 7.5% benefit rise for each year
Work-pension link	No	Yes	No	ERP: Yes FRP: No
Flat-rate scheme replacement ratio	-	-	-	Accrual 20 %
Other minimum provisions	social assistance	guaranteed minimum	guaranteed minimum	guaranteed minimum
Averaging period	career	best 10 years	last 5 years	career
Minimum contribution period	5	3 months	15	quarter of working life
Contribution period for full pension	working life	37.5	40	nine-tenths of working life
Accrual factor	1.5 %	1.75 %	2 %	0.4 %
Maximum replacement ratio	50 %	50 %	80 %	20 % (ERP)
Replacement ratio in unemployment	34.3 %	30.1 %	7.7 %	15.4 %
Spouse supplement	25 % ≤ age 45 60 % ≥ age 45	52 % of pension	60 % of pension	60 % of pension
Indexation	wages	wages	wages	prices

[a] In Italy, normal retirement age is being increased by one year for every two over the period 1993 to 2002 from age 60(55) to age 65(60) for men(women).
[b] The normal retirement age for women in the United Kingdom is to increase from 60 to 65 over the period 2010 to 2020.
Source: Foster (1994), Van den Noord and Herd (1993).

Table 3.3. Baseline Parameterisation.

Parameter	Symbol	Value
Utility Function Parameters		
Subjective discount rate	δ	--
Elasticity of intertemporal substitution	α	0.90
Consumption-leisure elasticity of substitution	ρ	1.10
Consumption-leisure parameter	α_L	--
Bequest preference parameter	α_B	0.50
Maximum life-span (assuming adult life begins at 20)	T	75.00
Industry Parameters		
Production elasticity (traded)	ε_1	0.92
Production elasticity (nontraded)	ε_3	0.71
Adjustment cost parameter	κ	0.05
Adjustment cost parameter	ξ	20

Note: δ and α_L are determined by the model calibration.

Table 3.4. Macro Variable Parameterisation.

Parameter	Germany	France	Italy	UK
Population	79.5	56.4	57.7	57.4
GDP	1488.2	1190.8	1090.8	975.1
Capital/output ratio	2.8	2.8	3.0	3.2
Labour income/GDP	54.5	52.0	45.1	57.7
Output share of nontraded sector	64.9	73.4	61.7	70.8
Capital share of nontraded sector	53.0	42.3	32.6	50.0
Labour share of nontraded sector	63.5	73.4	61.7	70.8
Exports/GDP	26.2	18.3	15.5	31.4
Imports/GDP	23.1	20.9	15.5	39.5
Net foreign assets/GDP	23.4	-3.9	-10.4	-0.6
Government Expenditure/GDP	46.0	49.9	43.1	42.1
Education/GDP	9.1	10.2	9.4	11.4
Health/GDP	12.8	13.1	11.0	12.4
Government bond stock/GDP	22.8	25.0	98.9	28.5
Interest rate	4.58	5.56	5.92	4.76

Source: OECD (1992b), OECD (1991a) and OECD (1991b).

Table 3.5. Summary of Pension Harmonization.

Policies:	Germany	France	Italy	UK	Average
Contributions Rates					
Employee rates	18.2	17.1	9.0	7.6	13.0
Employer rates	18.2	43.8	50.1	10.4	30.6
Total	36.4	60.9	59.1	18.0	43.6
Replacement ratios	60.0	50.0	80.0	33.0	55.8
Retirement ages	65	60	60	65	65
Averaging Periods					
First year	20	35	45	20	20
Final year	60	50	55	60	60

Table 3.6. Long-Run Simulation Results.

Country:	C	S	L	K	Y	w	r	er	U
(1) Contribution rate harmonisation									
Germany	-0.8	0.1	-0.9	0.2	-0.5	-9.0	-1.1	-0.4	-0.0
France	6.6	6.0	6.0	5.3	5.7	9.8	-0.7	4.7	0.3
Italy	3.2	1.8	3.3	1.8	2.5	13.9	0.7	1.7	0.1
UK	-13.3	-11.6	-10.8	-10.8	-10.8	-15.5	2.6	-8.6	-0.7
(2) Replacement rate harmonisation									
Germany	0.2	0.9	0.0	0.9	0.4	0.4	-1.1	0.3	0.0
France	-0.3	-1.0	0.1	-1.1	-0.5	-0.5	1.2	-0.4	-0.1
Italy	0.8	2.2	-0.2	2.5	1.2	1.6	-2.6	1.6	0.2
UK	-1.3	-4.1	0.0	-4.1	-1.9	-2.2	4.3	-2.3	-0.2
(3) = (1) + (2)									
Germany	-0.7	1.0	-0.9	1.1	-0.1	-8.7	-2.1	-0.1	0.0
France	6.3	4.9	6.2	4.0	5.1	9.2	0.6	4.2	0.2
Italy	4.1	4.5	3.0	4.8	3.9	16.0	-2.4	3.7	0.3
UK	-14.3	-14.7	-10.7	-13.9	-12.3	-17.1	6.3	-10.2	-0.9
(4) Retirement age harmonisation									
Germany	0.0	-0.0	-0.0	0.0	0.0	0.0	0.0	0.0	0.0
France	2.0	2.8	1.3	2.8	2.0	0.6	-1.7	1.6	0.2
Italy	2.5	2.4	2.0	2.5	2.3	0.3	-1.0	2.0	0.2
UK	-0.0	0.0	0.0	0.0	0.0	0.0	0.0	0.0	-0.0

(5) Averaging period harmonisation									
Germany	0.0	0.0	0.0	0.0	0.0	0.0	0.0	0.0	0.0
France	0.4	1.4	-0.2	1.6	0.7	0.7	-1.6	0.5	0.1
Italy	-1.7	-4.5	0.5	-5.2	-2.4	-3.3	5.6	-3.2	-0.4
UK	0.0	0.0	0.0	0.0	0.0	0.0	0.0	0.0	0.0
(6) = (3) + (4) + (5)									
Germany	-0.7	1.0	-0.9	1.1	-0.1	-8.7	-2.1	-0.1	0.0
France	9.2	10.3	7.4	9.5	8.4	10.9	-3.6	7.1	0.7
Italy	4.8	4.7	3.8	4.9	4.4	15.6	-1.9	4.0	0.4
UK	-14.3	-14.7	-10.7	-13.9	-12.3	-17.1	6.3	-10.2	-0.9
(7) = (6) without capital mobility									
Germany	-0.5	0.8	-0.7	1.3	-0.1	-9.3	-2.4	-0.1	0.0
France	9.8	8.9	8.0	10.1	8.8	12.4	-4.1	7.7	0.8
Italy	5.4	4.1	4.2	5.3	4.9	17.8	-2.3	4.6	0.5
UK	-16.2	-16.8	-11.6	-15.0	-13.3	-18.9	7.1	-11.7	-1.0

Table 3.7. Sensitivity Analysis of Long-Run Effects.

Country:	C	S	L	K	Y	w	r	er	U
Central case ($\alpha = 0.9$, $\rho = 1.1$, $\alpha_B = 0.5$)									
Germany	-0.7	1.0	-0.9	1.1	-0.1	-8.7	-2.1	-0.1	0.0
France	9.2	10.3	7.4	9.5	8.4	10.9	-3.6	7.1	0.7
Italy	4.8	4.7	3.8	4.9	4.4	15.6	-1.9	4.0	0.4
UK	-14.3	-14.7	-10.7	-13.9	-12.3	-17.1	6.3	-10.2	-0.9
High intertemporal elasticity ($\alpha = 1.2$)									
Germany	-0.8	0.5	-1.0	0.7	-0.3	-8-8	-1.6	-0.3	0.0
France	8.6	9.4	7.1	8.7	7.8	10.7	-3.1	6.5	0.7
Italy	4.3	4.0	3.6	4.2	3.9	15.3	-1.4	3.4	0.4
UK	-14.0	-13.8	-10.7	-13.1	-11.8	-16.7	5.3	-9.8	-0.9
Low intertemporal elasticity ($\alpha = 0.6$)									
Germany	-0.4	2.0	-0.8	2.0	0.3	-8.3	-3.1	0.4	0.0
France	10.2	12.0	8.1	11.3	9.6	11.4	-4.7	8.1	0.7
Italy	5.9	6.4	4.4	6.8	5.6	16.4	-3.3	5.4	0.4
UK	-15.1	-16.2	-10-9	-15.6	-13.1	-17.9	8.0	-11.1	-0.9
High intratemporal elasticity ($\rho = 1.4$)									
Germany	-0.8	0.8	-1.1	0.9	-0.3	-8.7	-2.1	-0.2	0.0
France	10.7	11.8	8.9	10.8	9.8	10.8	-3.8	8.2	0.7
Italy	5.4	4.9	4.5	5.2	4.8	15.3	-1.7	4.3	0.4
UK	-17.4	-16.4	-13.5	-15.5	-14.4	-16.5	5.5	-11.7	-0.9

Low intratemporal elasticity ($\rho = 0.8$)									
Germany	-0.5	1.1	-0.8	1.2	0.0	-8,7	-2.1	0.1	0.0
France	7.4	8.6	5.8	8.1	6.9	11.1	-3.5	5.7	0.7
Italy	4.0	4.1	3.0	4.4	3.7	15.8	-2.0	3.5	0.4
UK	-11.0	-12.9	-7.7	-12.4	-9.9	-17.8	7.2	-8.7	-0.9
Flat wage profile (same wage for all ages)									
Germany	-0.6	0.9	-0.8	1.0	-0.1	-8.7	-2.0	-0.0	0.0
France	9.7	8.7	9.0	7.4	8.3	9.4	-0.7	6.8	0.7
Italy	6.6	6.3	5.4	6.6	6.0	15.6	-2.4	5.4	0.4
UK	-13.7	-14.6	-10.0	-13.9	-11.9	-17.5	6.8	-10.0	-0.9
High bequest parameter ($\alpha_B = 1.0$)									
Germany	-0.6	1.0	-0.9	1.1	-0.1	-8.7	-2.1	-0.1	0.0
France	9.3	10.3	7.6	9.5	8.5	10.8	-3.5	7.1	0.7
Italy	5.0	4.9	4.0	5.2	4.6	15.6	-2.1	4.2	0.4
UK	-14.3	-14.6	-10.8	-13.9	-12.3	-17.1	6.2	-10.2	-0.9
Low bequest parameter ($\alpha_B = 0.25$)									
Germany	-0.7	1.0	-0.9	1.1	-0.1	-8.7	-2.1	-0.1	0.0
France	9.1	10.3	7.3	9.5	8.4	11.0	-3.7	7.0	0.7
Italy	4.7	4.5	3.7	4.8	4.3	15.6	-1.9	3.9	0.4
UK	14.3	14.7	10.7	-14.0	-12.2	-17.2	6.3	-10.2	-0.9

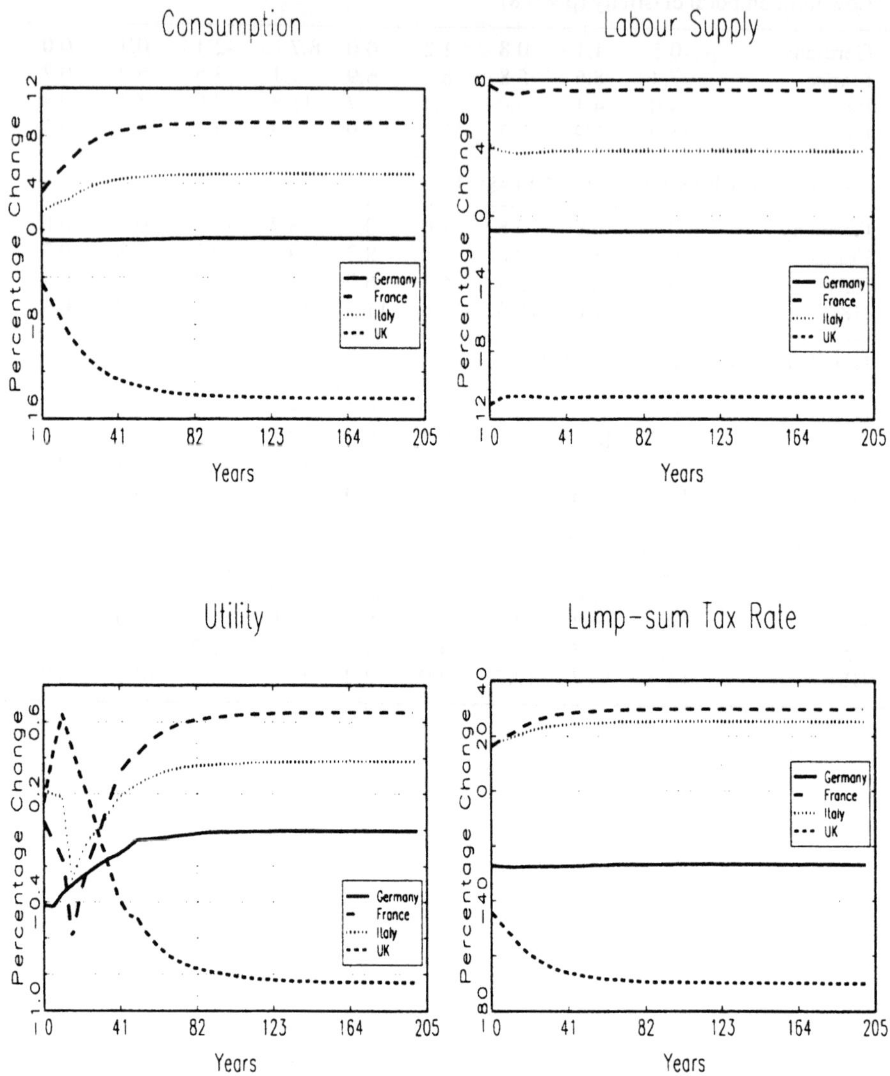

Figure 3.1. Macroeconomic Effects.

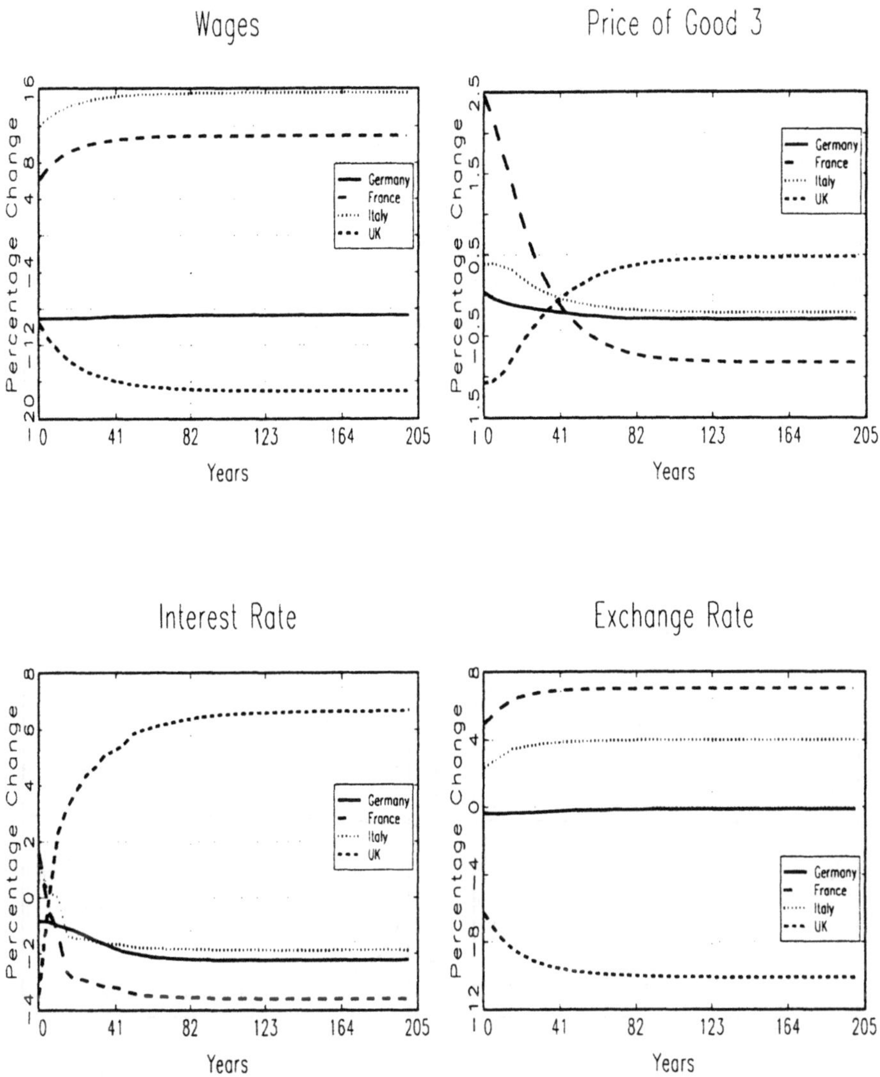

Figure 3.2. Price Effects.

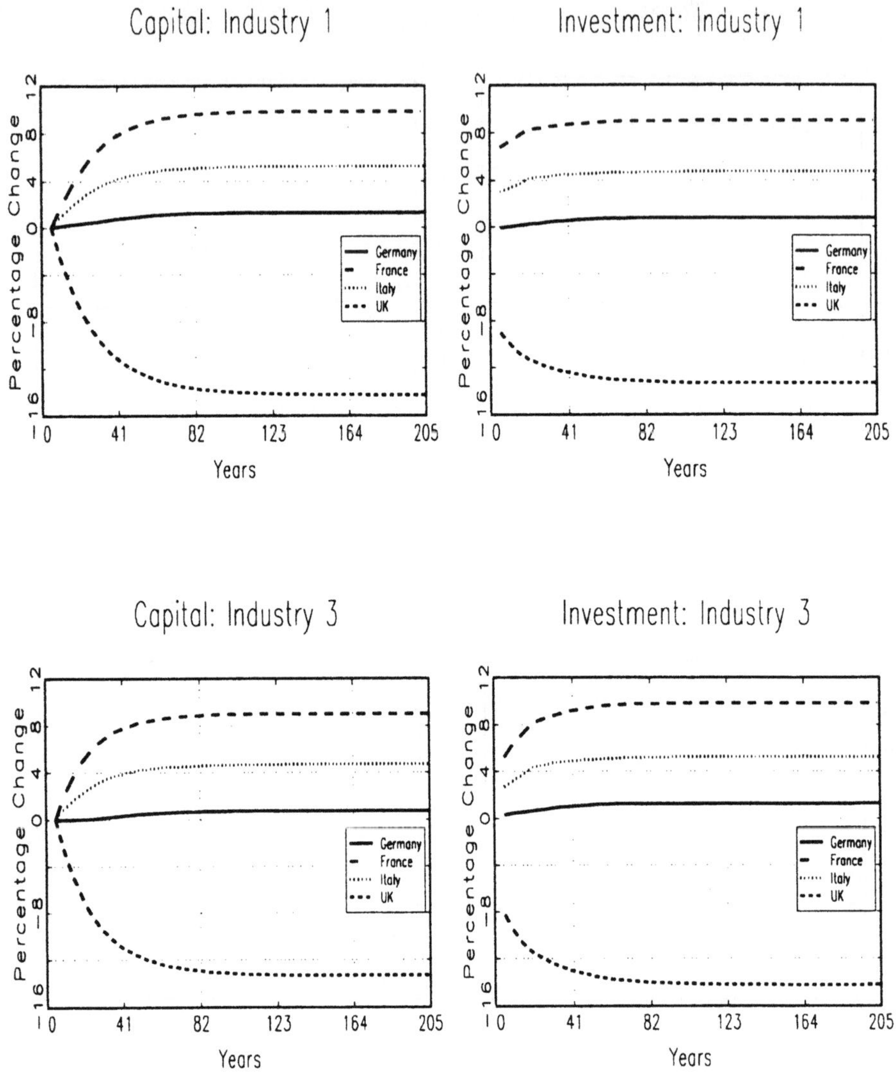

Figure 3.3. Capital Accumulation Effects.

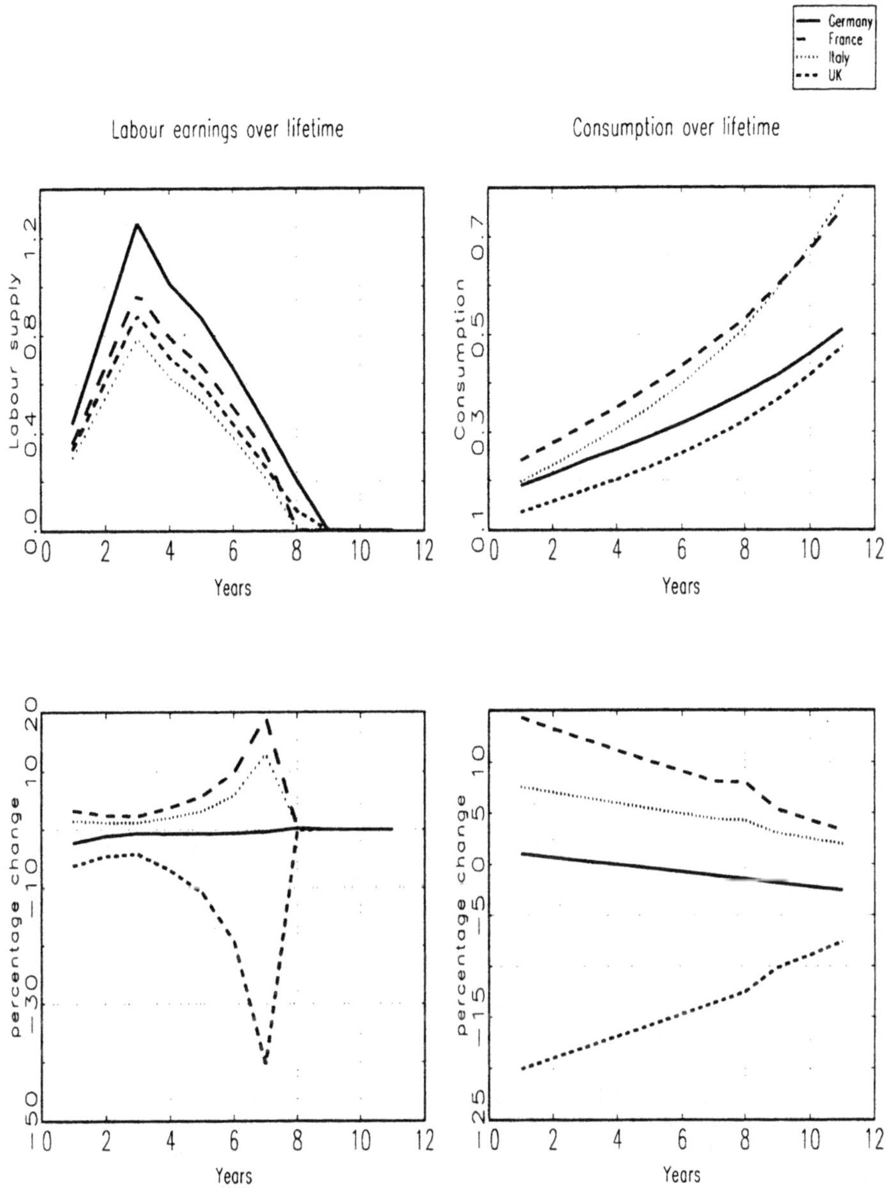

Figure 3.4. Lifetime Effects.

References

Artus, J. (1984): "The Disequilibrium Real Wage Hypothesis: An Empirical Evaluation," *IMF Staff Papers*, 31(2), 249–302.

Auerbach, A., L. J. Kotlikoff (1987): *Dynamic Fiscal Policy*. Cambridge University Press, Cambridge.

Barro, R. J., G. M. MacDonald (1979): "Social Security and Consumer Spending in an International Cross Section," *Journal of Public Economics*, 11(3), 275–289.

Bayoumi, T. (1990): "Financial Innovation with Staggered Price Setting," Working Paper 95, IMF.

Bös, D., R. von Weiszäcker (1989): "Economic Consequences of an Aging Population," *European Economic Review*, 33, 345–354.

Boskin, M. J. (1978): "Taxation, Saving, and the Rate of Interest", *Journal of Political Economy*, 86, S3–527.

Breyer, F., M. Straub (1993): "Welfare Effects of Unfunded Pension Systems when Labour Supply is Endogenous," *Journal of Public Economics*, 50, 77–91.

Broer, D. P., E. W. M. T. Westerhout, A. L. Bovenberg (1994): "Taxation, Pensions and Savings in a Small Open Economy," *Scandinavian Journal of Economics*, 96(3), 403–424.

Chauveau, T., R. Loufir (1995): "The Future of Public Pensions in the Seven Major Economies," mimeo.

Craig, B., R. G. Batina (1991): "The Effects of Social Security in a Life Cycle Family Labor Supply Simulation Model," *Journal of Public Economics*, 46(2), 199–226.

Cutler, D. M., J. M. Poterba, L. M. Scheiner, L. H. Summers (1990): "An Aging Society: Opportunity or Challenge?," *Brookings Papers on Economic Activity*, (1), 1–73.

Davies, S. (1992): "Cross-Country Patterns of Change in Relative Wages," in *NBER Macroeconomics Annual*, ed. by O. J. Blanchard, S. Fischer, pp. 238–292. MIT Press, Cambridge and London.

Diamond, P. A., J. A. Hausman (1984): "Individual Retirement and Savings Behavior," *Journal of Public Economics*, 23(1-2), 81–114.

EC Commission (1993): *Old Age Raplacement Ratios, Volume I: Relation Between Pensions and Income from Employment at the Moment.* EC Commission, Brussels.

Feldstein, M. (1974): "Social Security, Induced Retirement, and Aggregate Capital Accumulation," *Journal of Political Economy*, 82(5), 905–926.

Feldstein, M. S., A. Pellechio (1979): "Social Security and Household Wealth Accumulation: New Microeconometric Evidence," *Review of Economic Studies*, 61(3), 361–368.

Feldstein, M. S. (1982): "Inflation Tax Rules and Investment: Some Econometric Evidence", *Econometrica*, 50(4), 825-862.

Foster, H. (1994): *Employee Benefits in Europe and USA*. Longman, London.

Gottschalk, P., M. Joyce (1992): "Changes in Earnings inequality – An International Perspective," Working Paper 66, The Luxembourg Income Study.

Hageman, R. P., G. Nicoletti (1989): "Aging Populations: Economic Effects and Implications for Public Finance," *OECDES*, 12, 59–110.

Hall, R. E. (1988): "Intertemporal Substitution in Consumption," *Journal of Political Economy*, 96, 339–357.

Homburg, S. (1990): "The Efficiency of Unfunded Pension Schemes," *Journal of Institutional and Theoretical Economics*, 146(4), 640–647.

Hum, D., W. Simpson (1994): "Labour Supply Estimation and Public Policy," *Journal of Economic Surveys*, 8(1), 57–81.

Kenc, T., W. R. M. Perraudin (1995): "European Pension Systems: A Simulation Analysis," Working Paper 9505, Department of Applied Economics, University of Cambridge.

Kotlikoff, L. G. (1979a): "Social Security and Equilibrium Capital Intensity," *Quarterly Journal of Economics*, 93(2), 233–254.

Kotlikoff, L. J. (1979b): "Testing the Theory of Social Security and Life Cycle Accumulation," *American Economic Review*, 69(3), 396–410.

Kotlikoff, L. J., J. Gokhale (1992): "Estimating a Firm's Age-Productivity Profile using the Present Value of Worker's Earnings," *Quarterly Journal of Economics*, 107(4), 1214–1242.

Kotlikoff, L. J., L. H. Summers (1981): "The Role of Intergenerational Transfers in Aggregate Capital Accumulation," JPE, 89, 706–732.

Lawrance, E. C. (1991): "Poverty and the Rate of Time Preference: Evidence from Panel Data," *Journal of Political Economy*, 99(1), 54–77.

Mankiw, N. G., J. J. Rotemberg, L. H. Summers (1985): "Intertemporal Substitution in Macroeconomics," *Quarterly Journal of Economics*, 100, 225–251.

McCarty, T. A. (1990): "The Effect of Social Security on Married Women's Labor Force Participation," *National Tax Journal*, 43(1), 95–110.

OECD (1988): *Aging Populations: The Social Policy Implications*. OECD, Paris.

– (1991a): *Revenue Statistics of OECD Member Countries and National Accounts*. OECD, Paris.

– (1991b): *Taxing Profits in A Global Economy: Domestic and International Issues*. OECD, Paris.

– (1992a): *Private Pensions and Public Policy*. OECD, Paris.

– (1992b): *The Tax and Benefit Position of Production Workers*. OECD, Paris.

– (1993): *Economic Outlook*.

Patterson, K. D., B. Pesaran (1992): "The Intertemporal Elasticity of Substitution in Consumption in the United States and the United Kingdom," *The Review of Economics Statistics*, 74(4), 573–584.

Perraudin, W. R. M., T. Pujol (1991): "European Tax Harmonization and the French Economy," *IMF Staff Paper*, 38(2), 399–440.

Pestieau, P. (1992): "The Distribution of Private Pension Benefits: How Fair Is It?," in (OECD 1992a).

Summers, L. H. (1981): "Taxation and Corporate Investment: A q Theory Approach," *Brookings Papers on Economic Activity*, Spring, 67–127.

Törmä, H., T. Rutherford, and T. Vaittinen (1995): "What Will EU Membership and the Value-Added Tax Reform Do to Finnish Food Economy? – A Computable General Equilibrium Analysis," Research Report 88, VATT, Helsinki.

Van den Noord, P., R. Herd (1993): "Pension Liabilities in the Seven Major Economies," WP 142, OECD Department of Economics and Statistics.

4 Pension Policies and Lifetime Uncertainty in an Applied General Equilibrium Model

D.P. Broer[1,2]
E.W.M.T. Westerhout[1]
[1]Central Planning Bureau, P.O. Box 80510, 2508 GM The Hague, The Netherlands.
[2]Erasmus University, Department of Economic Policy, P.O. Box 1738, 3000 DR Rotterdam and Research Centre for Economic Policy (OCFEB), Erasmus University, P.O. Box 1738, 3000 DR Rotterdam, The Netherlands.

Abstract

This paper uses an overlapping generations model of a small open economy to explore the efficiency effects and intergenerational redistribution effects of several policy options aimed at reducing the burden of pay-as-you-go (PAYG) contributions on labor income. Both the policy option of subjecting the retirement benefits to PAYG contributions and that of cutting PAYG benefits succeed in improving efficiency, but only the latter one proves to be Pareto-welfare improving. In addition, the paper performs a sensitivity analysis to test whether simulation results depend on the assumption used with respect to the survival profile of households. It appears that assumptions about survival rates do not affect overall efficiency conclusions, but they do make a difference for the distribution of the gain across generations.

4.1 Introduction

The prospect of rising public spending on public pensions has led many industrialized countries to re-evaluate their pension schemes (see Bös and von Weizsäcker (1989)). Public pensions are typically financed by levying taxes or premiums on labor income which may have profound efficiency effects (see Marchand and Pestieau (1991)). In addition, pay-as-you-go (PAYG) pension schemes have important distribution effects as they distribute wealth from young working generations to older generations that are retired (see Nelissen (1987)). The projected ageing of the population in industrialized countries will only reinforce the role of both efficiency and distribution effects.

To explore the effects of different types of pension policies, intertemporal general equilibrium models with overlapping generations of households are a natural candidate. These models base the behaviour of economic subjects on a solid microfoundation. They also recognize the intertemporal dimension of not only saving and investment decisions, but also labor supply decisions. Furthermore, these models allow for the evaluation of the welfare consequences of policies for different generations, which is a prerequisite for a proper analysis of both the efficiency effects of pension policies and their distributional consequences.

This paper uses a Computable General Equilibrium (CGE) model to explore the effects of different types of pension policies. The model is a small open economy version of the well-known model of Auerbach and Kotlikoff (1987), extended with a pension sector.[1] The model is used to calculate the effects of two types of pension policies that are aimed at reducing the burden of contributions to the PAYG pension scheme.

The first policy subjects pension benefits to those who are retired to PAYG contributions. The second policy reduces the burden of PAYG contributions by cutting PAYG benefits. The analysis demonstrates the potential of general equilibrium models with overlapping generations. In particular, both policies will be shown to improve economic efficiency, but only in the latter case all generations share in the efficiency gain.

The Auerbach-Kotlikoff model makes a simplistic assumption on the survival profile of households. Households face a zero probability of death during their entire life and a probability of one when they have reached a certain age. This assumption does not recognize that in reality lifetimes are uncertain. In order to find out whether this biases our simulation results, we also perform simulations under two alternative assumptions. The first alternative assumption is one which is popular in analytical general equilibrium models and which is due to Blanchard (1985). In the Blanchard approach, households face a constant probability of death during their entire economic lives. The second alternative is that of an age-dependent probability of death, which allows for a more realistic modelling of the household's survival profile.

The remainder of the paper is structured as follows. Section 4.2 discusses the pension fund sector while the household sector is reviewed in section 4.4. Section 4.4 provides a brief overview of the rest of the model.[2] Section 4.5 describes the

[1] This part of the analysis draws heavily upon earlier work reported in Broer *et al.* (1994), to which we refer for a more elaborate description. Auerbach *et al.* (1989) and Bovenberg *et al.* (1993) also study ageing issues in an open-economy version of a CGE model with overlapping generations.

[2] See Broer and Westerhout (1993) for a more detailed description of the model.

policy simulations.[3] Section 4.6 explores the role of different assumptions on lifetime uncertainty. Finally, section 4.7 draws conclusions.

4.2 The Pension Sector

This section discusses the pension sector that consists of two kinds of pension schemes. The two schemes represent actual pension institutions in the Netherlands. They differ with respect to their financing structure, the formulas that define the benefit levels and their contribution bases. The PAYG scheme employs PAYG financing to provide a flat minimum benefit to residents who are 65 years and older. The contributions to this scheme are levied on the labor and capital income of those below 65 years of age. Residents aged 65 years or older are exempt from PAYG contributions.

The funded collective (FC) scheme involves capital funding. It provides benefits that supplement the benefits from the PAYG scheme. Therefore, they are based on final pay (i.e. the wage prevailing in the year before the household becomes eligible for pension benefits) only in so far as this pay exceeds a threshold linked to the PAYG benefit. The rights to FC benefits are accumulated during the working life. In particular, the benefit depends on the number of hours worked when younger than 65 years. FC contributions are levied on the labor income above a certain threshold - the franchise. Contributions to the FC scheme are deductible for both the income tax and PAYG contributions but FC benefits are subject to income taxation.

For the purpose of the PAYG and FC schemes, the model divides each household's economic life into two distinct periods. Generations who are in the first n_y years of their economic lives are called 'young' generations, while those in the last $n_T - n_y$ years of their lives are the 'old' generations. Young generations contribute to both the PAYG and the FC schemes. Old generations are entitled to the benefits from both these pension schemes.[4] The generation reaching working age in year t_0 is defined as generation t_0. Following Auerbach and Kotlikoff (1987), we will set n_y at 44. Assuming that households enter the model at the age of 21, they thus become eligible for pension benefits at the age of 65. Furthermore, we will adopt the parameterization used by Auerbach and Kotlikoff (1987)

[3] See Broer *et al.* (1993) for policy simulations of other measures that broaden the tax and PAYG contribution bases.

[4] In contrast to the *statutory* retirement age (i.e. the age at which benefits are first paid), the *actual* retirement age (i.e. the age at which the individual stops working) is endogenously determined (see section 4.3).

$n_T = 55$ in most of the analysis. Only in section 4.6 we will use two alternative assumptions that extend n_T to infinity.

All old generations collect the same per capita PAYG gross benefit, y_{PAYG}, which is linked to wages net of taxes and PAYG contributions:

$$y_{PAYG}(t) = \varepsilon(t) \frac{1 - t_l(t) - \pi^y_l(t)}{1 - t_l(t)} p_l(t) \tag{1}$$

where p_l represents the gross wage rate, which is the same for all generations, and t_l stands for the tax rate on labor income and pension benefits. The PAYG contributions levied on labor income of the young are denoted by π^y_l. ε represents a policy parameter that governs the ratio of net PAYG benefits to net wages.

The PAYG scheme applies the defined benefit principle, i.e. contributions rather than benefits absorb shocks that unbalance the PAYG budget. Hence, the parameter ε linking benefits to wages is set exogenously and the contribution rate π^y_l adjusts endogenously to meet the budget constraint of the PAYG scheme.

The FC scheme differs from the PAYG scheme in that benefits paid to the old generations are not flat but depend on the pension rights that each generation has accumulated when being young. In particular, per capita benefits paid by the FC scheme at time t to generation t_0, $y_{FC}(t, t_0)$, are determined according to the following formula:

$$y_{FC}(t,t_0) = [\, p_l(t) - f(t)\,]\, ac \sum_{\tau = t_0}^{t_0 + n_y - 1} l(\tau, t_0) \qquad t_0 \le t - n_y \tag{2}$$

For each unit of work $l(\tau, t_0)$ in year τ, a young household of generation t_0 accumulates the right to an annuity. After statutory retirement, this annuity pays a share ac of (before-tax) final pay in excess of a franchise f. The annuity is indexed to wages as FC benefits rise with the average wage level in the economy. In the Netherlands, ac is 0.0159. Accordingly, after 44 (n_y) years of full labor-market participation, a household has earned the right to an aggregate pension benefit of 70 % of (gross) final pay for a full work week.

The franchise is linked to the PAYG benefit in the same year:

$$f(t) = \phi\, y_{PAYG}(t) \tag{3}$$

This franchise structure implies that, if ε is cut, benefits from the FC scheme rise to ensure that overall pension benefits are not affected.[5]

[5] Broer *et al.* (1994) also analyse the case where the franchise is determined in the last year before retirement. In that case, old generations suffer an income loss if the PAYG benefit is reduced by lowering ε.

Just as the PAYG scheme, the funded plan applies the defined-benefit principle. Benefits are given by expression (2) and premiums adjust endogenously to ensure intertemporal budget balance. In particular, the funded scheme adopts a strategy of premium smoothing, i.e. the contribution rate is set at a level that the pension fund expects to be able to maintain forever. Contributions to the FC scheme are proportional to labor income of the young generations in excess of the franchise f. The contribution per unit of labor supply reads as $w(t)\,(p_l(t) - f(t))$ where w denotes the contribution rate of the FC scheme.

4.3 The Household Sector

Households maximize expected lifetime utility subject to a lifetime budget constraint. We assume that lifetime utility is time separable and exhibits a nested CES structure:

$$U(t,t_0) = (1 - 1/\gamma) \sum_{\tau=t}^{t_0+n_T-1} (1+\beta)^{t-\tau}\, u(\tau,t_0)^{1-1/\gamma} \qquad \gamma > 0 \tag{4}$$

Here γ denotes the intertemporal elasticity of substitution while β stands for the rate of time preference. $U(t, t_0)$ represents lifetime utility of generation t_0 as of period t and u stands for utility per year. (4) describes the general case where lifetimes may be certain or uncertain. In case of lifetime uncertainty, we use (4) to define the expected value of lifetime utility:

$$E\left[U(t,t_0) \mid t\right] = (1 - 1/\gamma) \sum_{\tau=t}^{t_0+n_T-1} (1+\beta)^{t-\tau} \left(\frac{\Lambda(\tau - t_0 + 1)}{\Lambda(t - t_0 + 1)}\right) u(\tau,t_0)^{1-1/\gamma} \tag{5}$$

where $\Lambda(t - t_0)$ denotes the survival rate of generations of age $t - t_0$. Hence, $\Lambda(\tau\text{-}t_0\text{+}1)/\Lambda(t\text{-}t_0\text{+}1)$ is the conditional probability of survival up to period τ, given that the household has survived to period t. The hazard rate $\lambda(t)=(\Lambda(t)\text{-}\Lambda(t\text{+}1))/\,\Lambda(t)$ measures the probability of dying in year t. Consequently, $\Lambda(\tau\text{-}t_0\text{+}1)/\,\Lambda(t\text{-}t_0\text{+}1)$ can be written as $\prod_{s=t-t_0+1}^{\tau-t_0} (1 - \lambda(s))$. The effective discount rate can be defined as $1 - (1 - \lambda(t - t_0 + 1))/(1 + \beta)$, which is approximately equal to the sum of the rate of time preference and the hazard rate, i.e. $\beta + \lambda(t - t_0 + 1)$.

We assume that, though individual households are in general uncertain about their time of death, the population is sufficiently large to ensure that every year a certain fraction of each generation dies with probability one. As in Yaari (1965), we assume that there are insurance companies that pay premiums to households on their financial assets upon receiving these assets in the case the household dies. The absence of uncertainty at the aggregate level combined with perfect competition among insurance companies ensures that profits in this industry will be zero. This condition implies that the life insurance companies can pay a premium to households of age $t - t_0 + 1$ on their financial assets equal to $\lambda\,(t - t_0 + 1)$. Note that this premium varies with age as the mortality rate is in general age-dependent.

Below, we will explore three possible assumptions on the age profile of survival rates. Under the sudden death assumption used by Auerbach and Kotlikoff, households live for n_T years with certainty. This assumption implies that $\lambda(t - t_0) = 0$ $(\Lambda(t - t_0) = 1)$ for $t - t_0 < n_T$ and $\lambda(t - t_0) = 1$ $(\Lambda(t - t_0) = 0)$ for $t - t_0 = n_T$. Under this assumption, the expected utility function (5) reduces to the utility functional in (4). Second, under the Blanchard (1985) assumption, λ is positive for all $t - t_0 < n_T$ and age-independent. At each age, households expect to live for the same remaining number of years, given by l/λ. Consequently, this assumption is frequently referred to as perpetual youth. Finally, we distinguish the more general case of an age-dependent mortality rate. The age profile of mortality rates as observed in the Netherlands seems to be best described by a rather small and constant mortality rate for economic age $t - t_0 \leq 24$ and a suitably chosen Gompertz distribution for $t - t_0 > 24$.[6] For convenience, we assume the mortality rate of young adults to be zero. This implies the following survival function:

$$\Lambda(t - t_0) = 1 \qquad t \leq t_0 + 24 \tag{6a}$$

$$\Lambda(t - t_0) = \exp\{-0.003(\exp[0.1(t - t_0 - 24)] - 1)\}\,\Lambda(t - t_0 - 24) \qquad t > t_0 + 24 \tag{6b}$$

Figure 4.1 illustrates the pattern of the survival distribution under the assumptions of perpetual youth and age-dependent mortality. The survival rates are truncated to zero after 150 and 80 adult years respectively, which is at ages of 170 and 100.

Instantaneous utility is defined as a function of the consumption of commodities and leisure:

$$u(t, t_0) = [(\theta_v(t, t_0)\, v(t, t_0))^{-\rho} + c(t, t_0)^{-\rho}]^{-1/\rho} \qquad \rho > -1 \tag{7}$$

Here, v denotes the consumption of leisure, and c the consumption of (produced) commodities. θ_v depends on time and the age of the household in such a way that it generates constancy of labor supply in the state of balanced growth as well as a

[6] Note that economic age equals actual age plus 20, as households enter the model at the age of 21.

decreasing labor supply over the life-cycle of generations.[7] The intratemporal elasticity of substitution between leisure and other commodities is given by $1/(1+\rho)$. Households leave no bequests. Thus, with produced goods as the numeraire, generation t_0 faces the following intertemporal budget constraint:

$$\sum_{\tau=t}^{t_0+n_T-1} R_h(\tau,t,t_0)\,[\,p_v(\tau,t_0)\,v(\tau,t_0)+(1+t_c(\tau))\,c(\tau,t_0)\,] \le W(t,t_0) \tag{8}$$

where W denotes lifetime wealth and p_v represents the price of leisure. $R_h(\tau, t, t_0)$ corresponds to the discount factor for generation t_0 which is defined as follows:

$$R_h(\tau,t,t_0) = \frac{1}{(1+r_h(\tau,t_0))}\prod_{s=t}^{\tau-1}\frac{1-\lambda_h(s,t_0)}{(1+r_h(s,t_0))} \tag{9}$$

where

$$r_h(t,t_0) = [1-t_k(t)-\pi_l^y(t)]\,r(t) \qquad t_0 > t-n_y$$

$$r_h(t,t_0) = [1-t_k(t)]\,r(t) \qquad t_0 \le t-n_y$$

$$\lambda_h(t,t_0) = [1-\phi_\lambda\,(t_k(t)+\pi_l^y(t))]\,\lambda(t-t_0+1) \qquad t_0 > t-n_y$$

$$\lambda_h(t,t_0) = [1-\phi_\lambda\,t_k(t)]\,\lambda(t-t_0+1) \qquad t_0 \le t-n_y$$

Here, $r_h(t, t_0)$ stands for the rate of return on nonhuman wealth at time t that applies to generation t_0 and t_k stands for the tax rate on interest income. r denotes the world interest rate. The rate of return on nonhuman wealth differs between young and old generations as only young generations contribute to the PAYG scheme. The parameter ϕ_λ determines whether the premiums distributed by life insurance companies are subject to capital income taxes and to PAYG contributions in the case of the young. Due to the contributions that the young make to the PAYG scheme, the life insurance premium is identical for young and old generations only if this premium is not part of the tax and PAYG contribution base ($\phi_\lambda = 0$).

An important aspect of the Dutch pension system is that the price of leisure, $p_v(t, t_0)$, differs between old and young generations. For old generations, the opportunity cost of leisure simply amounts to the wage net of taxes:

$$p_v(t,t_0) = [\,1-t_l(t)\,]\,p_l(t) \qquad t_0 \le t-n_y \tag{10}$$

[7] See also Auerbach *et al.* (1989). An alternative is to assume separability between consumption of commodities and leisure (King *et al.* (1988)).

The expression for the price of leisure that young generations face is more complicated:

$$p_v(t, t_0) = [1 - t_l(t) - \pi_l^v(t)][p_l(t) - w(t)(p_l(t) - f(t))]$$

$$+ ac \sum_{\tau = t_0 + n_y}^{t_0 + n_T - 1} R_h(\tau, t, t_0)[1 - t_l(\tau) - \pi_b(\tau)][p_l(\tau) - f(\tau)] \qquad (11)$$

$$t_0 > t - n_y$$

In addition to taxes, young generations pay retirement contributions to both the PAYG and the funded pension plans. The contributions to the funded plan are deductible for the labor income tax and the PAYG contributions on labor income. These pension contributions thus cut the cost of leisure of the young. However, more leisure also reduces pension rights being accumulated in the funded scheme. The last term at the right-hand side of (11) represents the present value of pension rights corresponding to one additional unit of work. This accumulation of pension rights raises the price of leisure of the young. This present value is higher the closer is the household to retirement and thus differs for different young generations. π_b denotes the PAYG contribution rate on pension benefits which is zero in the Netherlands and in the model's benchmark case.

4.4 The Rest of the Model

The model can be closed by adding the equations for firms, the government and the foreign sector. As Broer *et al.* (1994) give a full description of the relevant equations, we will only briefly review this part of the model.

The representative firm produces commodities by combining labor, capital and raw materials into a nested CES type constant-returns-to-scale production function. The firm maximizes its market value. Due to investment adjustment costs, the adjustment of investment to its steady-state level is spread over time. As to its financing structure, the firm is assumed to maintain its debt-equity ratio at an exogenously given constant level.

The government finances its public consumption by collecting taxes and by issuing debt. It adopts a policy of tax smoothing, i.e. it responds to a shock by making a once-and-for-all adjustment in one of its instruments, such that per capita government debt converges to a constant in the new steady state.

The economy under consideration imports consumption goods, investment goods and raw materials from abroad. Goods are perfect substitutes for foreign goods and private and government bonds are perfect substitutes for foreign bonds and equity.[8]

The full model is calibrated on the Dutch economy in 1989. Some of the parameter values are taken from Auerbach and Kotlikoff (1987), whereas other parameters and the exogenous variables are chosen such as to reflect the Dutch economy in 1989. For details on the calibration procedure, see Broer and Westerhout (1993). The calibration of the three survival profiles considered in the paper is such that the population shares of young and old generations are the same in the three model versions.

To explore intergenerational welfare implications, we compute the compensating variation, both for generations alive at the time of implementation of the policy measure and for all generations that are born at that time and thereafter. Efficiency is measured by the aggregate compensating variation, which is the sum of the generational compensating variations, discounted at the world interest rate.

4.5 Widening the Income Tax and PAYG Premium Base

This section explores two policy options designed to reduce the burden of PAYG contributions on the labor income of young generations. It first focuses on a measure that broadens the PAYG contribution base and next analyses the consequences of a cut in PAYG benefits. Both policy shocks are implemented in year 1 and are unanticipated. Before the policy shock occurs, the economy exhibits balanced growth. All variables are measured relative to the benchmark of the initial steady state. By adjusting the PAYG premium rate, $\pi_l^y(t)$, the PAYG budget is continuously balanced. The government budget, in contrast, may feature surpluses or deficits as the government smooths the tax rate on labor and pension income, t_l, over time so as to meet its intertemporal budget constraint. Also the FC fund may be unbalanced as it smooths the pension contribution rate, w, over time so as to meet its intertemporal budget constraint. The once-and-for-all adjustments in t_l and w are presented underneath Tables 4.2 to 4.6, that contain the results of the policy simulations. The tables themselves contain the time paths of $\pi_l^y(t)$. In both simulations, household's lifetimes are certain, as in Auerbach and Kotlikoff (1987).

[8] Note that equity provides a higher net rate of return to old generations than to young generations, as only the young pay contributions to the PAYG scheme on their interest and dividend income. In order to avoid problems of shareholder unanimity, we assume that all equity is held by the young.

4.5.1 Levying PAYG Premiums on Pensions Benefits

Contributions to the FC scheme are subject neither to the income tax nor PAYG contributions. However, the government collects income tax on the retirement benefits paid by the FC plans. In this way, the government in fact defers income tax on FC pension provisions until retirement. In contrast to the income tax, PAYG premiums are not levied on FC benefits (i.e. $\pi_b = 0$). Hence, FC pension plans escape PAYG contributions altogether. This sub-section explores the impact of collecting not only income tax but also PAYG contributions on FC benefits ($\pi_b = \pi_l^y$).

Efficiency and Intergenerational Distribution

In the present case, the discounted value of the compensated variations is negative, indicating an overall welfare gain. The intuition is that the government imposes an unanticipated capital levy on the pension rights that have been accumulated in the past. This capital levy is of a lump-sum nature and hence does not produce any efficiency losses. The revenues are used to reduce the distortionary rate of PAYG premium on the incomes of the young, thereby improving overall efficiency.

Despite the efficiency gain, older generations are hurt. Obviously, these generations suffer from the PAYG contributions they pay on their (FC) retirement benefits. Moreover, they collect lower gross pensions because pensions are indexed to wages, which fall as a result of higher labor supply (see below). In contrast, younger generations and those born after the policy shock are better off. These generations benefit from the lower PAYG contribution rate on labor income made possible by the wider contribution base.

The Labor Market

Labor supply exceeds its benchmark value during the first 30 years after the policy shock. Both income and substitution effects explain the initial boost to labor supply. As far as the substitution effect is concerned, the PAYG contribution rate on labor income falls, which raises the opportunity cost of leisure. This provides an incentive to substitute away from leisure and hence stimulates labor supply. The income effect explains why the labor supply response is strongest initially. In particular, the intergenerational redistribution away from older to younger generations hurts most generations alive during the initial period. The associated adverse income effect boosts the initial labor supply. As younger, richer generations enter the labor force, the demand for leisure gradually expands. In the long run, the positive income effect more than offsets the substitution effect upon leisure and labor supply thus falls.

Capital Accumulation

The initial boost to labor supply depresses gross wages and raises the return on the domestic capital stock. Consequently, the capital stock expands during the first decade. However, about a decade before labor supply falls below its initial equilibrium value, the capital stock is already smaller than in the initial steady state. Intuitively, forward-looking investors anticipate the decline in labor supply.

Saving

Three factors cause national saving to rise relative to national income. First, current consumption declines as income is redistributed away from older generations that have a higher propensity to consume than younger generations. Second, PAYG contributions are shifted from the beginning toward the end of the life cycle. Accordingly, young households save part of the additional disposable income produced by the reduction in PAYG premiums in order to smooth consumption over their life cycle. Thirdly, the increase in the net rate of return on nonhuman wealth implied by the decline in the PAYG contribution rate induces households to adopt a steeper consumption life-cycle pattern.

The External Accounts

The external current account improves due to a stronger saving performance. The ratio of the current account to GNP rises the most (by more than 0.35 percentage points) between years 10 and 30. Intuitively, the additional saving is invested abroad as the anticipation of lower labor supply depresses the expected return on domestic investment. Over time, the current account surplus strengthens the net foreign asset position. The trade balance turns from surplus into deficit around year 30; at that time, richer, young generations start to consume part of the return earned on the additional net foreign assets.

4.5.2 Reducing PAYG Benefits

An alternative way to mitigate the PAYG burden on labor income is to cut PAYG benefits. This sub-section investigates an unanticipated reduction in PAYG benefits of 10 percent (i.e. the parameter ε in expression (1) is decreased by 10 percent).

Efficiency and Intergenerational Distribution

The cut in PAYG benefits turns out to be Pareto-improving and hence clearly enhances efficiency. The policy shock raises the weight of the FC scheme at the expense of the PAYG scheme in the overall system of retirement provision. The FC scheme is more efficient than the PAYG scheme because it provides a link between labor supplied and the accumulation of pension rights, thereby improving labor-supply incentives. All generations, including the oldest, benefit. In fact, the oldest generations gain the most. The FC scheme protects these generations from the cut in PAYG benefits by raising FC benefits. At the same time, the old generations escape the higher FC contributions that are required to finance the additional FC benefits because these contributions are levied only on young generations.

Labor Market

The cut in PAYG benefits allows for a lower PAYG premium on labor income. At the same time, the FC contribution rate rises to finance larger FC benefits. Overall, the incentives to supply labor increase because, in contrast to the PAYG benefit, the FC benefit depends on hours worked. The expansion of labor supply reduces wages and boosts the return on the domestic capital stock. Consequently, capital accumulation is stimulated.

Saving

The saving ratio drops immediately in the year in which the policy is implemented. Intuitively, the older generations are made better off, which stimulates consumption. Moreover, consumption smoothing causes younger generations to save less; these generations pay the additional FC contributions only when young but benefit from lower PAYG contributions also when old (as PAYG benefits are indexed to wages *after* PAYG contributions, see expression (1)). Accordingly, disposable income collected when old rises relative to that received when young. In anticipation of the relatively high retirement incomes, households save less in order to smooth consumption.

The External Accounts

The current account reflects the time path of the saving ratio. The trade balance turns into deficit immediately after the shock and is in surplus in the new steady state. The initial deficit reflects the rise in consumption. In year 20, labor supply has risen so much that the country has become a net exporter of commodities. The eventual surplus corresponds to the servicing of net foreign debt that has resulted from a series of current account deficits.

4.6 The Role of the Survival Profile Assumption

Up till now, we have used the Auerbach-Kotlikoff assumption that all households live for the same number of n_T years. This section explores the effects of two alternatives that assume that lifetimes are uncertain and that have been discussed in section 4.3.

4.6.1 Perpetual Youth

Table 4.4 contains the effects of the same policy shock as analyzed in Table 4.3, i.e. a cut in PAYG benefits, but now under the assumption of perpetual youth. Households are not subject to taxation and PAYG contributions on their life-insurance annuities ($\phi_\lambda = 0$). Qualitatively, the results are similar to those in Table 4.3. Quantitatively, there are some important differences.

First, the labor supply response is larger in the first years following the policy shock but also in the new steady state. As discussed in the previous section, the policy of cutting PAYG benefits is efficiency-increasing because it enhances the role of the FC scheme in the provision of pensions and therefore strengthens the link between contributions to and benefits from the pension schemes. Replacing the sudden death assumption with that of perpetual youth affects the weight with which pension rights enter the price of leisure faced by different generations. Generations that have just entered the labor force face a high probability of death before being entitled to pensions, so that they will not gain much from the strengthening of the link between pension contributions and benefits. Consequently, their labor supply responses are smaller than under sudden death. On the other hand, generations that are close to retirement expect to live much longer under perpetual youth. For these generations, pension fund contributions yield a more than actuarially fair return. Hence, they increase their labor supply more when the policy shock changes the mix of PAYG and FC pension benefits.

Figure 4.2 demonstrates graphically how the labor supply reactions of different generations under the perpetual youth assumption differ from those under the sudden death assumption. It also shows that the latter of the two elements dominates. Hence, in the aggregate, labor supply increases most under the assumption of perpetual youth. Due to its beneficial effect upon the productivity of capital, the capital accumulation effect is also much stronger. The current account is relatively unaffected since the savings ratio falls less under the assumption of perpetual youth. Intuitively, the changes in expected lifetimes of older generations cause these households not only to supply more labor, but also to increase their saving by more because the longer horizon strengthens the consumption smoothing incentive. Accordingly, the economy faces smaller deficits on its current account and builds up a smaller stock of foreign debt.

As in Table 4.3, generations that are close to retirement benefit more than those that have just entered the labor force. The reason is that the older generations largely escape the increase in FC premiums that are paid by working generations. However, the gain for generations that are retired is smaller. As these generations are out of the labor force, they do not exploit the opportunities provided by the strengthened labor supply incentives. On balance, they still gain, due to the decrease of the labor income tax and the PAYG contribution rate.

Along with the introduction of the perpetual youth assumption, we have left the annuities from life insurance companies untaxed. One might argue that there is no reason to leave these annuities out of the tax base. Therefore, we have performed a second simulation under the assumption of perpetual youth, now assuming that $\phi_\lambda = 1$.

Table 5 contains the effects upon the relevant variables. The effects are in general much larger than in the previous simulation. All generations gain more than before, but the distribution of the extra gain is very uneven: old generations benefit about 50 % more than in the previous simulation, whereas the benefit for generations in the new steady state is almost three times their benefit in the previous simulation.

The reason that the effects are aggravated lies again in the effects of the policy shock upon the present value of pension benefits per unit of labor supply. An increase in the expected lifetime raises this present value. However, any increase in the mortality rate, which is higher under perpetual youth than under sudden death, reduces this present value as it raises the rate of return that is used for discounting future pension benefits. In the previous simulation, the two effects were of relatively similar magnitude. With annuities being taxed and subject to PAYG contributions, the rate of return on nonhuman wealth is lower however, so that the expected lifetime effect dominates the discount rate effect. This explains the stronger effect upon labor supply and other variables.

4.6.2 Age-dependent Mortality

The perpetual youth assumption seems more attractive than the sudden death assumption as it recognizes that people die at different ages and that the lifetime is uncertain ex ante. However, it neglects the effect of age on household behaviour. Therefore, we now turn to the general case of age-dependent mortality rates. Again, we assume that life-insurance annuities are left untaxed.

The outcomes of this experiment appear to deviate little from those in Table 4.3, the only exception being the stock of foreign debt which is somewhat smaller under age-dependent mortality. The explanation must be found in the expected lifetime effect and the discount rate effect, which work in opposite direction. Young generations have a somewhat shorter expected lifetime under age-dependent mortality than under sudden death and discount the future more heavily. Consequently, for them the policy shock raises the price of leisure less than under sudden death. Older generations expect to live longer than under sudden death, so to them the value of pension benefits is larger. In the aggregate however, the effects upon different generations vanish almost completely.

Summarizing, we conclude that the assumption one makes about the survival profile of generations matters less in the aggregate than for individual generations. The general direction of efficiency effects is not sensitive to the exact form of the survival distribution, but the sizes of the welfare effects of young and old generations may be very different. In addition, care must be taken with respect to the way the annuities of life-insurance companies are treated before taxes.

4.7 Conclusions

This paper has explored several types of pension policies aimed at reducing the burden of income taxes and PAYG contributions on labor income. Subjecting the retirement benefits to PAYG contributions succeeds in improving efficiency in general and labor-market incentives in particular. However, this policy option harms the oldest generations. This is in contrast to reducing PAYG benefits which proves to be Pareto-welfare improving. The FC scheme improves intratemporal efficiency by linking retirement benefits to hours worked, thereby mitigating the disincentives to labor supply originating in the income tax and the PAYG scheme. Furthermore, the FC plans in effect provide for intergenerational redistribution protecting the older generations. Moreover, these conclusions do not hinge upon specific assumptions on the survival profile of generations, although the size and distribution of the efficiency gain over generations are dependent upon the precise survival profile used.

References

Auerbach, A.J. and L.J. Kotlikoff (1987), *Dynamic Fiscal Policy*, Cambridge: Cambridge University Press.

Auerbach, A.J., L.J. Kotlikoff, R.P. Hagemann and G. Nicoletti (1989), "The Economic Dynamics of an Ageing Population: The Case of Four OECD Countries," *OECD Economic Studies*, no. 12, pp. 97130.

Blanchard, O.J. (1985), "Debts, Deficits, and Finite Horizons," *Journal of Political Economy*, Vol. 93, pp. 223–247.

Bös, D. and R.K. von Weizsäcker (1989), "Economic Consequences of an Aging Population," *European Economic Review*, Vol. 33, pp. 345–354.

Bovenberg, A.L., D.P. Broer and E.W.M.T. Westerhout (1993), "Public Pensions and Declining Fertility in a Small Open Economy: An Intertemporal Equilibrium Approach," in B.L. Wolfe (ed.), *On the Role of Budgetary Policy During Demographic Changes*, Supplement to *Public Finance*, Vol. 48, pp. 43–59.

Broer, D.P., and E.W.M.T. Westerhout (1993), "Taxation in an Intertemporal General Equilibrium Model of a Small Open Economy, *Economic Modelling*, Vol. 10, pp. 64–80.

Broer, D.P., E.W.M.T. Westerhout and A.L. Bovenberg (1993), *The Tax Treatment of Pension Savings in a Small Open Economy*, Research Centre for Economic Policy, Research Memorandum 9303.

Broer, D.P., E.W.M.T. Westerhout and A.L. Bovenberg (1994), "Taxation, Pensions, and Saving in a Small Open Economy," *Scandinavian Journal of Economics*, Vol. 96, pp. 403–424, 1994.

Fair, R., and J.B. Taylor (1983), "Solution and Maximum Likelihood Estimation of Dynamic Nonlinear Rational Expectations Models," *Econometrica*, Vol. 51, pp. 1169–1185.

King, R.G., C.H. Plosser and S.G. Rebelo (1988), "Production, Growth and Business Cycles," *Journal of Monetary Economics*, Vol. 21, pp. 195–232.
Marchand, M., and P. Pestieau (1991), "Public Pensions: Choices for the Future," *European Economic Review*, Vol. 35, pp. 441–453.
Nelissen, J. (1987), "The Redistributive Impact of the General Old Age Pensions Act on Lifetime Income in the Netherlands," *European Economic Review*, Vol. 31, pp. 1419–1441.
Shoven, J.B., and J. Whalley (1992), *Applying General Equilibrium*, Cambridge: Cambridge University Press.
Yaari, M.E. (1965), "Uncertain Lifetime, Life Insurance and the Theory of the Consumer," *Review of Economic Studies*, Vol. 32, pp. 137–150.

Appendix

Model Structure and Solution Algorithm

Before discussing the solution algorithm of the model, this appendix first provides an overview of the equations. Here we shall provide only sparse comments. For an extended discussion of the individual equations the reader is referred to Broer and Westerhout (1993) and Broer *et al.* (1994).

A) The Household Sector

We use t to denote the current year and t_0 to denote the year of birth of the generation. The definitions of other symbols may be found in the Glossary.

The utility function:

$$E\left(U(t,t_0)\mid t\right) = (1-1/\gamma)\sum_{\tau=t}^{t_0+n_T-1}(1+\beta)^{t-\tau}\frac{\Lambda(\tau-t_0+1)}{\Lambda(t-t_0+1)}u(\tau,t_0)^{1-1/\gamma} \qquad \gamma>0 \quad \text{(A1)}$$

$$u(t,t_0) = \left[\left(\theta_v(t,t_0)\,v(t,t_0)\right)^{-\rho} + c(t,t_0)^{-\rho}\right]^{-1/\rho} \qquad \rho > -1 \quad \text{(A2)}$$

$$\theta_v(t,t_0) = \theta_0(1+\theta)^{t-t_0}(1+\alpha)^{t_0} \qquad \text{(A3)}$$

The survival function:

$$\Lambda(\tau) = 1 \qquad \tau \le 24 \quad \text{(A4)}$$

$$\Lambda(\tau) = \exp\left\{-0.003\left(\exp\left[0.10(\tau-24)\right]-1\right)\right\}\Lambda(\tau-24) \qquad \tau > 24 \quad \text{(A5)}$$

$$\lambda(\tau) = \left(\Lambda(\tau)-\Lambda(\tau+1)\right)/\Lambda(\tau) \qquad \text{(A6)}$$

The budget restriction:

$$\sum_{\tau=t}^{t_0+n_T-1} R_h(\tau,t,t_0)\,[\,p_v(\tau,t_0)\,v(\tau,t_0) + (1+t_c(\tau))\,c(\tau,t_0)] \leq W(t,t_0) \qquad \text{(A7)}$$

$$W(t,t_0) = A(t,t_0) + \sum_{\tau=t}^{t_0+n_T-1} R_h(\tau,t,t_0)\,[\,p_v(\tau,t_0)\,l_{\max} + T(\tau,t_0)] \qquad \text{(A8)}$$

$$+ \sum_{\tau=\max(t,\,t_0+n_y)}^{t_0+n_T-1} R_h(\tau,t,t_0)\,(1-t_l(\tau))\,y_{PAYG}(\tau) + P_R(t,t_0)$$

$$A(t+1,t_0) \qquad \text{(A9)}$$

$$= (1+r_h(t,t_0))\,A(t,t_0) + (1-t_l(t)-\pi_l^y(t))\,(p_l(t) - w(t)\,(p_l(t)-f(t))\,)\,l(t,t_0)$$

$$+ \lambda_h(t,t_0)\,A(t+1,t_0) + T(t,t_0) - c(t,t_0) \qquad t < t_0+n_y$$

$$= (1+r_h(t,t_0)\,A(t,t_0) + (1-t_l(t))\,(p_l(t)\,l(t,t_0) + y_{PAYG}(t) + y_{FC}(t,t_0))$$

$$- \pi_b(t)\,y_{FC}(t) + \lambda_h(t,t_0)\,A(t+1,t_0) + T(t,t_0) - c(t,t_0) \qquad t \geq t_0+n_y$$

$$R_h(\tau,t,t_0) = \frac{1}{(1+r_h(\tau,t_0))} \prod_{s=t}^{\tau-1} \frac{1-\lambda_h(s,t_0)}{(1+r_h(s,t_0))} \qquad \text{(A10)}$$

$$\lambda_h(t,t_0) = [1-\phi_\lambda\ (t_k(t)+\pi_k^y(t))]\,\lambda(t-t_0+1) \qquad t_0 > t-n_y \qquad \text{(A11)}$$

$$\lambda_h(t,t_0) = [1-\phi_\lambda\ t_k(t)]\,\lambda(t-t_0+1) \qquad t_0 \leq t-n_y \qquad \text{(A12)}$$

$$r_h(t,t_0) = [1-t_k(t)-\pi_k^y(t)\,]\,r(t) \qquad t_0 > t-n_y \qquad \text{(A13)}$$

$$r_h(t,t_0) = [1-t_k(t)\,]\ r(t) \qquad t_0 \leq t-n_y \qquad \text{(A14)}$$

The value of pension rights accumulated in the past:

$$P_R(t,t_0) = \sum_{\tau=\max(t,\,t_0+n_y)}^{t_0+n_T-1} R_h(\tau,t,t_0)\,[1-t_l(\tau)]\,[p_l(\tau)-f(\tau)]\,ac \sum_{s=t_0}^{\min(t_0+n_y-1,\,t-1)} l(s,t_0) \qquad \text{(A15)}$$

$$l(t,t_0) = l_{\max} - v(t,t_0) \geq 0 \qquad \text{(A16)}$$

The price of leisure:

$$p_v(t,t_0) = [1-t_l(t)]\,(p_l(t) \qquad t_0 \leq t-n_y \qquad \text{(A17)}$$

$$p_v(t,t_0) = [1-t_l(t)-\pi_l^y(t)]\,[p_l(t) - w(t)\,(p_l(t)-f(t))] \qquad \text{(A18)}$$

$$+\ ac \sum_{\tau=t_0+n_y}^{t_0+n_T-1} R_h(\tau,t,t_0)\,[1-t_l(\tau)-\pi_b(\tau)]\,[p_l(\tau)-f(\tau)] \qquad t_0 > t-n_y$$

The optimal consumption plan of the household in period t for $\tau \geq t$:

$$\mu(\tau, t_0)(l_{\max} - v(\tau, t_0)) = 0; \qquad \mu(\tau, t_0) \geq 0 \tag{A19}$$

$$p_v^*(\tau, t_0) = \mu(\tau, t_0) + p_v(\tau, t_0)/\theta_v(\tau, t_0) \tag{A20}$$

$$p_u^*(\tau, t_0) = [\, p_v^*(\tau, t_0)^{1-\sigma} + (1 + t_c(\tau))^{1-\sigma}\,]^{1/(1-\sigma)} \tag{A21}$$

$$p_W^*(\tau, t_0) = \Big(\sum_{s=\tau}^{t_0+n_T-1} (1+\beta)^{\tau-s} \big(p_u^*(s,t_0)\, R_h(s,\tau,t_0)/(1+\beta)^{\tau-s} \big)^{1-\gamma} \Big)^{1/(1-\gamma)} \tag{A22}$$

$$u^*(\tau, t, t_0) = \tag{A23}$$

$$\Big(\frac{p_u^*(\tau, t_0)\, R_h(\tau, t, t_0)/((1+\beta)^{t-\tau}\, \Lambda(\tau - t_0 + 1)/\Lambda(t - t_0 + 1))}{p_W^*(t, t_0)}\Big)^{-\gamma} \frac{W^*(t, t_0)}{p_W^*(t, t_0)}$$

where

$$W^*(t, t_0) = W(t, t_0) + \sum_{s=t}^{t_0+n_T-1} R_h(s, t, t_0)\, \mu(s, t_0)\, l_{\max} \tag{A24}$$

$$v(\tau, t_0) = \frac{u^*(\tau, t, t_0)}{\theta_v(\tau, t_0)} \Big(\frac{p_v^*(\tau, t_0)}{p_u^*(\tau, t_0)} \Big)^{-\sigma} \tag{A25}$$

$$c(\tau, t_0) = u^*(\tau, t, t_0) \Big(\frac{1 + t_c(\tau)}{p_u^*(\tau, t_0)} \Big)^{-\sigma} \tag{A26}$$

Aggregates over households

$$L_s(t) = \sum_{t_0=t-n_T+1}^{t} l(t, t_0)\, gen(t_0)\, \Lambda(t - t_0) \tag{A27}$$

$$L^y(t) = \sum_{t_0=t-n_y+1}^{t} l(t, t_0)\, gen(t_0)\, \Lambda(t - t_0) \tag{A28}$$

$$c(t) = \sum_{t_0=t-n_T+1}^{t} c(t, t_0)\, gen(t_0)\, \Lambda(t - t_0) \tag{A29}$$

$$A(t) = \sum_{t_0=t-n_T+1}^{t} A(t, t_0)\, gen(t_0)\, \Lambda(t - t_0) \tag{A30}$$

$$A^y(t) = \sum_{t_0=t-n_y+1}^{t} A(t, t_0)\, gen(t_0)\, \Lambda(t - t_0) \tag{A31}$$

$$N^o(t) = \sum_{t_0 = t - n_T + 1}^{t - n_y} gen(t_0)\, \Lambda(t - t_0) \tag{A32}$$

Size of new-born generation

$$gen(t) = \sum_{i=20}^{39} fert(i)\, gen(t-i)\, \Lambda(i - 19) \tag{A33}$$

B) The Firm Sector

$$y(t) = F(t) - \frac{1}{2} c_I \frac{I^2(t)}{K(t)} \tag{B1}$$

$$F(t) = [\, \zeta_M M(t)^{-\rho_y} + \zeta_H H(t)^{-\rho_y} \,]^{-1/\rho_y} \qquad \rho_y > -1 \tag{B2}$$

$$H(t) = [\, \zeta_K K(t)^{-\rho_H} + \zeta_L (L(t)(1+\alpha)^t)^{-\rho_H} \,]^{-1/\rho_H} \qquad \rho_H > -1 \tag{B3}$$

$$\Pi(t) = y(t) - p_M(t) M(t) - p_l(t) L(t) - r(t) B(t) \tag{B4}$$

$$Div(t) = \Pi(t) - T_b(t) - I(t) - B(t+1) - B(t) \tag{B5}$$

$$T_b(t) = t_b(t) \left(\Pi(t) - cr(t) I(t) - \sum_{\tau = t - T_D + 1}^{t} \Lambda(t-\tau) I(\tau) \right) \tag{B6}$$

$$B(t) = \beta_K K(t) \tag{B7}$$

$$(V(t+1) - V(t))/V(t) + (1 - t_d(t) - \pi_k^y(t))\, Div(t)/V(t) \tag{B8}$$

$$= (1 - t_k(t) - \pi_k^y(t))\, r(t)$$

$$K(t+1) = I(t) + (1-\delta) K(t) \tag{B9}$$

$$V(t) = \sum_{\tau = t}^{\infty} R_f(\tau, t)(1 - t_d(\tau) - \pi_k^y(\tau))\, Div(\tau) \tag{B10}$$

$$R_f(\tau, t) = \prod_{s=t}^{\tau} [\, 1 + (1 - t_k(s) - \pi_k^y(s))\, r(s) \,]^{-1} \tag{B11}$$

$$q(t) = (1 - t_d(t) - \pi_k^y(t)) \left((1 - t_b(t))\, c_I \frac{I(t)}{K(t)} + 1 - t_b(t)\, cr(t) \right) - depr(t) \tag{B12}$$

$$depr(t) = \sum_{\tau = t}^{t + T_D - 1} (1 - t_d(\tau) - \pi_k^y(\tau))\, t_b(\tau)\, \Delta(\tau - t)\, R_f(\tau, t) \tag{B13}$$

$$(1 - t_d(\tau) - \pi_k^y(\tau))\,(1 - t_b(\tau))\left(\frac{\partial F(\tau)}{\partial K(\tau)} + \frac{1}{2}c_I\left(\frac{I(\tau)}{K(\tau)}\right)^2\right) \tag{B14}$$

$$+ (1-\delta)\,q(\tau) = q(\tau-1)\,\frac{R_f(\tau-1,t)}{R_f(\tau,t)} \qquad \tau > t+1$$

$$\frac{\partial F(t)}{\partial M(t)} = p_M(t) \tag{B15}$$

$$\frac{\partial F(t)}{\partial L(t)} = p_l(t) \tag{B16}$$

C) The Government

$$T_T(t) = t_l(t)\left(p_l(t)\,L(t) - w(t)\,(p_l(t) - f(t))\,L^y(t) + N^o(t)\,(y_{PAYG}(t) + y_{FC}(t))\right) \tag{C1}$$
$$+ T_b(t) + t_k(t)\,r(t)\,(A(t) - V(t)) + t_d(t)\,Div(t) + t_c(t)\,c(t)$$

$$T(t) = \sum_{t_0 = t - n_T + 1}^{t} T(t, t_0)\,gen(t_0) \tag{C2}$$

$$\sum_{\tau = t}^{\infty} R_g(\tau, t)\,[\,g(\tau) + T(\tau) - T_T(\tau)\,] = D(t) \tag{C3}$$

$$R_g(\tau, t) = \prod_{s=t}^{\tau} (1 + r(s))^{-1} \tag{C4}$$

D) The Pension Sector

The Pay-As-You-Go Scheme:

$$y_{PAYG}(t)\,N^o(t) = \pi_l^y(t)\,[\,p_l(t) - w(t)\,(p_l(t) - f(t))\,]\,L^y(t) \tag{D1}$$

$$+ \pi_b(t) \sum_{t_0 = t - n_T + 1}^{t - n_y} y_{FC}(t, t_0)\,gen(t_0)\,\Lambda(t - t_0)$$

$$+ \pi_k^y(t)\,[\,r(t)\,(A^y(t) - V(t)) + Div(t)\,]\,L^y(t) + \pi_p(t)\,r(t)\,A_p(t)$$

$$y_{PAYG}(t) = \varepsilon(t)\,\frac{1 - t_l(t) - \pi_l^y(t)}{1 - t_l(t)}\,p_l(t) \tag{D2}$$

The Funded Collective Scheme:

$$y_{FC}(t, t_0) = [\,p_l(t) - f(t)\,]\,ac \sum_{\tau = t_0}^{t_0 + n_y - 1} l(\tau, t_0) \qquad t_0 \le t - n_y \tag{D3}$$

$$f(t) = \phi \, y_{PAYG}(t) \tag{D4}$$

$$A_p(t) + w(t) \sum_{\tau=t}^{\infty} R_p(\tau, t) \left[p_l(\tau) - f(\tau) \right] L^y(\tau) = \tag{D5}$$

$$\sum_{\tau=t}^{\infty} R_p(\tau, t) \sum_{t_0=\tau-n_T+1}^{\tau-n_y} y_{FC}(\tau, t_0) \, gen(t_0) \, \Lambda(t-t_0)$$

$$R_p(\tau, t) = \prod_{s=t}^{\tau} (1 + r_p(s))^{-1} \tag{D6}$$

$$r_p(t) = \left[1 - t_p(t) - \pi_p(t) \right] r(t) \tag{D7}$$

E) The Foreign Sector

$$TB(t) = y(t) - c(t) - I(t) - g(t) \tag{E1}$$

$$A_e(t) = \sum_{\tau=t}^{\infty} R_g(\tau, t) \, TB(\tau) \tag{E2}$$

F) Equilibrium

$$L_s(t) = L(t) \tag{F1}$$

$$y(t) = c(t) + I(t) + g(t) + b(t) - p_M(t) M(t) \tag{F2}$$

$$A(t) + A_e(t) + A_p(t) = D(t) + B(t) + V(t) \tag{F3}$$

$$r(t) = r_e(t) \tag{F4}$$

Solving the Model

Most computational methods for the solution of general equilibrium models rely either on some version of Scarf's simplex algorithm or a version of Newton's method (for an exposition of these methods, see *e.g.* Shoven and Whalley (1992)). Scarf's method, while guaranteed to converge, is slow to converge and can be computationally demanding, while Newton's method requires the computation of the Jacobian of the system of equations of the model. This can be an important drawback if the number of equations is large and the Jacobian is not sparse, *i.e.* if there is a lot of interdependence in the system. Furthermore, an automatic differentiation procedure for the computation of the partial derivatives may not be available. In that case, both the computation of the Jacobian and the solution of the linear equation system may be very time-consuming. Typically, intertemporal computable general equilibrium models with perfect foresight fall into this category. At any given level of aggregation, the solution of the model for any given period requires knowledge of all future prices. For an annual model with an effective horizon of, say, 100 years, this implies a model size one hundred times that of the corresponding static equilibrium model. In overlapping generations models (or in any type of model with heterogeneous agents), this is further increased by the necessity to keep track of the defining characteristics of the different generations. This implies that the present model, though very small in terms of the number of sectors and the degree of sectoral disaggregation, is fairly large in terms of the number of feedback variables. A back-of-the-envelope calculation yields a dimension of approximately 12000 if no further attempt is made at dimension reduction (200 periods[9], in each period the wage rate, a tax rate, a PAYG contribution rate, an FC contribution rate, the capital stock, and 55 asset positions of households). To avoid these problems, the solution method used in this paper uses a more heuristic approach, in which the computation proceeds agent by agent. First the household model is solved for all periods and generations, conditional on a given vector of market prices, then the firm model, *etc.* The updating of the market prices and tax rates is on the basis of excess demand and budget deficits, using a Gauss-Jacobi type updating rule.

The benchmark solution of the model is defined as the steady state path starting in the base year (t=1). This steady state path is conditional on the initial size of government debt, the assets of the pension fund, and the size of the population. The age distribution of the population must be in agreement with a balanced growth path. The steady-state solution produces values for all the endogenous variables, including the state variables $K(t)$, $A_e(t)$ and $A(t,t_0)$, over the model horizon.

Because the growth rate of the economy is exogenously determined from the rate of technical progress and the population growth rate, the solution for the base year defines the steady-state growth path as well. The steady state solution of the model can thus be computed recursively, conditional on the values of p_l, T, π_l^y, w, and y in the base year. For the household sector, the life cycle model produces explicit solutions, given by (A20)-(A26), conditional on the Lagrange multiplier of the leisure constraint, μ. This part of the model is solved first, iterating over μ. The basic idea is that typically the household will retire only once, so that the Kuhn-Tucker condition in (A19) can be replaced by equality restrictions. The combinatorial aspect of the problem is then reduced to finding the year in which the restriction (A16) first becomes binding. The macro variables for the household sector are then obtained by applying the steady-state growth conditions to (A27)-(A31). The solution of the model as a whole in the base year is computed by a

[9] We have used a horizon of 200 periods in most applications as an approximation on infinity.

Newton-Rhapson type algorithm in the variables p_l, T, π_l^y, w, and y, using finite differences.

Given a steady-state benchmark solution path, the transition path in response to a shock in the exogenous variables is computed. For this transition path, the initial conditions for the state variables $K(1)$, $A_e(1)$ and $A(1,t_0)$ are as on the steady-state growth path. The solution of the household decision problem proceeds exactly as for the steady-state case, *i.e.* conditional on a given path for wages and taxes household decisions are computed for each generation and for all time periods. This results in time paths for the household decision variables c, L, A, plus labour taxes and pension premium payments.

Household decisions with respect to labour supply are then used in the sub-model for the firm, that is solved conditional on the time path for L (the actual values used are updated from L_s using relaxation). This is done iteratively by applying the method of Fair and Taylor (1983) to the expected marginal return on investment, q, in (B12). This yields time paths for p_l, V, y, M, I, and T_b.

The decisions of the private sector are then used to obtain new values for the tax rates and pension premiums from the budget restrictions (C2), (D1), and (D5). Again, it is necessary to use relaxation. For the government budget restriction, either an appropriate tax rate has to be selected to balance the budget, or balancing is automatic through adjustment of the transfers T. All three public sectors may also apply tax or premium smoothing. In that case the relevant budget constraint is the steady-state restriction, e.g. for the government $(r(\infty) + \psi(\infty)) D(\infty) = g(\infty) + T(\infty) - T_y(\infty)$, where $\psi(\infty)$ is the steady-state growth rate of output. The relevant tax rate is kept constant at a level that satisfies this equation over *the whole* simulation period. Given the updated time paths for taxes, a new iteration round starts.

Glossary and Calibration of the Model

Table 4.1. Variables and Parameters.

Variables	
λ	hazard rate (0.03)
λ_h	net premium rate life insurance companies
Λ	survival rate
μ	Lagrange multiplier of leisure constraint households
π_b	PAYG contribution rate on pension benefits
π_k^y	PAYG contribution rate on dividend and interest income of the young
π_l^y	PAYG contribution rate on labor income of the young
π_p	PAYG contribution rate on capital income FC pension funds
Π	profits
A	financial wealth of households
A_e	financial wealth foreign sector

Table 4.1. (cont.)

Variables	
A_p	financial wealth FC pension funds
A^y	aggregate financial wealth of young households
b	net exports of commodities
B	bonds issued by firms
c	consumption of commodities
cr	investment tax credit rate
$cv\ (t_0)$	compensating variation of generation t_0
CA	current account
CV	aggregate compensating variation
$depr$	discounted value of deductible depreciations per unit of investment good
D	bonds issued by government
Div	dividends
f	franchise
$fert$	fertility rate
F	gross output
g	government consumption
gen	size of generation of households
H	index defined over labor and capital
I	investment
K	capital stock
l	labor supply
L	aggregate labor supply
L^y	aggregate labor supply of young households
M	input of raw materials
N^o	size of old generations
p_l	wage rate
p_M	price of raw materials
p^*_u	shadow price of instantaneous utility
p_v	price of leisure
p^*_v	shadow price of leisure
p^*_w	shadow price of household wealth
P_R	value of accumulated pension rights
q	marginal value investment goods
r	domestic interest rate
r_e	world interest rate (0.055)
r_h	interest rate households
r_p	interest rate FC scheme pension funds
R_f	discount factor of firms
R_g	discount factor of government
R_h	discount factor of households
R_p	discount factor of FC scheme pension funds
S	aggregate saving
t_b	tax rate on profit income (0.35)
t_c	tax rate on consumption (0.25)
t_d	tax rate on dividend income of households (0.25)
t_k	tax rate on interest income of households (0.25)
t_l	tax rate on labor income (0.25)
t_p	tax rate on capital income FC scheme pension funds
T	lump-sum government transfers to households
T_b	revenues from taxation of profits

Table 4.1. (cont.)

Variables	
T_T	tax revenues
TB	trade balance
u	instantaneous utility households
u^*	shadow value of instantaneous utility households
U	lifetime utility households
v	consumption of leisure
V	value of firm
w	FC contribution rate
W	total wealth (human and financial) of households
W^*	shadow value of total wealth (human and financial) of households
y	net output
y_{FC}	gross pension benefit provided under the FC scheme
y_{PAYG}	gross pension benefit provided under the PAYG scheme
Y	gross national product
Parameters	
α	rate of labor-saving technical progress (0.02)
β	rate of time preference (0.009)
β_K	debt-equity ratio (0.60)
γ	elasticity of intertemporal substitution (0.25)
δ	economic depreciation rate of capital (0.12)
Δ	fiscal depreciation scheme of capital (0.125)
ε	net replacement rate PAYG benefits (0.137)
$\theta_v(t, t_0)$	preference for leisure parameter of generation t_0 in year t ($\theta_v = \theta_0 (1.025)^{t-t_0} (1.02)^{t_0}$)
ζ_H	parameter measuring the productivity of labor and capital combined
ζ_K	parameter measuring the productivity of capital
ζ_L	parameter measuring the productivity of labor
ζ_M	parameter measuring the productivity of raw materials
ρ	parameter of intratemporal substitution between leisure and commodities (0.11)
ρ_H	parameter of substitution between labor and capital (1.00)
ρ_y	parameter of substitution between raw materials and labor and capital combined (1.00)
σ	elasticity of intratemporal substitution between leisure and commodities (0.90)
ϕ	ratio of franchise to PAYG benefit (6.21)
ϕ_λ	dummy stating whether life insurance premiums are subject to taxes and PAYG contributions
ac	rate at which FC pension rights are accumulated (0.0159)
c_I	parameter of investment adjustment costs (10.0)
l_{max}	maximum supply of labor (1.00)
n	rate of population growth (0.01)
n_T	length of economic life of households (55)
n_y	length of economic life during which households are young (45)
T_D	length of fiscal life of capital goods (8)

Table 4.2. Levying PAYG Premiums on Pension Benefits ($\pi_b = \pi^y$).[a]

	year	1	10	20	30	40	50	200
L	%	0.38	0.29	0.14	0.01	-0.07	-0.10	-0.11
K	%	0.00	0.13	0.04	-0.07	-0.15	-0.19	-0.20
S/Y	D %	0.27	0.32	0.26	0.20	0.15	0.11	0.10
I/Y	D %	0.03	-0.07	-0.13	-0.15	-0.15	-0.15	-0.15
TB/Y	D %	0.25	0.27	0.11	-0.03	-0.13	-0.19	-0.20
CA/Y	D %	0.24	0.39	0.38	0.34	0.30	0.26	0.25
A_e	%	0.00	-2.12	-4.24	-5.64	-6.38	-6.66	-6.65
$\pi_b = \pi^y{}_l$	D %	-0.26	-0.27	-0.27	-0.27	-0.27	-0.27	-0.27
p_l	%	-0.34	-0.15	-0.09	-0.08	-0.08	-0.08	-0.09
$cv(t_0)$	Δ %	-0.07	-0.09	-0.09	-0.09	-0.09	-0.09	-0.09
$cv(1-t_0)$	Δ %	-0.07	-0.03	0.02	0.10	0.25	0.36	

CV: -15.67 (%) t_l: -0.23 (D %) w: -0.11 (D %)

Table 4.3. Reducing PAYG Benefits.[a]

	year	1	10	20	30	40	50	200
L	%	0.33	0.45	0.52	0.57	0.59	0.60	0.59
K	%	0.00	0.17	0.26	0.32	0.34	0.35	0.34
S/Y	D %	-0.23	-0.18	-0.14	-0.12	-0.10	-0.09	-0.10
I/Y	D %	0.01	0.01	0.02	0.02	0.02	0.02	0.02
TB/Y	D %	-0.23	-0.09	0.00	0.05	.08	0.10	0.09
CA/Y	D %	-0.24	-0.19	-0.16	-0.14	-0.12	-0.11	-0.11
A_e	%	0.00	1.30	2.11	2.55	2.74	2.76	2.68
π_l^y	D %	-0.68	-0.68	-0.68	-0.68	-0.68	-0.68	-0.68
p_l	%	-0.29	-0.25	-0.23	-0.23	-0.23	-0.22	-0.22
$cv(t_0)$	Δ %	-0.03	-0.04	-0.04	-0.04	-0.04	-0.04	-0.04
$cv(1-t_0)$	Δ %	-0.04	-0.10	-0.15	-0.20	-0.27	-0.28	

CV: -38.98 (%) t_l: -0.08 (D %) w: 2.07 (D %)

[a] All variables are expressed either as percentual deviation of the variable from the baseline (%), or as absolute deviation of the variable from the baseline (D %), or as absolute deviation of the variable from the baseline in terms of household's lifetime wealth (Δ %). For the definition of the variables, see Table 4.1.

Table 4.4. Reducing PAYG Benefits, Perpetual Youth, $\phi\lambda = 0$.[a]

	year	1	10	20	30	40	50	200
L	%	0.62	0.87	0.95	0.96	0.95	0.93	0.92
K	%	0.00	0.49	0.66	0.70	0.69	0.68	0.67
S/Y	D %	-0.18	-0.06	-0.03	-0.02	-0.02	-0.02	-0.06
I/Y	D %	0.09	0.06	0.04	0.03	0.02	0.01	-0.00
TB/Y	D %	-0.24	0.06	0.15	0.16	0.14	0.12	0.04
CA/Y	D %	-0.27	-0.12	-0.07	-0.05	-0.04	-0.04	-0.06
A_e	%	0.00	0.18	0.15	0.05	-0.06	-0.15	-0.39
π_l^y	D %	-0.68	-0.69	-0.69	-0.70	-0.70	-0.70	-0.70
p_l	%	-0.56	-0.34	-0.26	-0.24	-0.23	-0.22	-0.23
$cv(t_0)$	Δ %	-0.09	-0.11	-0.12	-0.13	-0.13	-0.13	-0.13
$cv(1-t_0)$	Δ %	-0.09	-0.15	-0.20	-0.24	-0.25	-0.14	

CV: -69.49 (%) t_l: -0.40 (D %) *w:* 2.21 (D %)

Table 4.5. Reducing PAYG Benefits, Perpetual Youth, $\phi\lambda = 1$.[a]

	year	1	10	20	30	40	50	200
L	%	1.32	1.98	2.13	2.09	2.02	1.97	1.93
K	%	0.00	1.38	1.80	1.85	1.81	1.76	1.71
S/Y	D %	-0.37	-0.09	0.00	0.01	0.00	-0.02	-0.09
I/Y	D %	0.27	0.19	0.14	0.11	0.09	0.08	0.04
TB/Y	D %	-0.60	0.18	0.39	0.39	0.34	0.28	0.10
CA/Y	D %	-0.64	-0.28	-0.14	-0.10	-0.09	-0.09	-0.13
A_e	%	0.00	0.36	0.26	0.03	-0.18	-0.36	-0.88
π_l^y	D %	-0.58	-0.59	-0.60	-0.60	-0.61	-0.61	-0.61
p_l	%	-1.20	-0.55	-0.29	-0.21	-0.19	-0.19	-0.20
$cv(t_0)$	Δ %	-0.25	-0.32	-0.35	-0.36	-0.37	-0.37	-0.36
$cv(1-t_0)$	Δ %	-0.25	-0.29	-0.33	-0.35	-0.35	-0.20	

CV: -208.66 (%) t_l: -1.28 (D %) *w:* 2.70 (D %)

[a] All variables are expressed either as percentual deviation of the variable from the baseline (%), or as absolute deviation of the variable from the baseline (D %), or as absolute deviation of the variable from the baseline in terms of household's lifetime wealth (Δ %). For the definition of the variables, see Table 4.1.

Table 4.6. Reducing PAYG Benefits, Age-Dependent Mortality, $\phi_\lambda = 0$.[a]

	year	1	10	20	30	40	50	200
L	%	0.36	0.49	0.57	0.62	0.63	0.63	0.63
K	%	0.00	0.20	0.31	0.36	0.38	0.39	0.38
S/Y	D %	-0.22	-0.17	-0.14	-0.12	-0.10	-0.09	-0.10
I/Y	D %	0.02	0.02	0.02	0.02	0.02	0.02	0.02
TB/Y	D %	-0.23	-0.08	0.01	0.06	0.09	0.10	0.09
CA/Y	D %	-0.24	-0.18	-0.16	-0.14	-0.12	-0.11	-0.11
A_e	%	0.00	0.88	1.42	1.70	1.81	1.82	1.79
π_l^y	D %	-0.68	-0.68	-0.69	-0.69	-0.69	-0.69	-0.69
p_l	%	-0.32	-0.26	-0.24	-0.23	-0.23	-0.22	-0.22
$cv(t_0)$	Δ %	-0.04	-0.04	-0.04	-0.04	-0.05	-0.05	-0.05
$cv(1-t_0)$	Δ %	-0.04	-0.10	-0.15	-0.21	-0.27	-0.25	

CV: -40.51 (%) t_l: -0.10 (D %) *w:* 2.15 (D %)

[a] All variables are expressed either as percentual deviation of the variable from the baseline (%), or as absolute deviation of the variable from the baseline (D %), or as absolute deviation of the variable from the baseline in terms of household's lifetime wealth (Δ %). For the definition of the variables, see Table 4.1.

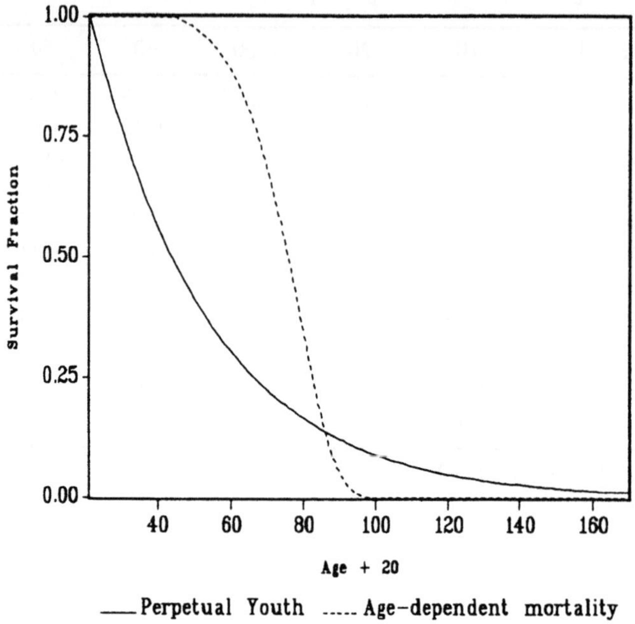

Figure 4.1. Survival Distributions.

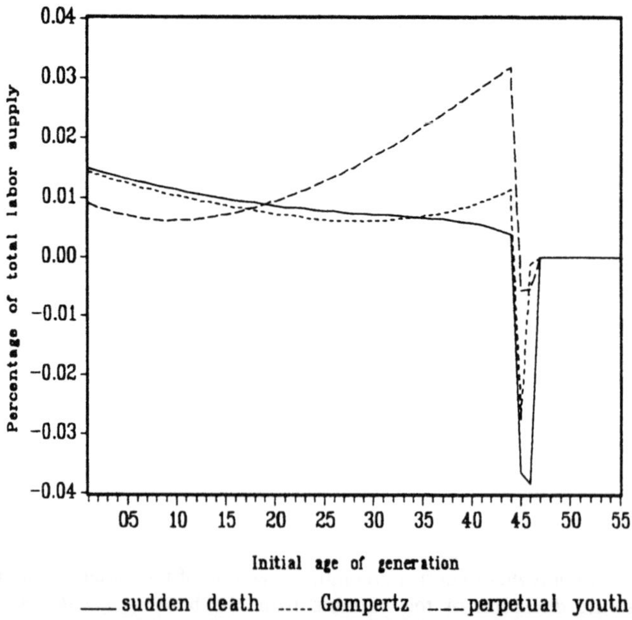

Figure 4.2. First-Year Labor Supply Effects of a PAYG Benefit Reduction.

5 Pension Policies and International Capital Mobility

Jukka Lassila, Heikki Palm and Tarmo Valkonen
The Research Institute of the Finnish Economy (ETLA)

Abstract

The effects of pension policies on households' and firms' behaviour depend on the international mobility of financial capital. We compare the policy effects between three regimes: a perfect capital mobility regime, a flow equilibrium regime where domestic interest rates react to current account developments, and a portfolio adjustment regime where the net foreign debt affects the domestic interest rate. We consider three different pension policies: an increase in the retirement age, a decrease in the pension benefit level and a temporary variation in the pension fund. The long-run policy effects are equal with perfect capital mobility and the flow equilibrium regime, but the short-run effects are different and the transition period is longer with the latter. In the portfolio adjustment regime even the long-run effects are different when the policy changes are permanent. Thus the degree of international capital mobility is important e.g. for the changes in intergenerational distribution. The effects on the pension contribution rate, on the other hand, are almost independent of the interest rate behaviour.

5.1 Introduction[1]

As in most industrialised countries, population ageing is expected to create problems also in Finland, in the form of rising social security costs. Pensions play

[1] The authors wish to thank D. Peter Broer and other participants of the workshop on Pension Systems, Taxation and Public Debt in Dynamic CGE Models, held at ETLA in April 1995, and John Rogers, for helpful comments. This research is part of the project 'Social Security and Future Generations', supported by the Ministry of Social Affairs and Health, the Academy of Finland, the Yrjö Jahnsson Foundation and ETLA. We thank D. Peter Broer, Svend Erik Hougaard Jensen, Søren Bo Nielsen, Peter Birch Sørensen and Ed W.M.T. Westerhout for valuable advice in early phases of the project, and Eija Kauppi for excellent model programming.

Pension Policies and Public Debt in Dynamic CGE Models

a key role in this respect, which increases the importance of studying the effects of pension system reforms. The need to ease the cost burden is strengthened by the high levels of public indebtedness, which makes it very difficult to reduce other taxes to leave room for rising social security payments.

The properties of the pension system affect private saving. Making changes in the system therefore changes saving behaviour, which has repercussions in the formation of productive capital and, further, to real wages and the welfare of all individuals. The link between saving and capital formation is, one the other hand, strongly dependent on international mobility of financial capital. Most previous studies have concentrated on the extreme cases of a closed economic system, where domestic saving must exactly match investment, or a small open economy which can borrow unlimited amounts from abroad without affecting the interest rate. Although these extreme descriptions are pedagogically instructive, we wish to focus explicitly on intermediate cases. Foreign borrowing is possible, but the more it is used the more domestic interest rates react. These reactions may be temporary or permanent. We show that these assumptions have important consequences for the speed that the economy adjusts to pension policy changes.

We consider three different pension policy instruments, a decrease in pension benefits, an increase in the retirement age and a fund-adjusting strategy. Both the macroeconomic effects and the intergenerational consequences of these policies are studied using a numerical overlapping-generations simulation model which is calibrated for the Finnish economy. We start by reviewing some closely related previous studies in section 5.2. Section 5.3 presents the model and discusses the determination of interest rates. Section 5.4 consists of the simulation results, and concluding comments are in section 5.5.

5.2 Some Related Studies

An increased interest to mitigate the unfavourable effects of population ageing and the development of CGE models have produced recently several pension policy simulation studies, most of which are somehow related to the pioneering work of Auerbach and Kotlikoff (1987).

Auerbach et al. (1989) studied the effects of the demographics and three policy options in the United States, Japan, Germany and Sweden. They used both a closed economy and a small open economy version of the Auerbach-Kotlikoff model in simulations. The first policy option was to fix the government outlays per member of the total population. The measure considerably eased the pressure to raise taxes. The second option was to raise the retirement age by one year in two stages. This lowered the social security contributions, raised wages and increased saving. The third measure was a 20 per cent cut in benefits. The effects were similar to those in the previous case, except that existing pensioners suffered and younger generations gained more because of this measure. In the open economy case where interest rates and wages were fixed, the demographic changes induced large capital movements to keep the factor returns intact. The assumption of no investment adjustment costs removed the possibility to study wealth effects induced by stock markets and produced large jumps in current account.

Also Chaveau and Loufir (1994) studied the effects of an increase in the retirement age and a cut in benefits with their model. The other options were favourable demographic developments and foundation of a transitory pension fund. The model describes a closed economy and includes no investment adjustment costs. Their main result is that increase in the retirement age produces the most favourable macroeconomic effects, but if the aim is intergenerational equity, the funding option should be used.

Bovenberg, Broer and Westerhout (1993) study the effects of a temporary decline in fertility in a small open economy, and several possible ways that the pension policy can help the economy to adjust. The demographic shock changes intergenerational income distribution markedly in the benchmark case in which pensions are financed by a PAYG system and the contribution rate adjusts. The studied policy options were contribution rate smoothing, broadening the base of contributions, a discrete cut in pension benefits and balancing the pension fund budget by adjusting the pension benefits. The authors stress the importance of the current account in smoothing the effects of demographic shocks.

Jensen and Nielsen (1993) also find that demographic shocks may have significant consequences for intergenerational distribution. These effects are strongly dependent on whether the pension benefits or contributions are used to adjust the system, or some intermediate path is chosen. Targeting net benefits in relation to net wages seems to be intergenerationally fair if one considers changes in consumption, whereas fixing the contribution rate and allowing benefits to vary seems to be acceptable considering discounted lifetime earnings. Their intertemporal model is somewhat different from that of Bovenberg et al., but it is a small open economy model, and the possibility to invest abroad is important also for their results.

5.3 The Model

5.3.1 Main Features

The model is an Auerbach-Kotlikoff-type perfect foresight numerical overlapping generations model. There are five sectors: households, enterprises, a government, a pension fund and a foreign sector. The labour, goods and capital markets are competitive and prices balance the demand and supply period-by-period. There is no money or inflation in the model.

The household sector consists of 14 overlapping generations. The households enter the model at the age of 20, participate in the labour markets until they are 60 years old, and live as pensioners thereafter. Their lifetimes are uncertain, but follow given constant probabilities. The expected remaining lifetime of those reaching 20 is 56.8 years. The households follow their utility maximising lifetime plans for consumption labour supply and bequests, which they have made when they are born. In the simulations the option of bequests was not used. After a simulated shock every household cohort revises its plan for the remaining lifetime.

The enterprise sector consists of small listed companies, which are forward looking and maximise the value of their shares. The representative firm decides about investments and the use of labour and intermediate goods. Investments cause adjustment costs and therefore the investment decisions are based on a tax adjusted version of Tobin's q theory. The increase in the capital stock is financed with retained earnings and debt in a given ratio.

The public sector collects taxes and uses them to hire workers and to pay the interest costs of the public debt. In the simulations the public debt is balanced period-by-period by the value added tax. The pension institution finances pensions with contributions levied in accordance with the wage bill and with capital income from the pension fund. The pension system is balanced period-by-period with the employers' contribution rate. Pensions are indexed partly to the wages and the pension wage is determined with a heavy weight on the last working period's earnings.

The households' working efficiency first increases and then decreases with age, which induces a hump-shaped life cycle earnings profile. The efficiency wage is formed in labour markets where the aggregate labour supply meets the exogenous public sector demand and the enterprises' demand, which is determined from the marginal productivity of labour rule.

There are two 'basic' goods in the model, one imported and one domestically produced. The goods are imperfect substitutes and are combined with a CES structure to form cost minimising composite intermediate, investment and consumption goods. The domestic good is also exported. The export demand depends on the real exchange rate with a constant price elasticity. The price of the imported good is given in international markets.

The capital markets are described more closely below. A more detailed description of the model can be found in the Appendix 2. The model has been calibrated so as to obtain certain features such as the ratios of investments and exports to gross domestic product and the public sector numbers roughly in line with the Finnish data. The parameter values used are listed at the end of the paper.

5.3.2 Capital Movements and Interest Rates

The way the foreign sector is modelled is important in the dynamic CGE models. Model building proceeded first from simple closed economy models to small open economy versions. In tax and trade policy analysis the foreign sector modelling has developed further to include imperfect substitution of domestic and foreign goods and assets[2]. The extremeness of the assumption of perfect capital movements have been noted also in some small open economy pension policy studies[3]. This study fills the gap by analysing pension policies with various assumptions about the degree of capital mobility.

How well the assumptions fit is, of course, an empirical question. One of the results indicating imperfect capital mobility is the strong correlation between national saving and investment found by Feldstein and Horioka (1980) in their famous study. But there are also additional explanations for the correlation. While the perfect capital movements assumption does equalise the interest rates expressed in a common numeraire, the real rates met by consumers and investors are different when the baskets of consumption and investment goods varies in different countries and consist of goods which are imperfect substitutes (Bovenberg 1989). These real interest rates speed up the balancing of the current account after a shock also in our case, even when the **fixed interest rate model** option, where capital mobility is perfect and the domestic interest rate is tied to the foreign one, is used.

In any case, it is a fact that lenders from various countries face different interest rates in international financial markets even when the debts are denominated in the same currency. We have developed two alternative formulations to describe the link between the external position of the country and the behaviour of investors, namely the flow equilibrium model and the portfolio adjustment model. The first mentioned is essentially the old Mundell - Fleming formulation of capital mobility, and the second follows the theory of portfolio selection developed by Markowitz and Tobin. The historical development of capital mobility formulations is described in Kenen (1985).

In the **flow equilibrium model** the current account surplus CA_t determines the interest rate differential between the domestic and the foreign interest rate:

$$r_t^D = r_t^F - \frac{CA_t}{\overline{\omega}} \tag{1}$$

When savings are larger than investment expenditures, the domestic interest rate r_t^D falls below the foreign rate r_t^F and vice versa. By changing the value of the parameter $\overline{\omega}$ various assumptions of the capital mobility can be introduced.

---

[2] From careful modelling of terms of trade in tax models, see e.g. Broer and Westerhout (1993) and in trade models e.g. Keuschnigg and Kohler (1994). Perraudin and Pujol (1991) and Goulder and Eichengreen (1989) represent tax models in which capital movements react to the interest rates. See also the article of Kenc and Perraudin in this book.

[3] See Steigum (1993) and Auerbach et al. (1989).

The **portfolio adjustment model** links the interest rate margin to the difference between current net foreign assets FA_t and the initial level of the foreign net assets FA_0:

$$r_t^D = r_t^F - \frac{FA_t - FA_0}{\overline{\omega}} \qquad (2)$$

Now the parameter $\overline{\omega}$ determines the elasticity of the domestic interest rate to the deviation of the stock of the foreign assets from its optimal level. When the value of the parameter is reduced enough, the model is financially closed, and with large values the model approaches to the small open economy case.

It is important to note the long-term properties of the various model versions. While there is no growth in the model, the budget constraints balance eventually the current account and in the flow adjustment model the domestic interest rate returns to the same level prevailing abroad. Therefore the steady state is the same as in the fixed interest rate version. In the portfolio adjustment model a permanent policy change produces a permanently different level of foreign assets, which leads to different steady state level of interest rates and all the other endogenous variables of the model. Besides the steady state differences, the interest rate elasticity affects also the speed of the adjustment of the economy, being faster the more perfect the capital markets are. The flow equilibrium model can be interpreted as an intermediate form between the portfolio adjustment model and the fixed interest rate model. The short-term effects of a policy change resemble those in the portfolio adjustment model and the long-term effects are the same as in the fixed interest rate model.

The various model versions have also different implications about welfare transfers induced by interest rate differences between the home country and foreign countries. In the fixed interest rate case there are, of course, no such transfers. In the other cases the welfare effects depend on the net external position of the home country. If the country is heavily indebted, as in our case, the higher domestic interest rate transfers welfare abroad. In the flow equilibrium model the welfare transfer initiated by the interest rate differential is temporary, but in the stock adjustment model a change in the country's net external position permanently changes the domestic interest rate and produces permanent welfare effects.

The introduction of the interest rate determination options to the model extends the possibilities to describe both current conditions in various countries and a changing environment of policy analysis in a single country. The international short-term money markets are already very efficient and the efficiency is improving also in the long maturities. For example, the liberalisation of the pension fund investments is continuously proceeding. Another important effect will possibly come through EMU, which abolishes part of the exchange rate risks, but also increases the transparency of the international financial markets.

5.4 Pension Policy Simulations

5.4.1 Justification and Description of the Pension Policy Measures

The ageing of the population affects considerably to the intergenerational equity and macroeconomic stability of the Western economies. The amount of the intergenerational transfer from young small generations to large older generations depends on the steepness of the demographic changes and the actuarial fairness of the pension system. The link between ageing and macroeconomic performance goes via changes in the labour supply, pension contribution rates and saving.

In most countries the public pension system is a pay-as-you-go scheme, in which the pension contribution rate adjusts yearly to cover the costs of defined pension benefits. Currently the large cohorts are in their most productive age and the contribution rate is low. After 10-20 years the baby-boomers will retire, which raises the contribution rate steeply because there are less payers and more beneficiaries. This trend has raised issues of intergenerational equity and credibility of the pension systems[4].

The age structure of the population has direct implications also on the national saving rate. Population ageing increases the number of old people who dissave and reduces the young saving generation's population share. This will weaken temporarily the balance of national saving and investments and induce variation in interest rates. Together with the variation in the labour supply and pension contribution rate it causes continuous changes in firms' operating environment. Furthermore, when changes in the capital stock induces adjustment costs, this development reduces also incomes.

We analyse three pension policy measures aimed to mitigate the unfavourable intergenerational and macroeconomic effects of population ageing. The two permanent measures are a reduction in the pension benefit level and an increase in the retirement age. The scale of these measures is fairly large in order to show clearly the macroeconomic effects. The third measure is a temporary increase in pension funding. Implementation of the pension policy measures is not announced beforehand. The pension system is described more closely in Appendix 2. A steady state path without growth and demographics was used as a baseline scenario in the simulations, because the focus was on the deviations caused by the measures.

We consider the openness of the economy being one of the main factors explaining the macroeconomic responses of the economy to changes in pension policy. While the degree of capital mobility is a disagreed empirical issue at least in the long maturities, we performed a sensitivity analysis using the three assumptions

[4] Lassila and Valkonen (1995) studies the credibility of pension policy when the replacement rate is determined by majority voting.

of interest rate determination described in the previous chapter. These proved to have considerable effects on the adjustment processes.

When the interactions of population ageing, capital mobility and interest rates are studied, one additional issue should be mentioned. The effects and timing of population ageing are largely similar in most OECD countries, which can produce common trends in national and international interest rates. These trends do not, however, change the interpretation of our results, because we study deviations from a baseline scenario.

5.4.2 Reducing the Pension Benefit Level

In the following we study the option in which the pension benefit level is reduced from 60 % to 40 % of the wages. Unlike most European countries the employment pension scheme in Finland is mainly financed by the employers' pension insurance contributions. In the simulations the budget of the pensions scheme is continuously balanced by adjusting the employers' contribution rate. Pensions are partly indexed to wages.

We first focus on the effects of reducing the pension benefit level in the case of perfect international capital mobility. The domestic interest rate is determined on the basis of the foreign interest rate.

When the pension benefit level is reduced by a third the households' pension wealth, pension institution's expenditure and the employers' pension contributions fall immediately. The labour costs of a firm consist of wages and employers' pension insurance contributions. The decreasing employers' pension insurance contribution raises wages in the short and long run, because the labour costs are determined by the marginal productivity condition of labour. The middle-aged households immediately increase the supply of labour as a reaction to reduced pensions and higher wages. In the longer run, as younger generations in the labour force will become wealthier and as new, high income generations enter the labour force, the demand for leisure gradually rises. Consequently, the supply of labour decreases in the long run because of the positive income effect more than offsets the substitution effect upon leisure.

The pensioners' consumption declines immediately. Initially the consumption of the generations near the retirement age drops also due to extra savings. The decrease in pension wealth is replaced by increasing the households' private savings. The consumption of young people and future generations increase because higher wages increase lifetime incomes more than the reduction of pensions decreases them. As a result, the total volume of consumption decreases initially but increases in the long run.

In the short run employment and domestic production increase. There will be excess supply of the domestic good and its price will fall immediately. The terms of trade initially weakens, which results in an increase in exports and a decrease in imports. The marginal productivity of capital and the market value of firms will rise. Consequently, investments and the capital stock expand.

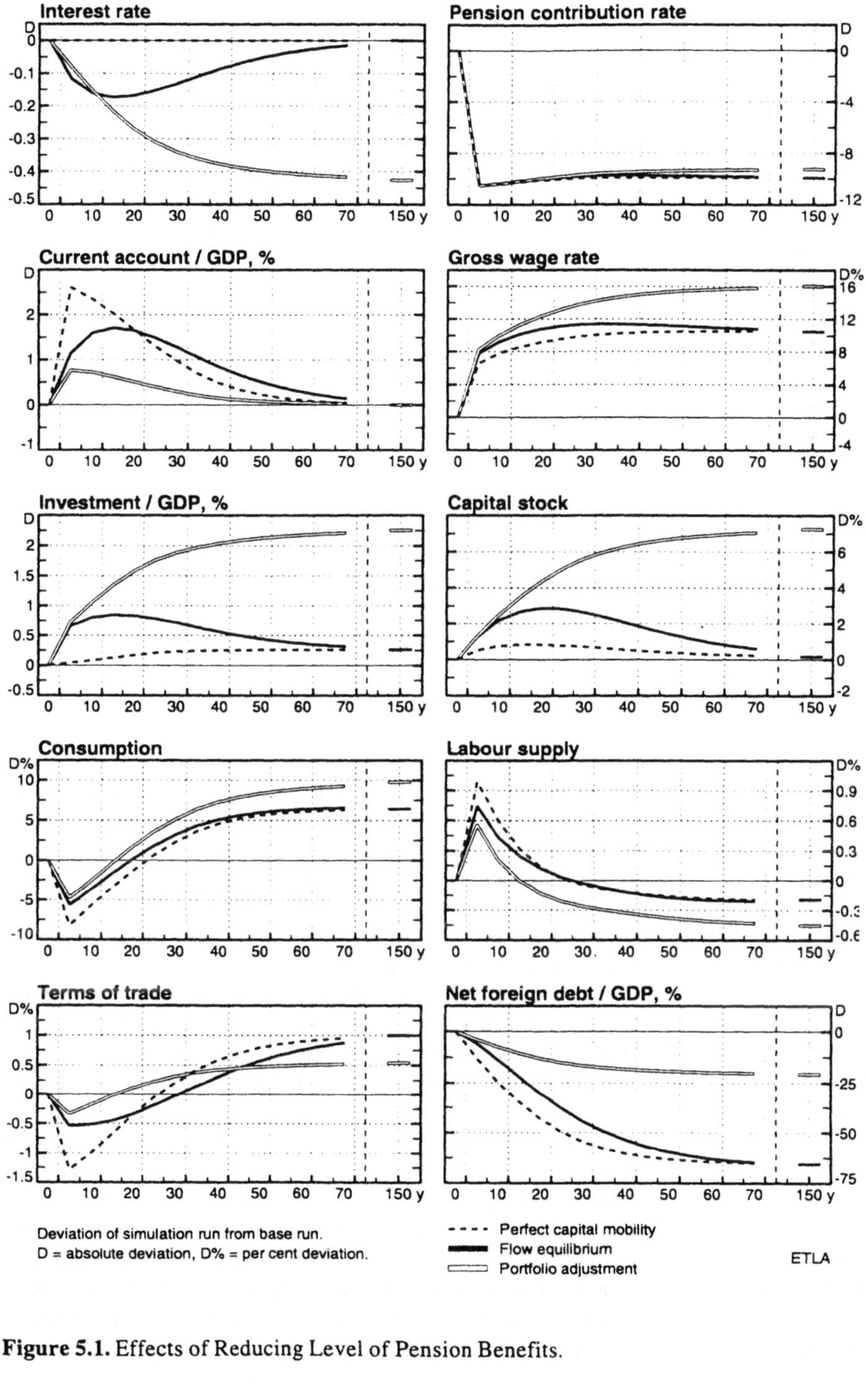

Figure 5.1. Effects of Reducing Level of Pension Benefits.

In the longer run, the effects are reversed. Investors anticipate the decline in the labour supply. The decline in the labour supply will lessen the marginal productivity of capital and that will dampen the investments. However, the capital stock per worker increases slightly also in the long run. The terms of trade improve and the trade balance will weaken.

In the economy with perfectly mobile capital, reducing the pension benefit level results in a temporary current account surplus and a permanently smaller foreign debt.

Secondly, we study the effects of cutting the pension benefit level in the cases where capital mobility is imperfect and depends on the difference between domestic and foreign interest rates. In the flow equilibrium model, where the interest rate is linked to the current account, the main difference is that the adjustment of the economy to the same stationary state takes place in a longer term. This has important consequences, for example, for the intergenerational welfare. Also the path of the capital stock and wages differ clearly in the transition period.

In the portfolio adjustment model the domestic interest rate decreases permanently when the pension benefit level is reduced because of the reduction in the net foreign debt. As a result of a decrease in the interest rate, savings and the households' wealth remain lower, but the capital per worker and investments are significantly higher than in a financially more open economy. The permanently high capital stock increases labour productivity and wages, but the labour supply decreases this time even more because of the larger income effect.

The current account surplus is smaller and foreign debt larger than in the case of perfect capital mobility. The difference between domestic and foreign interest rates is permanent and the economy's long-run equilibrium differs from that with perfect capital mobility.

The result of the interest rate remaining permanently lower is that the pension fund's interest income will remain smaller than in the case of a fixed interest rate. Consequently, pension contributions can be reduced less. Pension expenditure, too, remains higher because of the higher wages. The flexible interest rate has only small effects on the pension schemes. The reason is that pensions and pension contributions are strictly tied to wages. An important conclusion is that the pension insurance contribution rate is only slightly affected by the degree of capital mobility. The result is similar to the one of Auerbach et al. (1989).

The welfare effects of reducing the pension benefit level depend on the capital mobility. The existing pensioners always suffer from a pension cut. If capital is imperfectly mobile internationally the young and future generations gain, however, more from reducing the pension benefit level than in the case of perfect capital mobility.

The macroeconomic and the intergenerational welfare effects in the closed economy model of Chaveau and Loufir (1994) are very similar to the results of our portfolio adjustment model. Correspondingly, the effects produced by Bovenberg et al. (1994) with their small open economy model resemble our results in the fixed interest rate case. There are some differences, however. In Chaveau and Loufir an increase in wages is much lower and the supply of labour increases also in the long run. In Bovenberg et al. the result is a decrease in wages. This is explained by the differences between countries regarding who pays the pension contributions. The benefit from the decline in pension contributions is shared by employees and employers, so that net wages increase and labour costs decrease at the same time. If employers pay most of the contributions, as in Finland, the increase in net wages is achieved by increasing gross wages, but if employees pay the contributions, as in Holland, gross wages must decrease for the labour costs to decline. The French case is in between, but closer to the Finnish case.

5.4.3 Raising the Retirement Age

The retirement age is crucial to the contribution level, as it affects the worker - pensioner ratio in two ways. Raising the retirement age both increases the number of workers and decreases the number of pensioners. We assume that there is an exogenous retirement age which households take as given. An increase in this age from 60 to 65 is put into force instantaneously: those at the age of 60 who have planned to retire, have to work for five additional years, as does every younger generation also. Earlier, the age group 60 - 65 received pension benefits, but after the change they do not. We assume that pensions after age 65 are not affected directly: there is no change in the accrual system and in the averaging period. There are of course indirect effects, for instance the effects that changing wages have on pensions because of indexing.

For the economy, increasing the retirement age means that the available labour input increases. We assume that the labour markets function smoothly: wages adjust to equalise supply and demand in each period. The crucial thing then is how great the increase in the labour supply is. That depends on the effectiveness of those between 60 and 65 years. If they are as effective as younger generations the labour input increases substantially. In this case everybody seems to gain, even those who suddenly have to work for five more years than they earlier have thought. They get a good wage income for the work they do, and it more than compensates the loss of one period's pension. They suffer from reduced leisure in one period but gain from the fall in the price of consumer goods in all remaining periods. But if their work efficiency is low - as in our simulations - their wage income is small, and their lifetime utility may decrease. The gains of all other generations are also smaller in this case. Empirically this latter case is perhaps more plausible, especially if the pension level is high. But if there were no pension system, the former alternative would necessarily be better or at least as good: a household can work for one period more if it so chooses, without losing any pension income.

The pension contribution rate falls. The size of the fall is mainly determined by the relative amount of the population that belongs to the age group 60 - 65. To a lesser extent the fall is also affected by the work efficiency in that group. Interest rate behaviour has only a minimal effect on the size of the fall. This effect comes through the interest incomes of the pension fund. The steady state drop in the contribution rate is about 9 percentage points, and the drop in the first period is almost as much.

Even though the contribution rate is not sensitive to the interest rate behaviour, the adjustment of the economy in other respects to the increased retirement age is

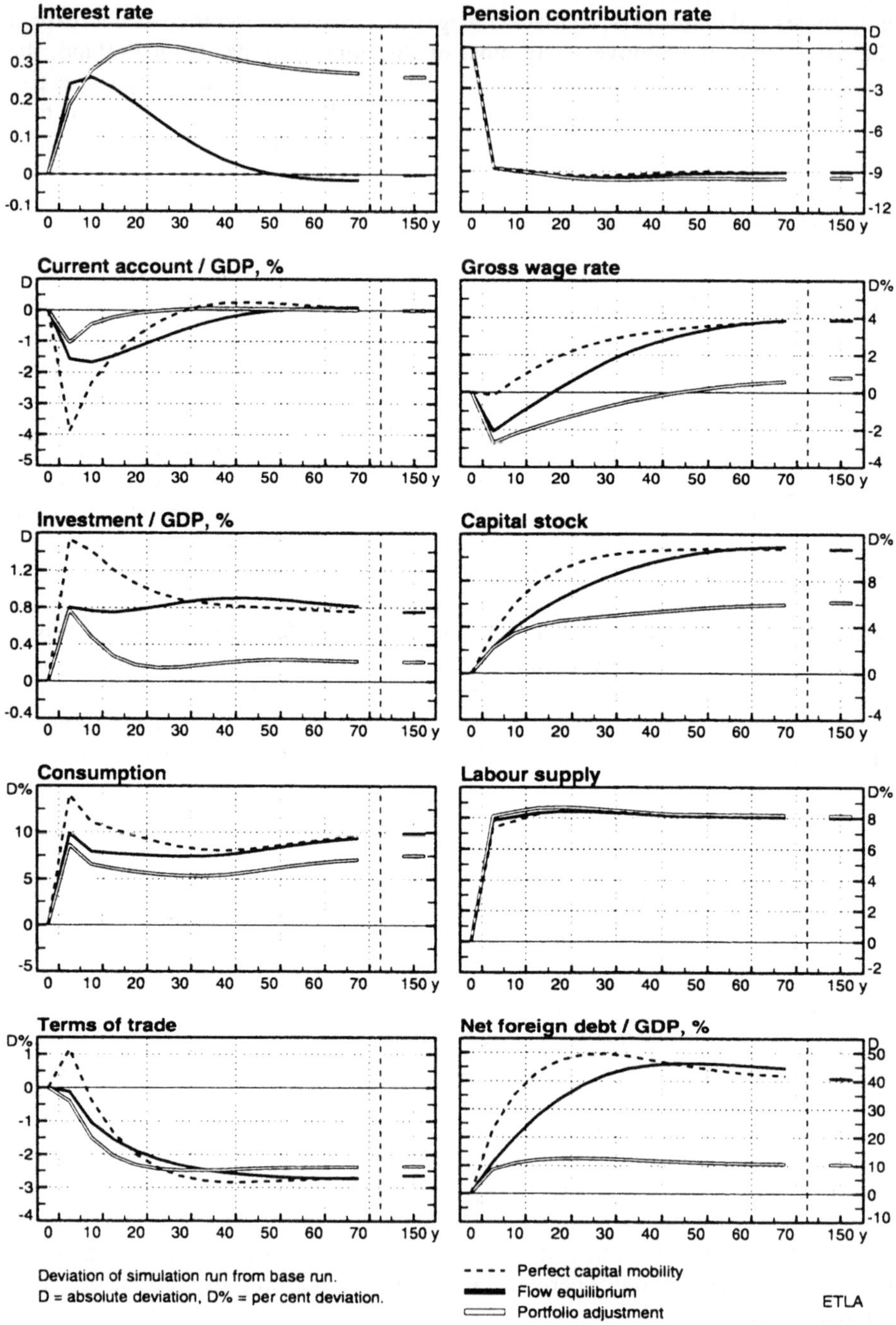

Figure 5.2. Effects of Increasing Retirement Age.

very sensitive. Consider first the case of perfect capital mobility (fixed interest rate). The decline in the pension contribution rate leaves room for higher wages. This together with a longer working period increases lifetime income. This increases the consumption of those at work and also of pensioners, as pensions are partly indexed to current wages. Another factor is wealth effects: share values react positively to the increase in the retirement age, and shareowners receive capital gains when the change is announced.

After the increase in the labour supply the capital-labour ratio is no longer optimal, and investments increase accordingly. Increased consumption and investment leads to a current account deficit and an increase in net foreign debt. The terms of trade deteriorate slightly.

If financial capital is less than perfectly mobile, the adjustment of the capital stock is slower. In the flow equilibrium case the capital stock eventually reaches the same new level as in the perfect capital mobility regime, but there may be marked differences during several decades of adjustment. These differences are reflected also in the labour market, where wages are lower than they would be with fixed interest rates, as a lower capital-labour ratio means lower labour productivity. Slower adjustment is also noted in the stock market, where the value of firms rise but less than it would have risen with fixed interest rates. This is further reflected in consumption which increases initially less, and in current account with smaller deficits that prevail for a longer period than with the case of perfect capital mobility.

A similar slow adjustment occurs also if capital mobility follows the portfolio adjustment model. An important difference from the flow equilibrium regime is that the final steady state is different. It has a higher interest rate and a lower capital stock. Investment and consumption grow less, current account deficits and the increase in net foreign debt are smaller.

Interest rate behaviour is important also for intergenerational distribution. In the flow equilibrium case, the less flexible the interest rate is, the quicker the economy adjusts towards the new equilibrium, and the better off everybody is during the beginning of the adjustment period. Generations born within a few years after the policy change will, however, gain less than they would if interest rates changed more. In the long run a new steady state is achieved; it is the same for the perfect capital mobility and flow equilibrium cases. Under the portfolio adjustment regime the welfare gains are smaller than with perfect capital mobility. In all cases part of the gains go abroad, in the form of deterioration of the terms of trade and higher interest rate.

The intergenerational welfare effects are similar to those in Chaveau and Loufir (1994). The first group whose pension period was delayed suffered in their analysis, while all others gained. In our analysis that age group also either suffers most or gains least, depending on their work effectiveness. Those already pensioned gained very little in Chaveau and Loufir's study, because their model does not include immediate stock revaluation effects; in our study this effect is important especially to pensioners as they usually have a rather large wealth. The results in Auerbach et al. (1989) are also similar except that a larger part of those working when the change is made suffer from the change.

Macroeconomic effects of increasing the retirement age on interest rate, wages, pension contribution rate, capital stock and labour supply are also very similar in the closed economy model of Chaveau and Loufir (1994) to our results with portfolio adjustment model. The path of consumption is different, however. We have a rapid increase in consumption in the first period. After that, consumption increase diminishes for a few periods as the wealth effect phases out, but after a while consumption again grows more due to increasing wages. In Chaveau and Loufir, consumption increases gradually, following the pattern of wages. The difference is again mostly the result of the wealth effect, which is not present in their model.

5.4.4 Temporary Increase in a Pension Fund

The third policy option is a temporary increase in a pension fund. This measure is aimed to mitigate the intergenerational income transfer produced by a pay-as-you-go pension finance, when there is a sharp turn in demographic trends[5]. The possibility to alleviate the unfavourable distribution effects of the PAYG system is, however, limited because the first generation who received the benefits without contributing to the system has passed and the current large generations near the retirement age have already participated in the financing of the previous generations' pension benefits.

There is no logical link between funding and labour supply distortions. Auerbach and Kotlikoff (1987) present a stylised model of the U.S. social security system, in which there exists a linkage between payments into and receipts from the pension system, even though it is not funded. It is this linkage that matters for the degree of distortion, not the absence or presence of funding. In our case the increased funding does not have any effect on that linkage.

We study the effects of a temporary increase in pension funding in the three regimes of the interest rate determination. In the baseline scenario the initial value of the pension fund is sustained by defining the contribution rate to cover pension benefits minus capital income from the pension fund. In the simulations a prespecified path to the fund is given and the employer's contribution rate adjusts. The path of the funding rate is planned to mitigate the effects of the large cohorts entering the pension age, so the fund grows 15 per cent per period (5 years) until the year 2010 and then decreases 6 per cent per period until it reaches again the initial level in the year 2050. This measure differs from earlier pension policy experiments in two ways: it defines a path of changes in a policy parameter and the value of the policy parameter returns to the initial level after 11 periods. The

[5] Funding reduces also variation in the pension contribution rate. This smoothing produces itself welfare gains, but the scale of this effect is minor compared to the intergenerational equity justification for funding, see Jensen and Nielsen (1995).

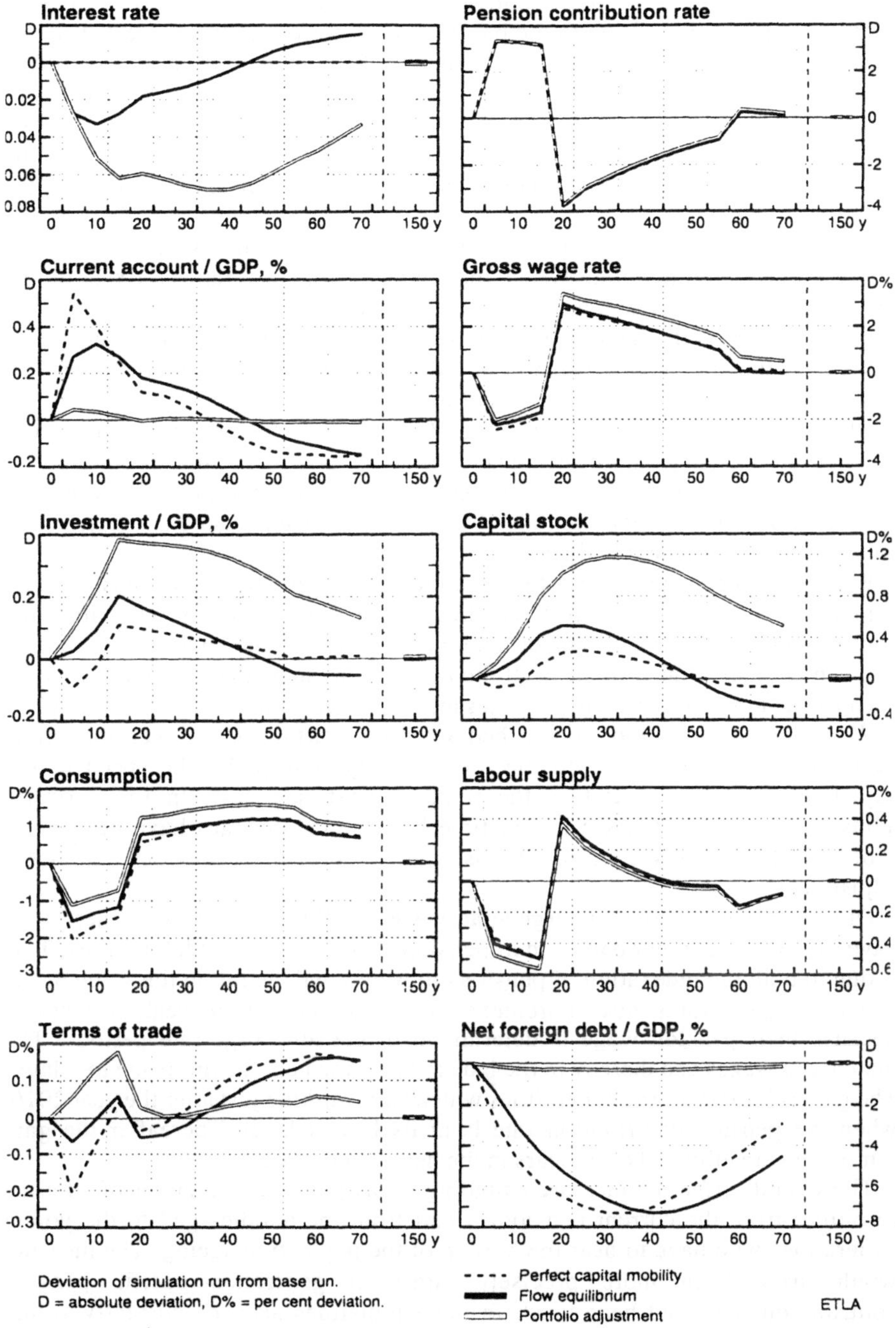

Figure 5.3. Temporary Increase in a Pension Fund.

employer's pension contribution rate rises during the first 15 years by nearly four percentage points compared to the baseline path to produce the requested rise in the funding rate. A major part of the burden of the higher contributions is shifted to wages in the labour markets. The households know that the wages will be higher after three periods and reduce their labour supply and saving temporarily. The national saving increases, however, above investment expenditures because of the increased pension saving. The consequent temporary current account surplus reduces foreign net debt.

The subsequent reaction of investments depends on the assumption of the interest rate determination. When the domestic interest rate is fixed to the international level, investments fall initially because of the lower productivity of capital induced by the reduction in the labour supply. In the flexible interest rate cases investments increase because of the fall in the domestic interest rate. The effect is more pronounced in the portfolio adjustment model.

After 15 years the effects are reversed. Running down the pension fund induces a temporary expansionary effect. The employers' pension contribution rate first falls sharply leading to a rise in wages and to an increase in the labour supply and consumption. This is supported also by a fall in the value added tax rate, which balances the government budget.

When the supporting effect to the contribution rate from the pension fund depletion and from the interest incomes of the fund decreases over time, the contribution rate rises again and the stimulation fades. In this stage the contribution rate is marginally higher in the portfolio adjustment model than in the other cases, because the lower interest rate produces less capital income to the pension fund.

When the pension fund has reached again the starting point level, the whole economy returns over time to the initial steady state path. The speed of the adjustment is again fastest in the fixed interest rate case. In the portfolio adjustment model it takes a longer time because the changes have been more profound. In the flow equilibrium case the overshooting behaviour delays the adjustment.

Did the measure increase intergenerational equity? The current pensioners, who have saved only a minor part of their pension benefits to the fund, lose most. This is due to both the indexation of pensions to wages and the fall in the value of the firms. The generations near retirement age lose because of the wealth effect and because their pension wage is determined in the low wage rate periods. The increase in wages and thereby in the indexed pension benefits limits the loss later. The gain is largest for the generations which start working just after the year 2010, when the pension contribution rate is at its lowest level. Thereafter the gain diminishes steadily and disappears in the new steady state.

The overall effect of increased funding is, as planned, a transfer of lifetime resources from the current pensioners and from the middle-aged to the young generations who have to bear the burden of the population ageing. The measure would have been more precisely aimed if generation-specific pension contribution rates had been used. In our simulations also the currently young generations had to participate in the costs of increased funding.

The degree of capital mobility does not affect markedly the pension contribution rate, but it has unquestionable utility impacts. In the stock equilibrium model the utility losses are smallest and gains largest because of the greatest positive terms of trade and interest rate effects, which transfer resources from abroad.

Chaveau and Loufir (1994) studied the effects of a temporary fund with their closed economy model. Their main results are the same: the temporary macroeconomic effects are not very large, but the welfare of the future generations can be considerably improved with funding. In their model the reactions of interest rate were greater, which led to a higher temporary increase in the capital stock and wages.

A related small open economy study is performed by Bovenberg et al. (1993), the focus of which was on the impacts of pension contribution smoothing. The fixed premium rate smoothens trends in the labour supply, investment and saving. The striking difference compared to our results is that in their model an increase in pension funds reduces national saving and weakens the current account balance. This is due to the households' stronger intertemporal shift of saving from the low-wage funding periods to the later high-wage periods.

5.5 Concluding Remarks

Pension policies have been extensively studied in recent years, because population ageing is expected to create financing problems in most industrialised countries. Studies that use numerical simulation models, like this study, usually assume that capital is perfectly mobile internationally. We relax that extreme assumption and study how the policy effects change when we move from perfect capital mobility to a flow equilibrium regime, where domestic interest rates react to current account developments, and to a portfolio adjustment regime where the net foreign debt affects the domestic interest rate.

The long-run policy effects are equal with perfect capital mobility and the flow equilibrium regime, but the initial effects are different and the transition period is longer with the latter. The interest rate reactions make the current account changes smaller, and the required long-run change in net foreign assets takes more time to accumulate. In the portfolio adjustment regime even the long-run effects are different when the policy changes are permanent. The degree of international capital mobility does not change qualitatively the intergenerational effects of pension policies but affects the size of gains and losses of different generations. The effects on the pension contribution rate, on the other hand, are largely independent of the interest rate behaviour. Pensions are generally both earnings-related and financed by payroll taxes, and this link is sometimes strengthened by the indexation of pensions to current wages. Although the wage effects of pension policies are quite different under different specifications of capital movements, the contribution rate does not vary much as changes in wages affect both pension benefits and their source of finance. A minor effect comes from differences in pension funds' interest incomes.

References

Auerbach, A.J. and L.J. Kotlikoff (1987): *Dynamic Fiscal Policy*. Cambridge University Press. Cambridge.

Auerbach, A.J., R.P. Hagemann, G. Nicoletti, and L.J. Kotlikoff (1989): The Economic Dynamics of an Ageing Population: The Case of Four OECD Countries. *OECD Economic Studies*, no. 12, pp. 97-130.

Bovenberg, A.L. (1989): The Effects of Capital Income Taxation on International Competitiveness and Trade Flows. *The American Economic Review*, Vol. 79, pp. 1045-1064.

Bovenberg, A.L., D.P. Broer and E.W.M.T. Westerhout (1993): Public Pensions and Declining Fertility in a Small Open Economy: An Intertemporal Simulation Approach. In B.L.Wolfe (ed.) *Proceedings of the 48th Congress of the International Institute of Public Finance*, Seoul 1992. Supplement to Public Finance, Vol. 48, pp. 43 - 59. 1993.

Bovenberg, A.L., D.P. Broer and E.W.M.T. Westerhout (1994): Taxation, Pensions and Saving in a Small Open Economy, *Scandinavian Journal of Economics*, Vol. 96, pp. 403-424.

Broer, D.P. and E.W.M.T. Westerhout (1993): Taxation in an Intertemporal General Equilibrium Model of a Small Open Economy. *Economic Modelling* Vol 10, pp. 64-80.

Chaveau,T. and R. Loufir (1994): Demographic Transition and Social Security Policies in France: a Welfare Analysis. OFCE Working Paper, no 94-2.

Feldstein, M. and C. Horioka (1980): Domestic Saving and International Capital Flows. *Economic Journal* 90 (June) pp. 314-329.

Goulder, L.H. and B. Eichengreen (1989): Savings Promotion, Investment Promotion and International Competitiveness. In R. Feenstra (ed.) *Trade Policies for International Competitiveness*. Chicago University Press. Chicago. 1989.

Jensen, S.E.H. and S.B. Nielsen (1993): Aging, Intergenerational Distribution and Public Pension Systems. In B.L. Wolfe (ed.) *Proceedings of the 48th Congress of the International Institute of Public Finance,* Seoul 1992. Supplement to Public Finance, Vol. 48, pp. 29 - 42. 1993.

Jensen, S.E.H. and S.B. Nielsen (1995): Population Ageing, Public Debt and Sustainable Fiscal Policy. *Fiscal Studies*, Vol. 16, pp. 1-20.

Kenen, P.B. (1985): Macroeconomic Theory and Policy: How the Closed Economy was Opened. In R.W. Jones and P.B. Kenen (eds.) *Handbook of International Economics*, Vol. 2, pp. 626-677. North-Holland.1985.

Keuschnigg, C. and W. Kohler (1994): Modeling Intertemporal General Equilibrium: An Application to Austrian Commercial Policy. *Empirical Economics*, Vol. 19, pp. 131-164.

Lassila, J. and T. Valkonen (1995): Policy Credibility in Numerical Overlapping Generations Models. Discussion Paper No. 545, The Research Institute of the Finnish Economy, Helsinki.

Perraudin, W.R.M. and T. Pujol (1991): European Fiscal Harmonization and the French Economy. *IMF Staff Papers*, Vol 38, No 2, pp. 399-440.

Steigum, E. Jr. (1993): Accounting for Long-run Effects of Fiscal Policy by Means of Computable Overlapping Generations Models. In S. Honkapohja and M. Ingberg (eds.) *Macroeconomic Modelling and Policy Implications*. pp. 45-67. Elsevier Publishers B.V. 1993.

Yaari, B.L. (1965): Uncertain Lifetime, Life Insurance and the Theory of the Consumer. *Review of the Economic Studies*, Vol 32, pp. 137-150.

Appendix 1[1]

Table 5.1. Effects of The Pension Policy Measures.

Reducing the Pension Benefit Level year	5	10	15	30	150
A. Fixed interest rate model					
Wage rate	6.60	7.84	8.64	9.94	10.48
Pension contribution rate	-10.48	-10.40	-10.24	-9.95	-9.92
Interest rate	0	0	0	0	0
Terms of trade	-1.28	-1.01	-0.69	0.20	0.99
B. Flow equilibrium model					
Wage rate	7.82	9.29	10.22	11.34	10.48
Pension contribution rate	-10.51	-10.34	-10.15	-9.79	-9.92
Interest rate	-0.12	-0.17	-0.18	-0.13	0
Terms of trade	-0.53	-0.51	-0.46	0	1.00
C. Portfolio adjustment model					
Wage rate	8.20	9.96	11.29	13.90	16.04
Pension contribution rate	-10.43	-10.31	-10.11	-9.63	-9.26
Interest rate	-0.08	-0.15	-0.22	-0.34	-0.43
Terms of trade	-0.36	-0.20	-0.05	0.30	0.54
Raising the Retirement Age year	**5**	**10**	**15**	**30**	**150**
A. Fixed interest rate model					
Wage rate	-0.16	0.66	1.37	2.79	3.87
Pension contribution rate	-8.84	-8.88	-9.05	-9.28	-9.03
Interest rate	0	0	0	0	0
Terms of trade	1.15	-0.40	-1.36	-2.67	-2.64
B. Flow equilibrium model					
Wage rate	-2.08	-1.25	-0.51	1.61	3.87
Pension contribution rate	-8.77	-9.03	-9.19	-9.45	-9.03
Interest rate	0	0.24	0.26	0.14	0
Terms of trade	-0.12	-1.06	-1.55	-2.32	-2.64
C. Portfolio adjustment model					
Wage rate	-2.70	-2.21	-1.83	-0.78	0.79
Pension contribution rate	-8.77	-8.96	-9.17	-9.61	-9.46
Interest rate	0	0.19	0.28	0.34	0.26
Terms of trade	-0.40	-1.51	-2.04	-2.49	-2.36

Table 5.1. (cont.)

[1] In the table the wage rate and terms of trade describe relative deviations from the steady state path in percents, while the pension contribution rate and interest rate describe percentage point deviations.

Table 5.1. (cont.)

Increase in a Pension Fund	year	5	10	15	30	150
A. Fixed interest rate model						
Wage rate		-2.44	-2.24	-1.90	2.26	0
Pension contribution rate		3.35	3.33	3.15	-2.63	0
Interest rate		0	0	0	0	0
Terms of trade		-0.21	-0.08	0.04	0.02	0
B. Flow equilibrium model						
Wage rate		-2.24	-2.02	-1.70	2.37	0
Pension contribution rate		3.33	3.29	3.17	-2.60	0
Interest rate		0	-0.03	-0.04	-0.02	0
Terms of trade		-0.07	0	0.06	-0.02	0
C. Portfolio adjustment model						
Wage rate		-2.03	-1.74	-1.33	2.92	0
Pension contribution rate		3.35	3.30	3.18	-2.53	0
Interest rate		0	-0.03	-0.06	-0.07	0
Terms of trade		0.06	0.13	0.18	0.01	0

Table 5.2. Generational Redistribution Measured by Relative Compensated Variation.

Reducing the Pension Benefit Level	age	80-84	60-64	40-44	20-24	-150
A. Fixed interest rate model		-26.2	-26.6	0.0	3.9	4.9
B. Flow equilibrium model		-21.7	-23.3	0.6	4.9	4.9
C. Portfolio adjustment model		-21.3	-22.9	0.9	5.0	8.3
Raising the Retirement Age	**age**	**80-84**	**60-64**	**40-44**	**20-24**	**-150**
A. Fixed interest rate model		15.4	-0.3	0.4	3.7	4.6
B. Flow equilibrium model		13.2	-2.0	0.2	3.3	4.6
C. Portfolio adjustment model		13.1	-2.2	-0.1	2.8	4.2
Increase in a Pension Fund	**age**	**80-84**	**60-64**	**40-44**	**20-24**	**-150**
A. Fixed interest rate model		-3.5	-2.1	-0.8	0.4	0
B. Flow equilibrium model		-2.8	-1.5	-0.7	0.6	0
C. Portfolio adjustment model		-2.4	-1.2	-0.5	0.9	0

Redistribution is measured by is 100* ($\ln E_s - \ln E_c$), where E denotes discounted lifetime consumption expenditure. Subscript s refers to the simulation run and c to the consumption necessary to achieve the baseline utility at simulation prices. The age row in the table refers to the age of various generations when the pension policy measure is implemented. Age -150 describes the utility result for a generation which will enter the labour force 150 years after the reform i.e. the utility effects in a new steady state.

Pension benefit reduction causes huge losses to pensioners. In practise, existing pensions would be unlikely to be fully reduced. The large gains to pensioners from increasing the retirement age come to a large extent from wealth effects and taxation: increasing labour income tax receipts are used to lower the VAT rate.

Appendix 2

The Model

Household Behaviour

Households maximise the utility from consumption and leisure in different periods, and a bequest they give. The lifecycle plan is the solution to the following problem.

$$\max_{C,L,B} \sum_{t=1}^{T} \frac{1}{1-\frac{1}{\gamma}} \frac{U_t^{1-\frac{1}{\gamma}}}{(1+\delta)^{t-1}} + \mu \frac{(B(1-\tau^B))^{1-\frac{1}{\gamma}}}{(1+\delta)^{T-1}}$$

subject to budget constraint

$$\sum_{t=1}^{T_w} (1-L_t)\, e_t w_t (1-\tau_t^w-\tau_t^e)\, R_t + \sum_{t=T_w+1}^{T} Z_t (1-\tau_t^w)\, R_t + R_7 B_7 (1-\tau_t^B) =$$

$$\sum_{t=1}^{T} C_t p_t^C (1+\tau_t^c) - R_T B_T$$

and subject also to the determination of pensions Z. U is the periodic utility

$$U_t = (C_t^{1-\frac{1}{\rho}} + \alpha_0 L_t^{1-\frac{1}{\rho}})^{1-\frac{1}{\rho}}$$

and R is the discount factor

$$R_t = \prod_{s=1}^{t-1} \frac{1}{(1+r_s(1-\tau_s^r))}$$

C is consumption, p^C its price, L is leisure, and of the constant parameters γ is the elasticity of intertemporal substitution, δ is the rate of time preference and ρ is the elasticity of substitution between consumption and leisure. The model includes a bequest motive. The households receive a net bequest $B(1-\tau^B)$ at the age of 55 (period 7) and give a bequest B before dying. The number of periods is 14: the unit period is five years. A life-cycle plan is made at the age of 20, people retire at 60 and live until 90. There is also a possibility of liquidity constraints on households, but this option is not used in this study.

The pension system relates pensions to earnings during working years. The normal pension is the share θ of a pension wage, which depends on the wage levels both during the persons' working years and pension years. The share θ depends on the number of working years but is here held constant. Let

$$1-L_p = \frac{1}{T_w} \sum_{t=1}^{T_w} (1-L_t)$$

and

$$w_p = \sum_{t=1}^{T_w} \beta_t (1 - L_t) e_t w_t / (1 - L_p) \quad \text{where} \quad \sum_{t=1}^{T_w} \beta_t = 1$$

The pension Z in period t is now

$$Z_t = \theta (1 - L_p) w_p^{\lambda} w_t^{1-\lambda} \quad \text{where} \quad 0 \leq \lambda \leq 1$$

The weights β determine the pension rights averaging period. If the worker stays in one firm, the averaging period consists of the last four years, which roughly would mean that β_8 is equal to unity and all other weights are zeros. In practice, due to moves between firms and also to some technical reasons all coefficients are positive, but β_8 is the largest. T_w is 8 in the baseline scenarios.

The term e_t describes work efficiency, which varies with age. It makes the life-cycle wage-income profile hump-shaped. Parameter λ describes pension indexing: $\lambda = 0$ means that pensions are fully indexed to current wages.

The budget constraint says that the discounted value of lifetime wage and pension incomes and received bequests equals discounted consumption expenditure and a given bequest. Households start with no wealth and leave no wealth upon death. The terms τ^w, τ^c, τ^B and τ^r are tax parameters and τ^e is the employees' pension contribution rate.

In the version described above all households live 14 periods. In the calculations of this paper, however, we have used a variant where the lifetimes are uncertain but follow given constant probabilities. Households now maximise expected utility. The population is large enough so that every period a given fraction of each cohort dies with probability one, so there is no uncertainty at the aggregate level. Following Yaari (1965) we assume that insurance companies pay premiums to households on their assets and receive these assets when the household dies. With perfect competition in the insurance industry its profits are zero. The premiums that households receive vary with age. The formulas above apply, except that the survival probabilities are included in the lifetime utility function and in the discount factor formula.

The actual equations of the model are the first-order conditions derived from the optimisation problem. The household sector consists of fourteen households, of different age, in each period. Total consumption, labour supply, pensions received and taxes paid are aggregated from individual household decisions.

Firms

A representative small firm produces the domestic good using capital inherited from the previous period, intermediate goods and labour. Infinite horizon decisions of investment, employment and use of intermediate goods are made to maximise firm's market value. The firm takes the prices, demand for production and supply of factors at given prices, production technology and taxation as given. Intermediate and capital goods are costs-minimising CES composites of domestic and imported goods. Investments are financed by retained earnings and debt.

The firm's gross production Y_t can be described as follows:

$$Y_t = \frac{F(K_{t-1}, L_t^f) - G(I_t, K_{t-1})}{1-\zeta}$$

$$G_t = \xi \frac{I_t^2}{K_{t-1}}$$

The use of the composite intermediate good is determined as a fixed proportion ζ of gross production. The production function F_t is a CES function of capital and labour. In the process of installing new capital some of the production is lost as investment adjustment costs G_t. These installation costs depend positively on the investments and negatively on the amount of capital. Both the adjustment costs and the substitutability of capital for labour are important determinants of the firm's reaction to unexpected changes in the external environment.

Domestic households consider bonds and firms' shares as perfect substitutes in their portfolios. The arbitrage condition between after-tax returns on bonds and shares is:

$$r_{t-1}^D (1-\tau_t^r) V_{t-1} = (1-\tau_t^d) D_t + (1-\tau_t^g)(V_t - V_{t-1})$$

where the left-hand side describes the invested amount yielding the domestic after-tax interest rate. Notice that the subscript in the interest rate refers to the period when the rate is determined. The corresponding interest payment is paid and received in the next period. On the right-hand side the first term is the after-tax dividend income and the second term the after-tax capital gain.

The arbitrage condition can be transformed to a form where the market value of the shares equals the present value of expected future dividends, adjusted for capital income taxes:

$$V_t = \sum_{s=t+1}^{\infty} \frac{1-\tau_s^d}{1-\tau_s^g} D_s \prod_{v=t+1}^{s} \frac{1}{1 + r_{v-1}^D \left(\frac{1-\tau_v^r}{1-\tau_v^g}\right)}$$

The dividends are a residual from the firm's cash flow identity:

$$D_t = (1-\tau_t^f) \left[p_t^F (F_t - G_t) - (1+\tau_t^l) w_t L_t - r_{t-1}^D B_{t-1}^c \right] -$$
$$p_t^K I_t + \tau_t^f d \, p_{t-1}^K K_{t-1} + (B_t^c - B_{t-1}^c)$$

where the dividend in period t is determined by after-tax profits before depreciation minus investment expenditure plus depreciation allowances, which corresponds to real depreciation plus any increase in corporate debt. In this simple version all other allowances are included by using an effective average corporate tax rate. Corporate debt is preferred when financing investments, but its use is limited to a fixed ratio of the replacement value of corporate capital.

The firm chooses the optimal path of investment, use of labour and intermediate goods to maximise the firm's value. If there are no unexpected shocks, there is no need to revise the optimal plan and it will be followed forever. Capital depreciates at a constant annual rate of d. The constraints of the maximisation are the initial capital stock and an equation describing its dynamics:

$$K_t = K_{t-1}(1-d) + I_t$$

Three of the four first order conditions of the constrained optimisation are used as model equations. The first implies that investments should be carried out until the marginal benefit from an additional unit of investment is as large as the marginal cost. The marginal cost includes the price of a unit of capital plus the installation cost. The condition can be transformed to a q-theory investment equation:

$$I_t = \frac{\left(\frac{1-\tau_t^g}{1-\tau_t^d}\, q_t - p_t^K\right) K_{t-1}}{(1-\tau_t^f)\, \xi\, p_t^F}$$

The optimality condition of capital says that capital should be installed until the after-tax return of an additional unit is large enough to cover the expenses of carrying the capital to the next period. These expenses include interest, depreciation and the change in the replacement price of capital. This condition is transformed to an equation describing the path of the shadow value of the capital:

$$q_t = \Big\{ \frac{1-\tau_{t+1}^d}{1-\tau_{t+1}^g} \big[(1-\tau_{t+1}^f)\,(p_{t+1}^F\,(F_{K,t+1} - G_{K,t+1}) - r_t^D\, b\, p_t^K) - b\, p_t^K + \tau_{t+1}^f\, d\, p_t^K\big]$$
$$+ \frac{1-\tau_t^d}{1-\tau_t^g}\, b\, p_t^K \left(1 + r_t^D\, \frac{1-\tau_{t+1}^r}{1-\tau_{t+1}^g}\right) + q_{t+1}(1-d) \Big\} \frac{1}{1 + r_t^D \frac{1-\tau_{t+1}^r}{1-\tau_{t+1}^g}}$$

In a steady state this marginal productivity condition of capital can be written as:

$$F_K - G_K = \frac{p^K}{p^F} \left[d + b\, r^D + (1-b)\, r^D \frac{1-\tau^r}{(1-\tau^g)(1-\tau^f)}\right] + r^D \frac{1-\tau^r}{1-\tau^g}\, \xi\, d + \xi\, d^2$$

Inside of the square brackets there is the depreciation rate d, the interest cost of debt-financed share b of the capital stock and cost of capital financed by retained earnings. The two terms after the brackets are based on adjustment costs linked to replacement investments.

The third condition says that the marginal benefit of an extra unit of labour should cover wage costs plus the employer's social security contribution:

$$p_t^F F_L = (1 + \tau_t^l)\, w_t$$

The fourth condition is a transversality condition ensuring that the discounted shadow value of capital goes to zero as time approaches infinity.

The market value of the firm is linked to the shadow value of the capital in the leveraged firm as follows:

$$V_t = K_t q_t - \frac{1-\tau_t^d}{1-\tau_t^g} B_t^c$$

where B_t^c is the firm's debt. This link has been derived using the homogeneity of production and capital installation technologies. The value of the firm jumps whenever unexpected news about the firm's future profitability comes to the market. Households are the sole owners of the firms and changes in their wealth changes life-cycle plans immediately.

Pension Institution

The pension institution finances pensions with contributions levied in accordance with the wage bill and with capital income from the pension fund. The pension system is balanced periodically with the employers' contribution rate. The assets of the fund are invested in domestic bonds. The funded amount is assumed to stay at the current level in the baseline scenario.

Government Sector

The government collects various taxes and uses the proceeds to pay interest on outstanding debt and to employ civil servants to produce public services. These services are provided free of charge and are not taken into account in individual utility considerations.

The model includes many possibilities to balance revenues and expenditures of the government every period. An endogenous value added tax rate is used most often, because it induces little changes in the intergenerational incidence of taxation. From the expenditure side it is possible to endogenise the number of government employees. There is also a possibility to let the government run a deficit or a surplus in the budget, but then a transversality condition must be determined so that the public debt does not expand indefinitely.

Foreign Sector

The model imitates a small open economy, where the export share of the total demand is large. The amount exported depends on the price elasticity of the foreign demand:

$$X_t = ex \left(\frac{p_t^D}{p_t^M} \right)^{\sigma^E}$$

A large negative value for the elasticity implies that a small country has to adjust to the price level of international markets.

The use of the imported good is determined as part of cost-minimising composite goods used in consumption, in investments and as an intermediate good in production. The price of the foreign good is determined in the international markets and used as a numeraire in the model.

Markets

The model includes four markets, which balance every period. In the labour markets the firms demand labour following the marginal productivity of labour rule. Households' aggregate labour supply is divided between public and private employment. The wage rate is determined so as to equate supply and demand in the labour markets.

In the markets of the domestic good the firms are the sole suppliers. The product is used by other firms as a part of the composite intermediate and investment goods, by households as a part of the composite consumption good and by foreign agents. The demand of the domestic agents is determined by a cost-minimising CES structure. The export demand conditions are explained above. The equilibrium condition which determines the price of the domestic good is thus:

$$Y_t = Y_t^D + I_t^D + C_t^D + X_t$$

The domestic demand for the fixed-price imported good is also determined by minimising costs of the composite goods. The perfectly elastic supply adjusts to demand in these markets:

$$M_t = Y_t^M + I_t^M + C_t^M$$

The fourth markets are the capital markets. In these markets savings and investment are balanced. The determination of the domestic interest rate is described in more detail in the section 5.3.2. The arbitrage condition of domestic households ensures that they are ex ante indifferent between investing their savings in bonds and in firms' shares. The foreign agents are restricted to participate only in the bond markets. Total savings are a sum of domestic savings and foreign portfolio investments. The parallel stock equilibrium can be written as:

$$W_t + H_t = V_t + B_t^c + B_t^g + FA_t$$

where W_t is the household wealth, H_t is the value of the pension fund assets, V_t is the market value of the firm, B_t^c is the firms' debt, B_t^g is the public debt and FA_t is the net foreign assets of the country.

List of Variables

K	capital stock of the firms
Y	gross production of the domestic good
G	installation costs
F	value added
V	value of the firms
D	dividends
B^c	firms' debt
I	aggregate investment
I^D	demand of the domestic good in investment use
I^M	demand of the imported good in investment use
C	aggregate consumption
C^D	demand of the domestic good in consumption use
C^M	demand of the imported good in consumption use
Y^D	demand of the domestic good in intermediate use
Y^M	demand of the imported good in intermediate use
E	exports
I	imports
CA	current account deficit
FA	net foreign assets
r^D	domestic interest rate
p^D	price of the domestic good
p^M	price of the imported good
p^C	price of the composite consumption good
p^K	price of the composite investment good
p^F	price of the value added
q	shadow price of the capital
τ^l	employer's pension contribution
H	value of the pension fund's assets
B^g	public debt
τ^C	value added tax
W	household wealth
L^f	firms' labour demand
L	leisure
w	wage rate
U	utility
Z	pension
B	bequest

Parameter Values

personal income tax	τ^w	0.30
dividend income tax	τ^d	0.00
interest income tax	τ^r	0.28
bequest tax	τ^B	0.10
capital gains tax	τ^g	0.28
corporate income tax	τ^f	0.28
employee's pension contribution	τ^e	0.05
depreciation rate	d	0.09
installation cost parameter	ξ	1.00
share of the value of firms' capital financed by debt	b	0.70
input-output coefficient for the composite intermediate good input	ζ	0.10
labour share parameter of the value added production fuction	ε	0.36
elasticity of substitution between labour and capital	β	0.80
share parameter of domestic good for consumption	υ^C	0.70
share parameter of domestic good for investment	υ^K	0.70
share parameter of domestic good for intermediate use	υ^I	0.70
elasticity of substitution between imported and domestic good in consumption	σ^C	0.99
elasticity of substitution between imported and domestic good in investment	σ^K	0.99
elasticity of substitution between imported and domestic good in intermediate use	σ^I	0.99
scale parameter of export demand	ex	0.60
price elasticity of export demand	σ^E	-4.00
foreign interest rate	r^F	0.03
sensitivity parameter of capital movements	$\overline{\omega}$	3.00
elasticity of intertemporal substitution of consumption	γ	0.50
elasticity of substitution between consumption and leisure	ρ	0.75
rate of time preference	δ	.015
share of full pension to pension wage	θ	0.60
pension indexing parameter	λ	0.50

6 Debt Reduction, Wage Formation and Intergenerational Welfare

Svend Erik Hougaard Jensen
Department of Economics, University of Copenhagen, and
Economic Policy Research Unit (EPRU),
Copenhagen Business School, Denmark

Abstract

The macroeconomic and cross-generational effects of policies aiming at public debt reduction are shown to depend crucially on how wages respond to the associated tightening of fiscal policy. In order to dampen the adverse transitional effects on the macroeconomy and in order to protect currently living generations against potentially severe drops in consumption possibilities, the paper argues in favour of a long-term strategy for debt reduction, achieved through a temporarily higher excise tax rate rather than raising the tax rate on labour income.

JEL Classification: E62, H3, H63
Keywords: Fiscal policy, Trade unions; Macroeconomic adjustment

6.1 Introduction[1]

Over the last couple of decades several OECD countries have seen their public debt rise rather dramatically. With or without formal debt targets, such as those implied by the Maastricht Treaty, debt accumulation seems to be ongoing. For example, the average debt-to-GDP ratio in the European countries has been

[1] I wish to thank Søren Bo Nielsen, Ole Risager and Peter Birch Sørensen for helpful comments. Thanks are also due to participants at the conference on Pension Systems, Taxation and Public Debt in Dynamic CGE Models, held in Helsinki, Finland, April 1995. Ninette Pilegaard Hansen has provided excellent research assistance. Financial support from the Danish National Research Foundation is gratefully acknowledged.

projected to rise from 74.0 percent in 1994 to 77.5 percent already in 1996 (OECD, 1994). It is no easy task to bring this process to a halt: economic growth rates are low relative to real interest rates, structural deficits have increased and in future the phenomenon of population ageing is likely to put additional strain on public finances.

Against this background, doubts over the sustainability of current fiscal policies have been voiced.[2] More restraint in the conduct of fiscal policy may therefore be expected. As to the design of a fiscal tightening, a number of questions arise: Should existing debt eventually be eliminated or should one just aim at consolidating debt-to-GDP ratios at current levels? What is the required fiscal adjustment if either debt elimination or debt consolidation is opted for? What is the short-term trade-off between debt reduction and unemployment? To what extent are short-term losses offset by long-term gains? What are the generational redistribution effects of alternative debt policies?

In the following we shall, in addition to try answering the above questions, focus on three aspects of debt policy. First, we look at the *timing* of a fiscal tightening. In particular, if a government decides to eventually eliminate its outstanding debt, at what pace should that happen? The second issue is concerned with the choice of tax base. In particular, should a higher tax rate be levied on labour income or consumption? The third issue is related to the link between debt policy and the structure of the labour market. In particular, what is the wage response to higher taxation?

Our device for addressing these issues is a computable general equilibrium (CGE) model of a small open economy. The model describes the behaviour of profit-maximizing firms, overlapping generations of intertemporally optimizing consumers with uncertain lifetimes, and a government equipped with a rich menu of fiscal instruments, including a public pension system. From the perspective of the themes discussed in this paper, an important feature of the model is a unionized labour market.[3]

The paper is organized as follows. Section 6.2 points out some important channels through which debt policy may affect the real economy and Section 6.3 outlines a model accounting for these channels. Section 6.4 then describes how fiscal policy may be designed in order to achieve a certain debt target. Section 6.5 goes on to consider the quantitative impact of such policies on the macroeconomy, both in the short run and in the long run. The intergenerational welfare effects are treated in Section 6.6 and, finally, Section 6.7 concludes.

---

[2] See, for example, Buiter and Kletzer (1992) for a discussion why a rising burden of the public debt may cause concern. Robson and Scarth (1994) provide a useful introduction to the debate on deficit reduction.

[3] Compared to most existing dynamic CGE models, this element of imperfect competition is a distinguishing feature. See, for example, Auerbach and Kotlikoff (1987), Steigum (1993), James (1994) and Macklem, Rose and Tetlow (1994).

6.2 Debt Policy and the Real Economy

Two Aspects of Debt Policy

We have in mind a world in which public debt (and hence debt policy) has real effects, operating through two main channels. First, changes in public debt act as an intergenerational transfer device and, second, with distortionary tax instruments debt policy has spillovers onto wage formation and employment.

Intergenerational redistribution comes in because households are assumed to have finite horizons. Hence the burden of public debt created by current generations will in part be carried by future generations.[4] Suppose a government aims at completely eliminating public debt over a certain period of time. If government expenditures (as a ratio-to-GDP) are held constant, a higher tax rate is required. However, in the new steady state, with zero interest payments, taxes are lower. While some currently living households will have to pay higher taxes, they foresee that some of the benefits of lower taxes will be enjoyed by future generations. More precisely, the present value of the fall in disposable income during the temporary period of higher taxes is greater than the present value of the rise in disposable income thereafter. Currently living generations of households therefore lower their consumption during the transition period when taxes are high. This, in turn, has wider macroeconomic repercussions.

The link between the fiscal policy rule and wage formation may also generate important real effects, by altering the incentives of economic agents. Empirically, our knowledge about how wages respond to tax changes is relatively poor. Even in theory, however, the *direction* of the wage response to higher marginal tax rates is far from clear. It depends, in particular, on the organization of the labour market. Suppose the marginal tax rate on labour income is raised, keeping the average tax rate constant so that the income effect is eliminated. In a standard neoclassical model of a competitive labour market the supply of labour will tend to fall if the marginal income tax rate is raised: an increase in the marginal wage tax will lower the opportunity cost of leisure, hence causing consumers to substitute away from labour market participation and towards leisure.

If the labour market is unionized, however, a rise in the marginal wage tax rate will actually lower the pre-tax real wage rate claimed by unions, thus stimulating the level of employment.[5] The reason is the following: to obtain some given

[4] If agents' planning horizons are infinite, income transfers across generations are by definition absent, and all the effects of intertemporal allocations through taxation and transfer payments are felt by the same infinitely-lived generation. In such a world debt policy would have no effect on, e.g., consumption and output, a result generally known as 'Ricardian equivalence' (Barro, 1974).

[5] See, e.g., Hersoug (1984), Malcolmson and Sartor (1987), or Lockwood and Manning (1993).

increase in employment, unions must accept a certain cut in the pre-tax real wage rate governing the labour demand of employers. The higher the marginal tax rate, the lower will be the loss of after-tax wage income implied by any given reduction in pre-tax wages. A higher marginal tax rate therefore makes it 'cheaper' for unions to 'buy' additional jobs by lowering the pre-tax wage rate, thereby strengthening the incentive for unions to display wage moderation.

While either the neoclassical setting or models with exogenous labour supply are the most frequent in the literature, in the following we assume a unionized labour market. This assumption seems particularly relevant in a Nordic context, where the degree of unionization is higher than anywhere else in the world, and where union densities continued to increase during the 1980s, despite falling rates of unionization in other parts of the OECD area (see Freeman, 1988). In Calmfors (1990), union models of wage formation have in fact been applied empirically with a reasonable degree of success to explain wage formation in the Nordic countries. As pointed out by Calmfors (op.cit.) and by Andersen and Risager (1990), the Danish labour market stands out by being dominated by craft unions rather than industry unions, and there has been a clear trend towards less centralised wage bargaining in Denmark. For this reason we have chosen to focus on a labour market with decentralised craft unions each of which is too small to be able to influence the general level of wages and prices.

6.3 A Dynamic CGE Model

General Features

The model solves for a full intertemporal equilibrium in which a private sector endowed with forward-looking rational expectations maximizes intertemporal objective functions.[6] The model is deterministic and specified in discrete time. There is no monetary sector in the model. Perfect mobility of financial capital and residence-based taxation of interest income serve to equate the domestic pre-tax interest rate with the foreign pre-tax interest rate which is exogenously fixed in units of a foreign tradable good.[7]

---

[6] Further details of the model are to be found in Jensen, Nielsen, Pedersen and Sørensen (1996). A model with the same behavioural structure has been used to evaluate the effects of a tax-cut-cum-base-broadening tax reform, see Jensen, Nielsen, Pedersen and Sørensen (1994).

[7] There is evidence suggesting that the larger debt and deficits are relative to the tax base, the higher is the real interest rate that governments must pay; see, for example, Alesina, Broeck and Tabellini (1993) and Missale and Blanchard (1994). However, given the absence of risk and uncertainty in the model we are so far unable to capture this effect.

In the following we provide a more formal treatment of individual household behaviour and wage formation.[8]

The Household Sector

The household sector comprises an infinite number of overlapping generations which are divided into workers and pensioners. The relative size of the two groups is determined by an exogenous retirement age (dictated by the social security system) indicating when an individual changes status from worker to pensioner. Despite our distinction between young and old, we retain Blanchard's (1985) simplifying assumption that the probability to survive into the next period is age-independent. Hence the expected remaining lifetime of each generation is the same. We also assume that the birth rate and the death probability are identical, implying a stationary population and a constant age structure.

An individual household derives utility from a consumption aggregate c (to be explained later) and incurs disutility $f(n^*)$ from its individual work effort n^*. The household strives to maximize its expected discounted lifetime utility which at time t is equal to

$$U_t = \sum_{s=t}^{\infty} \left(\frac{1-\rho}{1+\theta}\right)^{(s-t)} \cdot \frac{1}{1-\nu}\left(c_s - f(n^*)\right)^{1-\nu} \tag{1}$$

where ρ is the death probability, θ is the time preference rate, and ν is the intertemporal elasticity of substitution.

In the absence of an operative bequest motive, each consumer engages in a deal with a competitive life insurance company which agrees to pay a return on the sum of the consumer's financial and housing wealth on the condition that it may take over this wealth when the consumer dies. When the premium paid by insurance companies equals $\rho/(1-\rho)$ times the stock of wealth of those consumers who survive into the next period, profits in the insurance industry will be zero. Hence, with r denoting the interest rate, and t^r indicating the capital income tax rate, the

[8] There is also a production sector in the model, comprising a 'manufacturing' industry producing a tradable good, and a 'construction' industry producing a non-tradable good (housing units). Gross output in both sectors is a CES-function of an imported intermediate input and of a Cobb-Douglas aggregate of capital and labour, with the CD-aggregate representing domestic value-added. Labour is immobile internationally, but perfectly mobile between the two domestic industries. Output in both sectors is produced by a large number of identical competitive firms, being organized as joint stock companies.

dynamic budget identity facing the individual consumer in period t may be written as

$$(a_t + P_t^h h_t) = (\frac{1 + r_t (1 - t_t^r)}{1 - \rho}) (a_{t-1} + P^h_{t-1} h_{t-1}) + y_t - P_t c_t \qquad (2)$$

where a is the stock of financial wealth, P^h is the price of housing units, h is the physical housing stock, P is a general consumer price index including excise taxes and the user-cost of housing, and y is non-capital income. In specifying y, we have to distinguish between the non-capital income accruing to a pensioner, y^p, which is simply equal to an exogenous pension benefit, and the non-capital income earned by a worker, y^w. To keep aggregation problems down to a minimum, we assume that unemployment in each union is equally shared among all union members, since this is not essential to our qualitative results. Hence we may specify the non-capital income accruing to a worker as follows:

$$y_t^w = [w_t (1 - t_t^l) + d_t] n^*_t + [\upsilon_t (1 - t_t^\upsilon) + d_t] (H - n^*_t) + \tau_t \qquad (3)$$

The first term on the RHS of (3) represents disposable wage income, with w being the pre-tax wage rate, t^l being the marginal tax rate on labour income, and d indicating a tax credit available to wage earners (measured on an hourly basis). The second term on the RHS is the after-tax unemployment benefit, where υ is the benefit rate, H is an institutionally fixed maximum working time (so that $H - n^*$ is the worker's recorded amount of unemployment) and t^υ is the marginal tax rate on benefit income.

Note that employment, n^*, is exogenous to the individual consumer, since it is determined by the wage setting behaviour of unions. Individuals belonging to the labour force also receive a lump sum transfer, τ, represented by the third term on the RHS of (3). The income of pensioners consists of a pension benefit, b, which, like labour income, is augmented by a general transfer, τ. Neither τ nor b is subject to taxation.

The exact distribution of the individual's lifetime non-capital disposable income on wage income and pension benefits, respectively, is determined exogenously by the pension system.[9]

The consumer maximizes expected lifetime utility (1) subject to (2) and to the well-known 'no-Ponzi-game' condition, recalling that non-capital income will be given by (3) during the working period of life and by the pension benefit during the retirement period. The solution to this problem (available upon request) implies that total consumption in any period is proportional to the sum of the consumer's total non-human and human wealth, with the latter defined as the

[9] The share of workers to pensioners in the population is given by $s = 1 - (1 - \rho)^{a^r}$, where a^r is the retirement age. See Nielsen (1994) for further details.

present value of future non-capital income, and with the propensity to consume out of wealth depending on the after-tax interest rate, the time preference rate, the death probability, the intertemporal substitution elasticity, and the expected evolution of the consumer price index.

Once the consumer has optimized the time path of her total consumption, she further optimizes the allocation of total consumption in each period between consumption of housing services and non-durables and between foreign and domestic non-durables. This three-stage optimization procedure is valid because the consumer's sub-utility functions are homothetic. More specifically, we take total consumption to consist of a Cobb-Douglas aggregate of non-durables and housing services, while non-durables consist of a CES aggregate of foreign and domestic goods.

With individual consumption of the different goods being determined in this way, it is possible to derive aggregate consumption functions (including an aggregate demand for new housing), given our assumptions about the overlapping generations structure, including the assumptions of a constant death rate and a constant retirement age.

The Labour Market

Labour Demand

Since it is crucial to know how and by how much tax changes are transmitted to wages and employment, the features of the labour market are really the guts of the model.

We consider an imperfectly competitive labour market, modelled *ad modum* Blanchard and Kiyotaki (1987), here extended to allow for taxation and unemployment benefits. The number of unions in the economy is equal to the number of specific labour skills, with workers being organized according to their skill-type. While the labour market is thus characterized by monopolistic supply, there are no employers' associations, so the demand side is competitive. Unions may therefore dictate their wage rates to employers, subject to the labour demand curves for each individual skill. By choosing a wage rate, the union implicitly determines the overall level of employment for its members, and this amount of total employment is equally shared among all members. All unions have the same size. This assumption eliminates aggregation problems by allowing for symmetric equilibria. Furthermore, because we assume the number of different skills (unions) to be very large, each union has a negligible influence on the aggregate wage level and a similar negligible influence on the aggregate employment level. This simplifies the dynamic effects considerably, since it eliminates any effects of the individual union's wage claim on aggregate investment and hence on the future path of the general level of real wages.

The solution to the firm's optimization problem yields demand schedules for labour input. We abstract from any possible costs of adjusting the level of employment, assuming that firms can costlessly hire and fire labour. The different labour skills are imperfect substitutes in the production technology of the firm, and aggregate labour input L at time t is defined by the CES aggregate

$$L_t = (m^{1/(1-E)}) \left(\sum_{i=1}^{m} (n^i_t)^{(E-1)/E} \right)^{E/(E-1)}, \; E > 1 \tag{4}$$

where n^i is aggregate demand for labour with skill i, E is the (constant) elasticity of substitution between any two different skills of labour, and m is the total number of skills. The minimum-cost allocation of a given amount of total labour input L among the different skill categories can be shown to yield the following optimal demand for labour of skill i

$$n^i_t = \left(\frac{w^i_t}{W_t}\right)^{-E} \frac{L_t}{m} \quad \forall i; \quad W_t = \left(\frac{1}{m} \sum_{i=1}^{m} (w^i_t)^{(1-E)} \right)^{1/(1-E)} \tag{5}$$

where w^i is the wage rate of labour of skill i, and W is an index of the general wage level. The firm optimizes its labour demand by first optimizing the level of aggregate labour input in accordance with the standard marginal productivity condition (taking W as the price of 'aggregate' labour), and then allocating this aggregate labour input across the different skills in accordance with the cost-minimization rule (5).

Wage Formation

Having sketched labour demand we now turn to wage formation. Each union sets its wage rate with the aim of maximizing the expected lifetime utility of its representative member. Individual union members take the resulting wage rate and employment level and the resulting stock of human capital as given, and on this basis they optimize their individual consumption and housing decisions.

Formally, the problem for the union of workers with skill i is to maximize expected lifetime utility (1) with respect to the (time path of the) wage rate, subject to the consumer's dynamic budget constraint (given by (2) and (3)), and subject to the labour demand curve (5) for workers of skill i. Technically, the union performs this optimization on the assumption that its members will choose the optimum level and composition of consumption for any given wage rate and level of employment. The solution to the union's problem can be shown to imply a wage-employment relationship of the form

$$\frac{w^i_t}{P_t} = \left(\frac{E}{E-1}\right) \left[\frac{f'(n^*_t) + (1-t^{\upsilon}_t)(\upsilon_t/P_t)}{1-t^l_t}\right] \tag{6}$$

(6) sets out the factors which determine the degree of 'aggressiveness' of the union. It may be most easily interpreted if $t^{\upsilon} = t^l = 0$. The equation then says that the union - which is a monopoly seller of labour with skill i - will claim a real wage

rate which is a mark-up on the marginal cost of employment, with the latter being equal to the sum of the foregone real unemployment benefit, υ/P, and the marginal disutility of work, $f'(n^*)$. The tax parameters simply adjust for the asymmetric tax treatment of wage income and the two components of the marginal cost of employment. The mark-up itself depends entirely on the elasticity of substitution between skills (E). The closer substitutes are the different skills, the closer we get to the competitive labour market, and hence the lower is the mark-up. E is therefore also a proxy for the degree of monopoly power possessed by each union.[10] In implementing the model, the disutility of work has been specified as

$$f(n^*_t) = \frac{(n^*_t)^{1+\gamma}}{(1+\gamma)\,\xi} + k \;\rightarrow\; f'(n^*_t) = \frac{(n^*_t)^{\gamma}}{\xi} \qquad (7)$$

where γ is the elasticity of the marginal disutility of work and ξ is a scale parameter. In the general case, unions *have* market power (i.e. E is relatively small), and the disutility of work will be accounted for (i.e. ξ has a finite value). Hence, wages are responsive to changes in both the wage tax and the excise tax. The crucial question is how much weight unions attach to leisure. As a (polar) benchmark, suppose the union just maximizes the total after-tax wage and benefit income of its members, without accounting for the disutility of work (obtained by letting ξ tend to infinity). In this special case the consumer price index drops out and hence there will be no effect on the nominal wage of variations in the excise tax (which is contained in the consumer price index).[11] Note further that if labour income and unemployment benefits are taxed symmetrically (i.e. $t^{\upsilon} = t^{l}$), wages are also inflexible to changes in the wage tax. Effectively, the nominal wage rate will be set as a mark-up on the unemployment benefit rate, and is hence under the full control of the government.

Another (polar) benchmark to be considered is one where unions attach a high weight to leisure (i.e. ξ is very low). In this case wages respond heavily to tax adjustments. For example, if the wage tax is raised unions would prefer to take more time off, simply because leisure is a non-taxed 'good'. This behaviour is

---

[10] Notice that, in general, unions will set wage rates above the competitive level. Yet, because individual skills are perfectly substitutable within each union, the individual worker's notional labour supply may still be found by letting E tend to infinity. Thus, if the individual were not restricted by his union to supply only his proportional share of the total number of working hours within the union, he would like to work more at the going wage rate. On the other hand, for any given average level of wages and prices in the economy, workers with a particular skill will be better off by forming a union and exploiting their collective monopoly power rather than acting atomistically as individual competitive suppliers of labour.

[11] This wage rigidity result applies when the labour demand elasticity is constant and when the marginal disutility of work is zero, see also Oswald (1985).

reflected in higher wage demands which in turn reduce the demand for labour. In the following we shall refer to the two benchmarks as nominal wage rigidity (NWR) and nominal wage flexibility (NWF), respectively.

Calibration

The upper part of table 6.1 reports the values assigned to some important behavioural parameters and exogenous variables in the model. In calibrating the model, we have chosen parameter values which appear plausible and which generate an initial steady state of the model corresponding roughly to a set of benchmark data for the Danish economy around 1990. We have adopted a liberal interpretation of the parameter $1/\rho$, considering it as an index of the length of the planning horizon (the degree of 'far-sightedness') of consumers. Assuming a value of $\rho = .04$ implies a horizon of 25 years. Another liberal interpretation applies to our calibration of the retirement age, a^r, which is set at 36 years (after entrance on the labour market). The combination of the chosen values for ρ and a^r produces relative proportions of workers and pensioners corresponding to actual proportions in Denmark (77 percent).

Table 6.1. Parameterization of the Model.

	Key parameters	
v	Intertemporal elasticity of substitution in consumption	0.533
r	Rate of interest	0.050
θ	Rate of time preference	0.008
ρ	Probability of death	0.040
β	Share of housing consumption in total private consumption	0.170
E	Elasticity of substitution between different labour skills	9.000
γ	Elasticity of marginal disutility of work	5.000
ξ	Scale parameter concerning disutility of work	$2.577 \cdot 10^8$
	Selected policy variables	
d	Tax credit for employed workers	0.170
t^l	Marginal personal tax rate on labour income	0.600
t^b	Marginal personal tax rate on unemployment benefits	0.500
t^r	Marginal personal tax rate on capital income	0.500
t^p	Rate of ad valorem excise tax	0.200
a^r	Retirement age	36
b/w	Rate of pension benefit relative to the pre-tax wage rate	0.665
v/w	Rate of unempl. benefits relative to the pre-tax wage rate	0.691

A select of tax instruments and other policy instruments available to the government is indicated in the lower part of table 6.1. The tax rates stated in the table provide a rough estimate of the average value of the marginal tax rates on different types of income in the personal income tax system in Denmark in the early 1990s. The values of the tax rates relating to wage income and unemployment benefits imply that the tax system is progressive in the sense that the marginal tax rate on labour income exceed the marginal tax rate on unemployment benefits.

6.4 The Design of Fiscal Policy

Fiscal Policy

Fiscal policy is designed in terms of a target ratio of debt-to-GDP. The fiscal policy function is 'geared' so as to ensure that the debt ratio converges smoothly on its targeted rate. Rather than adjusting government consumption and transfer payments, the debt target is achieved through intertemporal tax adjustments.

If the government aims at bringing the public debt-to-GDP ratio down, a temporary tightening of fiscal policy is required (from the base-year to year n). As soon as the target debt ratio has been achieved, we assume that it is permanently fixed at that level (from year n to ∞). This allows for a relaxation of fiscal policy at the beginning of time $n+1$. Table 6.2 shows both the 'tough' and the 'soft' tax rates. The benchmark for comparison is the initial steady state (scenario I) and the tax adjustments are reported as absolute deviations from the rates prevailing in that state.

All scenarios involve a gradual elimination of public debt. The magnitude of the intertemporal tax adjustments needed to accomplish such an ambitious target is seen to display a high degree of sensitivity to the choice of tax base, the timing of the tax adjustments (the length of period 0 to n) and the wage response to the tax adjustments.

A distinction has been made between a medium-term approach (12 years) and a long-term approach (36 years) to debt elimination. Why these horizons? The medium-term has been 'quantified' to 12 years in order to conform with the official debt policy of the Danish government which is to eliminate public debt over a horizon of 10–15 years.[12] However, since a severe recession in the economy could well be an unacceptable side-effect of pursuing such an ambitious debt strategy, we also consider a stretched-out elimination period. A period of 36 years has simply been chosen because it is equivalent to the number of years that an individual is active on the labour market.

[12] Finansministeriet (1995).

Table 6.2. Intertemporal Tax Adjustments.

Horizon		Initial steady state		Debt elimination					
				baseline		NWR		NWF	
		τ^l	τ^c	τ^l	τ^c	τ^l	τ^c	τ^l	τ^c
	0	60.0	20.0	68.5	33.4	66.7	31.9	71.1	35.3
n=12	13	-	-	56.0	12.7	56.1	13.0	56.2	12.0
0		60.0	20.0	61.8	22.5	61.4	22.3	64.1	23.8
n=36	37	-	-	54.0	12.0	54.5	12.5	52.6	10.2

In scenario II the labour market has been calibrated according to the baseline assumptions stated in table 1. If public debt is settled through a more heavy taxation of labour income over a period of 12 years, the wage tax must be raised by 8.5 percentage points (from 60 percent) on impact. When the debt eventually has been settled, a cut of 12.5 percentage points can be implemented, corresponding to a new wage tax rate of 56 percent. If instead fiscal policy is tightened in the form of a higher excise tax rate, an initial rise from 20 percent to 33.4 percent is required. As soon as public debt has been eliminated, the rate can be cut to 12.7 percent. For obvious reasons, if the process is stretched over a longer time horizon, the intertemporal tax profile becomes smoother.[13] Similarly, we observe that the longer is the period with 'tough' tax rates the lower are the tax rates that may be enjoyed thereafter.

The question now arises as to how sensitive the tax adjustments are to alternative assumptions about wage formation. Scenario III shows the case with nominal wage rigidity (NWR) and Scenario IV marks the other polar case with nominal wage flexibility (NWF). To obtain comparability between the different scenarios, we have offset the effects of the change in ξ by adjusting the parameters E (in (6)) and γ (in (7)) such that the model generates exactly the same initial steady state in all cases.

The need for tax adjustment associated with achieving a certain debt target is seen to be very different in the two scenarios. Indeed, if the process of debt elimination is streched over 12 years, the wage tax should be increased by 6.7 percentage points under NWR, whereas an increase of nearly twice as much is required under NWF. The point is, of course, that in the latter case a higher wage tax triggers a more aggressive union behaviour, in turn causing economic reces-

[13] Since the deadweight loss imposed by a distortionary tax is known to increase by more than in proportion to the tax rate, tax smoothing can be motivated on efficiency grounds, Barro (1979).

sion and hence greater difficulties in bringing the debt ratio down. It is worth noting that a high degree of wage flexibility implies a very 'rugged' tax profile: when taxes are subsequently relaxed, large cuts must be implemented in order to prevent the debt-to-GDP ratio from getting negative!

We now turn to an evaluation of some macroeconomic and distributional effects of this policy framework.

6.5 Macroeconomic Effects

Baseline

The steady states predicted by the model are shown in table 6.3. In the top panel the results are reported as percentage differences from the initial steady state, while the bottom panel reports the results in levels as percentages of GDP. The rate of unemployment in each scenario is also reported.

Table 6.3. Steady State Effects of Debt Reduction.

	Initial st. state	Debt elimination					
		(baseline) II		(NWR) III		(NWF) IV	
(a) Percentage change from initial steady state	I	τ^l	τ^c	τ^l	τ^c	τ^l	τ^c
Output	0.0	2.5	0.8	0.8	0.3	7.4	2.8
Employment	0.0	2.6	0.9	0.9	0.3	7.9	3.0
Consumption	0.0	12.3	6.3	10.4	5.6	17.6	7.8
Investment	0.0	1.8	0.7	0.4	0.3	6.1	2.5
Nominal wages	0.0	-0.1	-0.1	0.0	0.0	-0.4	-0.1
Consumer price index	0.0	0.1	-4.6	0.1	-4.3	0.1	-5.6
(b) Percentage of GDP							
Total tax revenue	58.0	54.8	54.9	55.4	55.3	52.9	53.5
Public consumption	30.0	30.0	30.0	30.0	30.0	30.0	30.0
Public interest payments	3.0	0.0	0.0	0.0	0.0	0.0	0.0
Pension benefits	6.9	6.7	6.8	6.8	6.9	6.4	6.7
Unemployment benefits	5.3	3.9	4.8	4.8	5.1	1.3	3.7
Net foreign assets	-42.4	55.0	17.7	54.9	18.8	52.1	12.9
Public debt	60.4	0.0	0.0	0.0	0.0	0.0	0.0
(c) Unemployment rate	9.6	7.3	8.8	8.8	9.3	2.5	6.9

In the initial steady state (scenario I), the public debt-to-GDP ratio is 60.4 percent and the ratio of net foreign assets to GDP is -42.4 percent. The total tax revenue constitutes 58 percent of GDP. Hereof personal labour income taxes and commodity taxes are the most important contributors (33.7 and 22.1 percent, respectively). Government expenditures are set so that their share of GDP is held constant at 30 percent. Expenditures allocated to income transfers depend on the retirement age, the unemployment rate and the corresponding benefit rates. Given an unemployment rate of 9.6 percent and a compensation ratio of 69.1 percent, unemployment benefits amount to 5.3 percent of GDP. Similarly, with a retirement age of 36 years and a pension replacement ratio of 66.5 percent, the share of pension benefits to GDP is 6.9 percent. With a real interest rate of 5 percent p.a., public interest payments amount to 3 percent of GDP.

Against this background we next consider the steady states produced if the government undertakes to eliminate its outstanding debt. Scenario II describes the effects of debt elimination, given that wages adjust in accordance with the baseline calibration. While the qualitative effects are seen not to depend on the choice of tax instrument, the quantitative effects are strongest in the case of a lower wage tax. We observe that the lower tax rates lead to a minor downward pressure on wages. This stimulates demand for labour and hence employment. The capital stock is also higher in the new steady state; hence there is a boost to output. The effects on output and employment are relatively small, however, compared to the upsurge in consumption. The reason for this is that not only has public debt been eliminated; the country has changed its position vis-à-vis the rest of the world from being a net debtor (42.4 percent of GDP) to a net creditor. Rather than paying interest to foreigners as in the initial steady state, huge interest incomes are received from abroad so GNP exceeds GDP. Finally, an important long-term property of debt elimination is a significant fall in the rate of unemployment.

To what extent are these long-term gains offset by transitional losses? Like the steady state effects, the transitional effects depend on the choice of tax base and the assumptions made about wage formation, but also the timing of the process plays a role. Table 6.4 reports the (percentage) deviations in certain years of employment, output and consumption from their initial steady state level. The level of the current account is shown as a percentage of GDP.

Role of Timing and the Tax Base

We first consider the role of the tax base, given a medium-term horizon for elimination (n=12). Higher tax rates are seen to cause macroeconomic distress. For two reasons, this is most pronounced in the case of a higher wage tax. The first reason has to do with the broadness of the tax base. If a higher revenue is raised through a higher tax rate on consumption expenditures, *all* households are involved. The wage tax, however, is only levied on members of the workforce. Hence, a higher wage tax triggers a larger wage pressure than a higher excise tax. The second reason has to do with the distortionary nature of an excise tax. A previously unexpected and immediately implemented rise in the excise tax rate is equivalent to a tax on pre-existing wealth. With household decisions being based on pre-existing tax rates, the higher tax effectively operates as a lump sum tax. That is why we observe rather modest employment and output effects in this case (notice that there is in any case a negative income effect, but there is no excess burden of that part of the excise tax which falls on existing wealth.)

Table 6.4. Transitional Effects of Debt Reduction.

		Tax base and timing				Wage formation			
		n=12		n=37		NWR		NWF	
		τ^l	τ^c	τ^l	τ^c	τ^l	τ^c	τ^l	τ^c
Variable	Year	Percentage deviations from initial steady state							
Employment (hours)	2	-3.30	-1.56	-0.56	-0.20	-0.71	-0.43	-6.85	-2.78
	5	-3.55	-1.62	-0.62	-0.21	-0.81	-0.43	-7.49	-2.96
	12	-3.73	-1.75	-0.75	-0.20	-0.97	-0.57	-7.87	-3.13
	13	1.44	0.96	-0.76	-0.20	0.62	0.49	1.72	1.55
	25	1.73	0.88	-0.81	-0.21	0.62	0.26	2.64	1.66
	36	1.78	0.85	-0.65	-0.36	0.63	0.20	2.79	1.63
	37	1.78	0.85	2.31	0.99	0.63	0.20	2.79	1.63
	50	1.78	0.85	2.60	0.91	0.63	0.19	2.80	1.63
Output	2	-2.45	-1.09	-0.43	-0.14	-0.55	-0.27	-5.07	-1.97
	5	-2.92	-1.28	-0.53	-0.16	-0.68	-0.32	-6.16	-2.36
	12	-3.15	-1.49	-0.68	-0.18	-0.80	-0.50	-6.73	-2.66
	13	0.79	0.57	-0.69	-0.18	0.41	0.31	0.59	0.91
	25	1.57	0.81	-0.74	-0.19	0.58	0.24	2.35	1.51
	36	1.67	0.80	-0.47	-0.29	0.59	0.19	2.60	1.53
	37	1.67	0.80	1.80	0.75	0.60	0.19	2.61	1.53
	50	1.68	0.80	2.40	0.85	0.60	0.18	2.63	1.53
Consumption	2	-3.05	-4.80	-1.20	-1.19	-2.16	-4.13	-4.45	-5.54
	5	-3.07	-4.73	-1.29	-1.17	-2.13	-4.06	-4.56	-5.49
	12	-2.39	-4.46	-1.34	-1.02	-1.45	-3.79	-3.94	-5.22
	13	-1.89	2.34	-1.32	-0.99	-1.25	2.25	-3.10	2.52
	25	0.41	3.00	-0.66	-0.53	0.72	2.82	-0.40	3.27
	36	2.31	3.63	0.95	-0.05	2.36	3.38	1.81	3.96
	37	2.45	3.68	1.33	3.64	2.48	3.42	1.97	4.01
	50	3.95	4.20	3.44	4.06	3.78	3.89	3.71	4.59
		Percent of GDP							
Current Account	2	1.36	2.26	0.76	0.63	1.32	2.13	1.64	2.44
	5	0.85	2.38	0.84	0.67	1.30	2.44	0.38	2.32
	12	-1.30	2.86	0.91	0.80	0.63	3.43	-3.95	2.17
	13	0.92	0.47	0.91	0.83	1.30	0.71	0.37	0.20
	25	1.12	0.50	0.77	1.20	1.06	0.50	1.16	0.50
	36	0.97	0.36	-0.47	1.74	0.85	0.32	1.10	0.38
	37	0.96	0.35	0.76	0.39	0.84	0.31	1.09	0.38
	50	0.79	0.27	0.99	0.34	0.68	0.24	0.90	0.29

The two tax bases also have different effects on aggregate demand. As to domestic demand, a higher excise tax involves a strong intertemporal substitution effect, leading forward-looking households to postpone their consumption in anticipation of a future fall in the taxation of consumption. The fall in domestic demand is, however, nearly offset by a large boost to net exports, as observed by the huge surpluses on the current account. The income effect associated with a higher wage tax also causes a drop in consumption and improves the external position. However, as wages start rising, international competitiveness deteriorates and the surplus is turned into deficit. Note also that a higher wage tax generates a fairly smooth consumption path: the intertemporal tax adjustments are anticipated by households and hence consumption hardly changes at the time of implementation.

As to the role of timing, we find that a stretched-out elimination period (n=36) generates a much smoother macroeconomic outcome. While a tough approach may generate output and employment losses of nearly 4 percent relative to the initial steady state, the soft approach does at no time bring losses above 1 percent. If the elimination is financed through a higher excise tax, the losses are negligible.

Role of Wage Formation

Scenarios III and IV illustrate the importance of the wage formation process. If wages are rigid (scenario III), there is no responsiveness to lower tax rates and, consequently, the employment and output effects are rather modest. However, the elimination of public debt also reverses the net foreign asset position; hence consumption rises much more than output. If instead unions are willing to lower wages in return for tax cuts (scenario IV), the macroeconomy is burgeoning in the new steady state. For example, if the wage tax is lowered, consumption increases by almost a fifth. Note also that a lower wage tax implies that unemployment virtually disappears if wages are very flexible.

While the most expansionary steady state effects of debt reduction are obtained in the case with a heavy weight attached to leisure (NWF), the opposite holds during the transitional period. As we have seen, the more responsive wages are to tax changes, the stronger is the fiscal adjustment needed to achieve a certain debt target. This relationship is obviously reflected in the performance of the macroeconomy. Indeed, if wages are very responsive to higher tax rates, employment falls by almost 7 percent already in the second year, whereas if wages respond only sluggishly, the employment and output losses are almost negligible. As soon as the debt has been settled and the tax rates have been cut, this picture is turned upside-down. With flexible wages, a lower wage tax then raises output above its initial steady state level by almost two percent. From the last year with high tax rates to the first with low tax rates there is a gigantic boost to employment and output by about 10 percent. The combination of an ambitious debt strategy and flexible wages thus generates a very erratic macroeconomic behaviour.

The magnitude of the tax adjustments also has quite dramatic consequences for the impact effect on disposable income and hence for consumption and the current account. The income effect associated with higher taxes thus implies a fall in consumption by about 4.5 percent already in the second year if wages are flexible and by about 2.5 percent in the case of rigid wages. When tax rates have been cut again, the consumption gap gradually narrows. The process of wage formation also accounts for the rather diverse behaviour of the current account. Under NWR, the current account effect is dominated by the income effect on aggregate consumption, i.e. the current account is positive throughout the transitional period. Under NWF, however, the pressure on wages has implications for the country's international competitiveness: as wages rise, competitiveness and hence net exports fall. Specifically, after 12 years, just before the switch to lower taxes, the current account deficit is almost 4 percent of GDP. As soon as the wage tax has been cut again, wages fall, competitiveness improves and the country again accumulates claims vis-à-vis the rest of the world.

In sum, our analysis suggests that adherence to very ambitious debt strategies may undermine macroeconomic stability in the short run, in particular if wages are very sentitive to fiscal tightening.[14] Although a stretched-out elimination strategy is relatively lenient to the economy, there is in any case a trade-off between short-term and long-term performance. A less ambitious strategy of consolidating the debt ratio at current levels should therefore be considered as a serious alternative.

6.6 Welfare and Generational Redistribution

The desirability of alternative debt strategies may also be evaluated in another dimension, namely their effect on the intergenerational distribution of consumer welfare. For this purpose, we employ a dynamic compensating variation measure which is derived as follows: First, we calculate the level of discounted lifetime utility obtained by each generation in the initial steady state equilibrium. For each generation, we then calculate the minimum capitalized value of lifetime consumption expenditure (net of the disutility of work) which would yield a similar level of lifetime utility, given the after-tax prices and wages prevailing in each period after a specific debt policy has been set in motion. In this way, we obtain a measure of the stock of wealth which would enable the generation in question to maintain an unchanged level of welfare. To arrive at the net lifetime welfare gain, we subtract

[14] Our results thus in no way support the so-called 'expansionary fiscal contraction' hypothesis, as offered by Giavazzi and Pagano (1990).

this 'compensated' stock of wealth from the actual stock of human plus non-human wealth prevailing right after the introduction of a debt policy, given the evolution of the economy after the policy has been enacted.

In figures 6.1-6.2, the percentage welfare gains are measured along the vertical axis, while the different generations are ordered along the horizontal axis, with generations becoming successively younger as we move from left to right. Generation 0 is the generation entering the labour market in the period where the specific debt policy is initiated; generation -50 is the generation which entered the labour market 50 years before that time, while generation 25 comprises yet unborn individuals who will start their working careers in 25 years.

We first examine the role of the tax base, see figure 6.1. Irrespective of the choice of tax base, we note that debt elimination is certainly not a Pareto-improving arrangement: currently living generations lose and future generations win. The choice of tax base has, however, quite important consequences for the distribution of welfare. If debt elimination is financed using the excise tax, the loss of consumer welfare suffered by current generations is fairly equally distributed. This follows as a result of the assumption that the excise tax is levied on everybody and that each generation, whether young or old, has the same expected remaining lifetime. If the debt target is achieved over 12 years, all currently living generations experience a loss in lifetime welfare of about 1 percent, while the loss caused by a long-drawn-out elimination strategy (n=36) is almost negligible.

If the same debt target is achieved through a higher wage tax, the currently living generations of working-age are the real losers. However, since pension benefits go un-taxed, retired people are left unaffected. The most severely hit generation is clearly the one which entered the labour market 24 years before the introduction of a new debt policy and which has to pay the high wage tax each year over its remaining 12 years as a member of the workforce. Contrary to previously born generations, it never gains from a lower wage tax and its total loss amounts to about 5 percent.

Not all future generations win; indeed, generations born right after the higher tax rates have been introduced also lose. It is remarkable, however, that if a debt reduction is financed through higher excise taxes, the generations born later than 3 years after the programme has been initiated stand to gain. For generations born into the economy when public debt has been settled (generation 13 and younger), the welfare gain amounts to about 5 percent and even more for younger generations. Again, by stretching the elimination period over many years a much smoother welfare profile can be attained.

Figure 6.2 next considers the importance of the wage formation scheme for the intergenerational distribution. We can certainly verify the presumption that the extent to which wages respond to tax changes is crucial for the intergenerational distribution profile. If a higher wage tax is met by aggressive union behaviour (NWF), all generations of working-age taking full part in the programme (generations 0-24) suffer a welfare loss of almost 7 percent. The loss is only about half of that if taxes can be raised without triggering higher wages (NWR). Hence, with flexible wages it may be extremely difficult to get acceptance to bring public debt

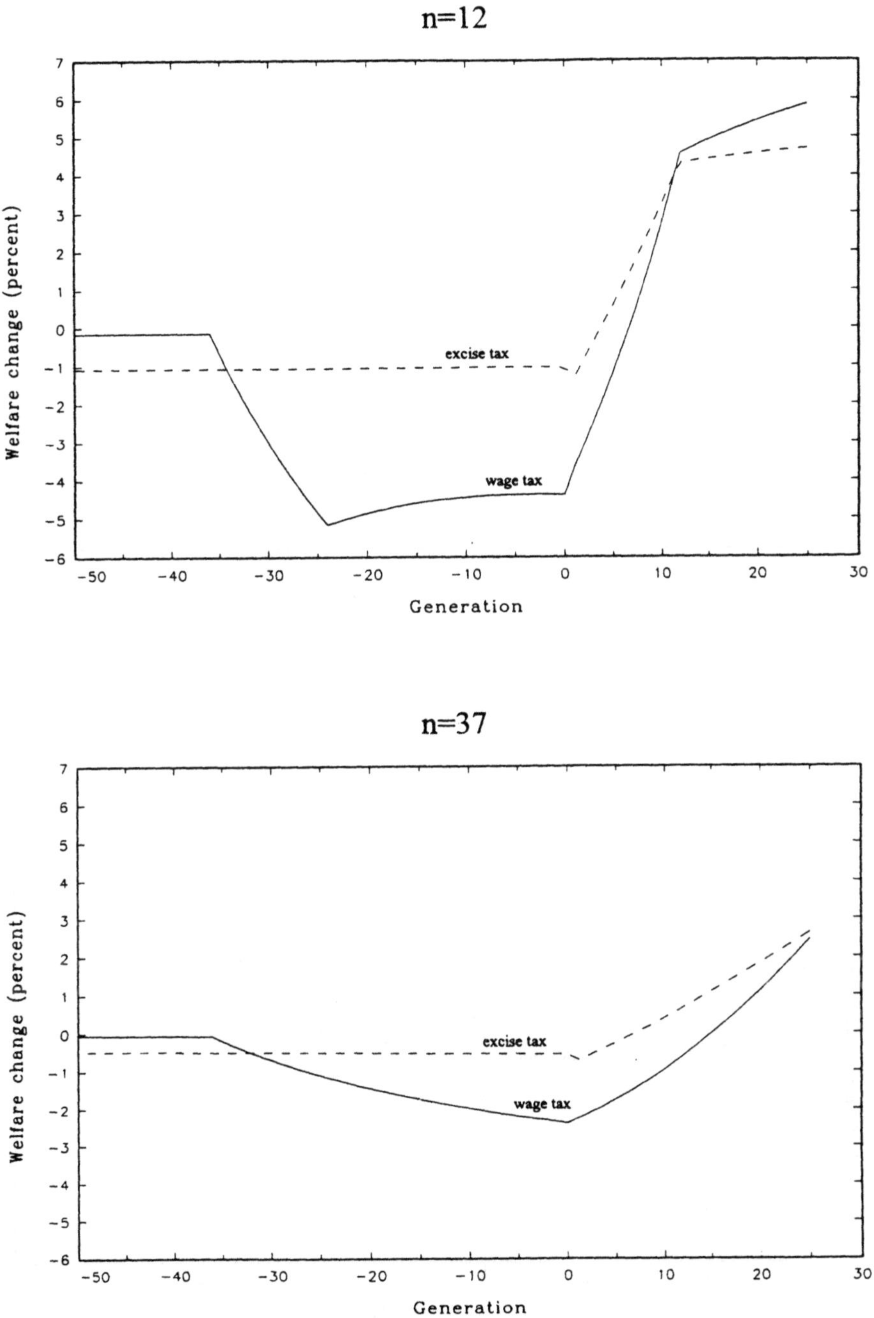

Figure 6.1. Debt Elimination under Alternative Tax Bases.

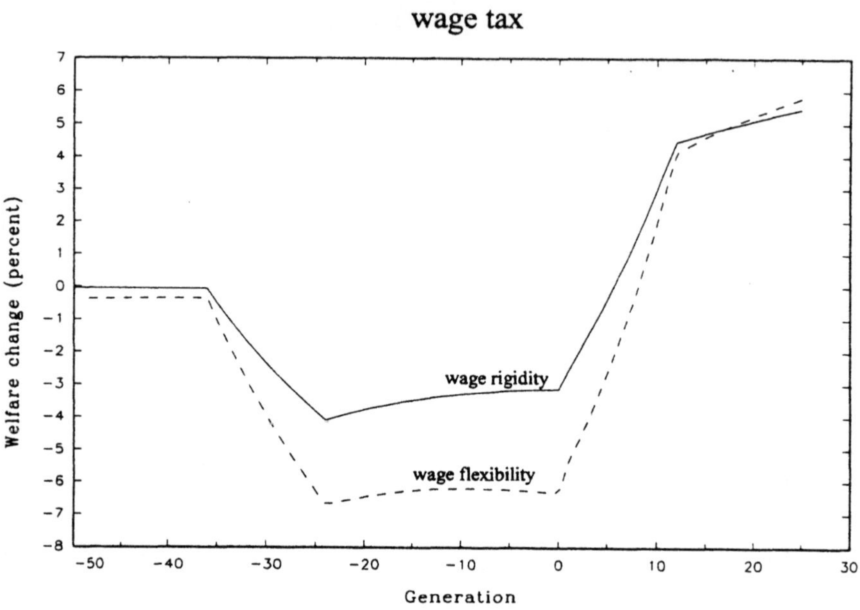

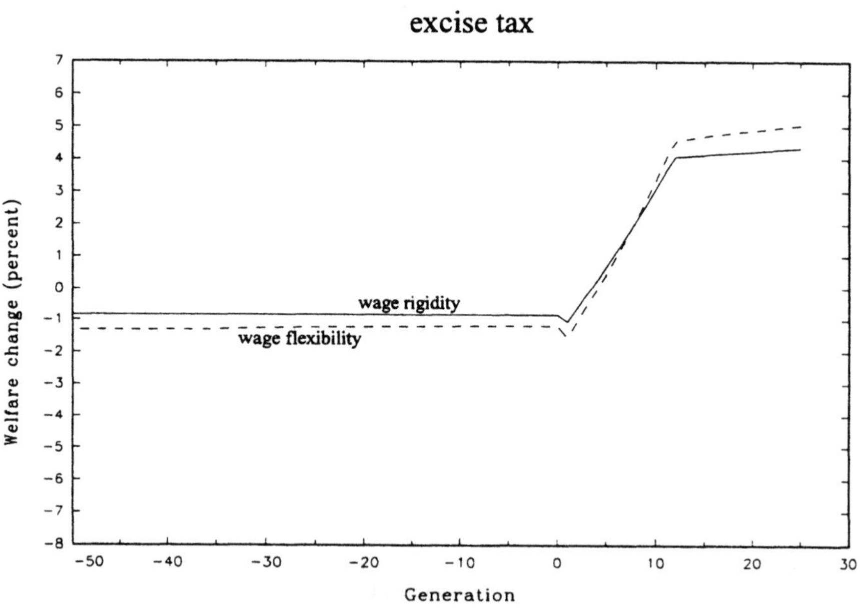

Figure 6.2. Debt Elimination under Alternative Wage Formation Schemes (n=12).

down by means of higher taxes on labour income. This point can be made even more forceful by noting that the generations born into the economy when it is free from public debt are likely to gain about 5 percent in welfare.[15]

It may therefore be comforting to know that, apparently, the same debt target can be achieved with current generations sacrifycing much less if taxes instead are levied on consumption expenditures. In this case *all* currently living generations are predicted to lose about 1 percent relative to the initial steady state, with future generations being as well-off as they would be if the debt target was achieved through higher wage taxes.

6.7 Conclusions

Across a broad political landscape the weight attached to debt reduction seems to have increased in recent years. In view of this observation, this paper has considered some macroeconomic and welfare effects of pursuing an ambitious debt target. While such a strategy involves adherence to a tight fiscal policy, for a shorter or longer period, it also provides room for a future relaxation of fiscal policy. Hence there will also be cross-generational redistribution involved.

We have shown that the macroeconomic and distributional profiles of such debt policies crucially depend on both the timing of the associated fiscal tightening and the choice of tax base to finance it. For example, a government striving to eliminate its outstanding debt within a decade or so may have to accept a dramatic tightening of fiscal policy. This is most pronounced if wages respond very flexibly to higher tax rates. In spite of a potential relaxation of fiscal policy when debt has been settled, the transitional effects may be quite significant. In particular, if debt reduction is accomplished through a temporarily higher wage tax, output losses may be severe and unemployment rates may reach unacceptable heights. Indeed, the wage response may seriously undermine the desirability of an ambitious debt strategy. Unless backed up by structural labour market reforms, a less ambitious strategy of debt consolidation strategy should therefore be considered.

Debt elimination can, generally, be seen as a 'gesture' from currently living generations to future generations. However, quite significant welfare losses may be inflicted upon current generations, in particular if the strategy is financed through a higher wage tax and implemented over a short time horizon. This is most obvious to elderly members of the workforce who may never enjoy the gains from

[15] It should be stressed that our model neglects income differentials within each individual generation. Such differentials will of course tend to be narrowed by a fiscal policy which increases the degree of tax progressivity.

lower tax rates when the debt target has been achieved. From the point of view of generational fairness, if the objective is to get rid of public debt the analysis of this paper suggests that this should be achieved through a higher excise tax and by stretching the elimination period over many years.

Future work will focus on the *intra*generational redistribution that might be associated with debt reduction, thereby allowing for a serious treatment of the costs of cutting down on the expenditure side of the government budget. An analysis of the international repercussions of debt policies is also on the research agenda.

References

Alesina, A, M. De Broeck and G. Tabellini. [1993]. 'Default risk on government debt in OECD countries', *Economic Policy*, no. 14, pp. 428–463.

Andersen, T.M. and O. Risager. [1990]. 'Wage formation in Denmark', in Calmfors, L. (ed.), *Wage formation and macroeconomic policy in the Nordic countries*, Oxford University Press.

Auerbach, A. and L. Kotlikoff. [1987]. *Dynamic fiscal policy*, Cambridge University Press.

Barro, R. [1974]. 'Are government bonds net wealth?', *Journal of Political Economy*, vol. 82, pp. 1095–1117.

Barro, R. [1979]. 'On the determination of public debt', *Journal of Political Economy*, vol. 87, pp. 940–71.

Blanchard, O. [1985]. 'Debt, deficits and finite horizons', *Journal of Political Economy*, vol. 93, pp. 223–247.

Blanchard, O. and N. Kiyotaki. [1987]. 'Monopolistic competition and the effects of aggregate demand', *American Economic Review*, vol. 77, pp. 647–666.

Buiter, W. and K. Kletzer. [1992]. 'Who's afraid of the public debt?', *American Economic Review*, vol. 82, pp. 200–294.

Calmfors, L. (ed.). [1990]. *Wage formationand macroeconomic policy in the Nordic countries*, Oxford University Press.

Finansministeriet. [1995]. *Finansredogørelse*, Copenhagen.

Freeman, R.B. [1988]. 'Labour market institutions and economic performance', *Economic Policy*, no. 6, pp. 63–80.

Giavazzi, F. and M. Pagano. [1989]. 'Can severe fiscal contractions be expansionary? Tales of two small economies', in Blanchard, O. and S. Fischer (eds.), *NBER Macroeconomics Review*, MIT Press, Cambridge, Mass.

Hersoug, T. [1984]. 'Union wage responses to tax changes', *Oxford Economic Papers*, vol. 36, pp. 37–51.

James, S. [1994]. 'Debt reduction with distorting taxes and incomplete ricardianism: A computable dynamic general equilibrium analysis', in Robson, W. and W. Scarth (eds.), *Deficit reduction - what pain, what gain?*, C.D. Howe Institute, Ontario,Canada.

Jensen, S.H. and S.B. Nielsen. [1993]. 'Aging, intergenerational distribution and public pension systems', *Public Finance*, vol. 48 (supplement), pp. 29–42.

Jensen, S.H., S.B. Nielsen, L.H. Pedersen and P.B. Sørensen. [1994]. 'Labour tax reform, employment and intergenerational distribution', *Scandinavian Journal of Economics*, vol. 96, pp. 381–401.

Jensen, S.H., S.B. Nielsen, L.H. Pedersen and P.B. Sørensen. [1996]. 'Tax policy, housing and the labour market: An intertemporal simulation approach', *Economic Modelling* (to appear).

Lockwood, B. and A. Manning. [1993]. 'Wage setting and the tax system. Theory and evidence for the UK', *Journal of Public Economics*, vol. 52, pp. 1–29.

Macklem, T., D. Rose and R. Tetlow. [1994]. 'Government debt and deficits in Canada: A macro simulation study',in Robson, W. and W. Scarth (eds.), *Deficit reduction - what pain, what gain?*, C.D. Howe Institute, Ontario, Canada.

Malcolmson, J. and N. Sartor. [1987]. 'Tax push inflation in a unionized labour market', *European Economic Review*, vol. 31, pp. 1581–1596.

Missale, A. and O. Blanchard. [1994]. 'The debt burden and debt maturity', *American Economic Review*, vol. 84, pp. 309–319.

Nielsen, S.B. [1994]. 'Social security and foreign indebtedness in a small open economy', *Open Economies Review*, vol. 5, pp. 47–63.

OECD, [1994]. *Economic Outlook*, vol. 56, december

Oswald, A. [1985]. 'The economic theory of trade unions: an introductory survey', *Scandinavian Journal of Economics*, vol. 87, pp. 160–193.

Robson, W. and W. Scarth. [1994]. 'Debating deficit reductions: Economic perspectives and policy choices', in Robson, W. and W. Scarth (eds.), *Deficit reduction - what pain, what gain?*, C.D. Howe Institute, Ontario, Canada.

Steigum, E. [1993]. 'Accounting for long run effects of fiscal policy by means of computable overlapping generations models', in Honkapohja, S. and M. Ingberg (eds.), *Macroeconomic modelling and policy implications*, Elsevier Science Publishers.

MIX
Papier aus verantwortungsvollen Quellen
Paper from responsible sources
FSC® C105338
FSC
www.fsc.org

If you have any concerns about our products,
you can contact us on
ProductSafety@springernature.com

In case Publisher is established outside the EU,
the EU authorized representative is:
Springer Nature Customer Service Center GmbH
Europaplatz 3, 69115 Heidelberg, Germany

Printed by Libri Plureos GmbH
in Hamburg, Germany